THE
GREAT
PHILOSOPHERS

Consulting Editors
Ray Monk and Frederic Raphael

Anthony Gottlieb

....

SOCRATES

Philosophy's Martyr

PHŒNIX

A PHŒNIX PAPERBACK

First published in Great Britain in 1997 by
Phoenix, a division of the Orion Publishing Group Ltd
Orion House
5 Upper St Martin's Lane
London, WC2H 9EA

Second impression 1998
Third impression 1999

A catalogue reference is available
from the British Library

ISBN 0 753 80191 4

Typeset by Deltatype Ltd, Birkenhead, Merseyside

Printed in Great Britain by
Clays Ltd, St Ives plc

The author is grateful to Sir Kenneth Dover for his comments on a draft of this work.

This text is part of a forthcoming history of western philosophy, to be published by Viking / Penguin.

SOCRATES

Philosophy's Martyr

ACKNOWLEDGEMENTS

The author and publishers wish to thank the following for permission to use copyright material:

Princeton University Press for excerpts from *The Collected Dialogues of Plato*, eds. E Hamilton and H Cairns (1961). Copyright © 1961, renewed 1989 by Princeton University Press;

Every effort has been made to trace the copyright holders but if any have been inadvertently overlooked the publishers will be pleased to make the necessary arrangement at the first opportunity.

PHILOSOPHY'S MARTYR: SOCRATES

Socrates is the saint and martyr of philosophy. No other great philosopher has been so obsessed with righteous living. Like many martyrs, Socrates chose not to try to save his life when he probably could have done so by changing his ways. According to Plato, who was there at the time, Socrates told the judges at his trial that '[y]ou are mistaken … if you think that a man who is worth anything ought to spend his time weighing up the prospects of life and death. He has only one thing to consider in performing any action – that is, whether he is acting rightly or wrongly.' But, unlike many saints, Socrates had a lively sense of humour; this sometimes appeared as playful wit, sometimes as pregnant irony. And, unlike the saints of any and every religion, his faith consisted not in a reliance on revelation or blind hope but in a devotion to argumentative reason. He would not be swayed by anything less.

His friends told stories about how strange he was. After dinner one night, according to a dialogue of Plato's, a young man who had been on military service with Socrates recounted how Socrates had

> started wrestling with some problem or other about sunrise one morning, and stood there lost in thought, and when the answer wouldn't come he still stood there thinking and refused to give it up. Time went on, and by about midday the troops … began telling each other

how Socrates had been standing there thinking ever since daybreak. And at last, toward nightfall, some of the Ionians brought out their bedding after supper … partly to see whether he was going to stay there all night. Well, there he stood till morning, and then at sunrise he said his prayers to the sun and went away.

Despite such uses of his spare time, Socrates had by all accounts an honourable military record.

Another friend described how, on the way to the dinner party at which the above story is told, Socrates 'fell into a fit of abstraction and began to lag behind'. Socrates then lurked in a neighbour's porch to continue thinking. 'It's quite a habit of his, you know; off he goes and there he stands, no matter where it is.' His other regular habits did not include washing; even his best friends admitted that it was unusual to see him freshly bathed and with his shoes on. He was shabby and unkempt, never had any money or cared where his next meal was coming from. He admitted to the court that 'I have never lived an ordinary quiet life. I did not care for the things that most people care about – making money, having a comfortable home, high military or civil rank, and all the other activities … which go on in our city.' But Socrates did not think that any of these trappings of a conventionally successful life were bad in themselves. Neither was he an ascetic in the ordinary sense of the term. He never preached abstinence (he could, said his friends, drink any of them under the table, though he was never seen to be drunk), nor did he urge others to live as simply as he did. A hardy and preoccupied man, he was just too busy to pay much attention to such things as clothing, food or money.

For most of the time he was busy talking to others, not just contemplating by himself. His discussions, it seems, were as intense as his fits of solitary abstraction. A distinguished general who knew him once said:

> anyone who is close to Socrates and enters into conversation with him is liable to be drawn into an argument, and whatever subject he may start, he will be continually carried round and round by him, until at last he finds that he has to give an account both of his present and past life, and when he is once entangled, Socrates will not let him go until he has completely and thoroughly sifted him.

Socrates was poor, had no conventional achievements to his name and was of humble birth – his father was a stonemason and his mother was a midwife. The fact that he nevertheless had an entrée to Athenian high society attests to his remarkable conversation. Alcibiades, who told the story of Socrates' vigil at camp, compared his speech to the music of Marsyas, the river god 'who had only to put his flute to his lips to bewitch mankind'. The 'difference between you and Marsyas,' Alcibiades tells Socrates, 'is that you can get just the same effect without any instrument at all – with nothing but a few simple words, not even poetry.' And:

> speaking for myself, gentlemen, if I wasn't afraid you'd tell me I was completely bottled, I'd swear on oath what an extraordinary effect his words have had on me … For the moment I hear him speak I am smitten with a kind of

sacred rage ... and my heart jumps into my mouth and the tears start into my eyes – oh, and not only me, but lots of other men ...

This latter-day Marsyas, here, has often left me in such a state of mind that I've felt I simply couldn't go on living the way I did ... He makes me admit that while I'm spending my time on politics I am neglecting all the things that are crying for attention in myself.

The young Alcibiades was indeed 'bottled' at this stage of the dinner, so no doubt he was getting carried away. It is a telling fact that everyone got carried away when they talked about Socrates, whether it was Alcidiades singing his praises or his enemies ranting against him.

Alcibiades also wanted Socrates to love him. It was fairly usual for dealings between Athenian philosophers and young men to be tinged with homo-eroticism, especially among Plato's circle. Attracted by the youthful beauty of boys, an older man would happily hold their attention by spooning them wisdom. But both Plato and Socrates criticized homosexual intercourse; Alcibiades had at first been mortified when Socrates refused to return his physical affections. As Socrates had tactfully explained at the time, he resisted the advances of Alcibiades for ethical reasons, not because he was not attracted to him. Alcibiades was famously handsome and Socrates was famously ugly. It was an inner beauty that Alcibiades saw in him: 'I've been bitten in the heart, or the mind, or whatever you like to call it, by Socrates' philosophy, which clings like an adder to any young and gifted mind it can get hold of.'

Socrates poked fun at his own ugliness, and he could

make something more than half-serious out of even such a lighthearted subject as that. Critobulus, a friend of Socrates, apparently once challenged him to a 'beauty contest' in which each man was to try to convince a mock jury that he was better looking than the other. Socrates begins the contest:

Socrates The first step, then, in my suit, is to summon you to the preliminary hearing; be so kind as to answer my questions ... Do you hold ... that beauty is to be found only in man, or is it also in other objects?

Critobulus In faith, my opinion is that beauty is to be found quite as well in a horse or an ox or in any number of inanimate things. I know, at any rate, that a shield may be beautiful, or a sword, or a spear.

Soc. How can it be that all these things are beautiful when they are entirely dissimilar?

Crit. Why, they are beautiful and fine if they are well made for the respective functions for which we obtain them or if they are naturally well constituted to serve our needs.

Soc. Do you know the reason why we need eyes?

Crit. Obviously to see with.

Soc. In that case it would appear without further ado that my eyes are finer ones than yours.

Crit. How so?

Soc. Because, while yours see only straight ahead, mine, by bulging out as they do, see also to the sides.

Crit. Do you mean to say that a crab is better equipped visually than any other creature?

Soc. Absolutely ...

Crit. Well, let that pass; but whose nose is finer, yours or mine?

Soc. Mine, I consider, granting that Providence made us noses to smell with. For your nostrils look down toward the ground, but mine are wide open and turned outward so that I can catch scents from all about.

Crit. But how do you make a snub nose handsomer than a straight one?

Soc. For the reason that it does not put a barricade between the eyes but allows them unobstructed vision of whatever they desire to see; whereas a high nose, as if in despite, has walled the eyes off one from the other.

Crit. As for the mouth, I concede that point. For if it is created for the purpose of biting off food, you could bite off a far bigger mouthful than I could. And don't you think that your kiss is also the more tender because you have thick lips?

Soc. According to your argument, it would seem that I have a mouth more ugly even than an ass's …

Crit. I cannot argue any longer with you, let them distribute the ballots …

Of course Socrates lost. He knew he could not really be said to be good-looking, and they were only having fun. This exchange (from a dialogue by another admirer, Xenophon) is not the sort of thing that would bring tears to the eyes of Alcibiades, unless perhaps they were tears of laughter. Nor yet does it show Socrates at his most sophisticated. Far from it: this is the Beginner's Socrates. But it is interesting to see how this simple banter has much of the Socrates that one meets in the weightier and better-known philosophical exchanges in Plato's dialogues.

First there is his characteristic method of interrogation.

Instead of proposing a thesis himself, Socrates lets the other man do so and then draws out its consequences. As always with Socrates, the business begins with a request for an enlightening definition of whatever is being discussed – in this case, of beauty. Critobulus takes the bait and offers as his definition: '[things are] beautiful and fine if they are well made for the respective functions for which we obtain them or if they are naturally well consituted to serve our needs'. Then Socrates reels him in. He has no difficulty in showing that if this is what beauty is, then he himself is beautiful. Unravelling the accounts of others is how Socrates always played the game of dialectic.

The contest also shows Socrates' complex irony. He knows that he is ugly. He knows that Critobulus' definition of beauty is faulty. Yet he proceeds as if neither of these things were so: he seems perfectly happy to adopt the definition and to use it to prove that he is in fact good-looking. But he is not just trying to exploit Critobulus' words to win the beauty contest by foul means. He is not really trying to win it at all. While pretending to fight the contest, Socrates is in fact doing something else. By playfully adopting Critobulus' definition, Socrates demonstrates that Critobulus has failed to get to the bottom of what beauty is. It cannot be defined in terms of fitness and usefulness alone, since this would imply that Socrates' features are beautiful, which everybody knows they are not. Thus, while ironically pretending to convince Critobulus of his beauty, Socrates has in fact established the negative result that beauty cannot be what Critobulus says it is.

Socrates frequently and tiresomely denied that he knew anything about beauty or virtue or justice, or whatever else was being discussed. Such avowed ignorance was his trademark. Like his playful claim to personal beauty, these denials were partly ironic, though with a more serious purpose. Although he always claimed to have nothing to teach, his activities looked very much like teaching – enough so to get him hauled before the courts as a teacher with a malign influence. I shall now turn to the trial of Socrates and his defence, which show just what it was that made him so unpopular with some conservative Athenians, and so popular with most subsequent philosophers.

The trial of Socrates took place in 399 BC when he was nearly seventy. The charges were that he refused to recognize the official gods of the state, that he introduced new gods and that he corrupted the young. There was a vivid political background to the trial, but this does not mean that the charges were a sham and that the trial was really a political one. Politics, religion and education were all intertwined in the matter, and, however you looked at it, Socrates was saying the wrong things at the wrong time.

In 404 BC, five years before the trial, a twenty-seven-year war between Athens and Sparta had ended with the defeat of Athens. The Athenian democracy was overthrown and replaced by a group of men, subsequently known as the Thirty Tyrants, who were installed by Sparta. In the course of earning their name, the Tyrants murdered so many people that they lasted for only a year, though it was not until 401 BC that democracy was fully restored. Understandably, the democrats were still feeling rather insecure in 399 BC.

There were plenty of reasons to be uneasy about the presence of Socrates in the city.

Two close former associates of his had been involved in the tyranny. One, Critias, was the leader of the Thirty and a particularly bloodthirsty man. The other, Charmides, was one of their deputies (both men were, incidentally, relations of Plato's). Alcibiades had also turned out to be rather a liability. A headstrong and arrogant aristocrat, he was accused of sacrilegious high-jinks and profanity – committed, perhaps, while 'bottled'. Alcibiades heard about these charges while he was on a military expedition to Sicily. Rather than return to face them, he defected and treacherously fought on the side of Sparta instead. None of this looked good for these men's former mentor, Socrates.

In 403 BC, however, a political amnesty had been declared in Athens, so it would not have been possible to indict Socrates on explicitly political charges, even if anyone had wanted to. Besides, there were deeper causes for concern about his influence. During the long war with Sparta, Athenians had grown increasingly nervous about the home front. It was felt that intellectuals were weakening Athenian society by undermining its traditional views and values. Well might a man who captivated idle youths with his questioning about justice have aroused suspicion. The fact that there had been a hilarious caricature of Socrates as a bumbling but subversive teacher in a play by Aristophanes, staged in Athens twenty-four years earlier, did not help matters. And whatever truth there was to the rumour that Socrates disbelieved in the traditional gods – he seemed to deny the charge, but not convincingly – there was no doubt that he had an unorthodox approach to divinity. The way he talked about his *daimonion*, his 'guardian spirit' or personal 'divine sign', gave reasonable cause for concern that he did indeed 'introduce new gods', as the indictment put it. That would have been a grievous sin against the shaky democracy. The state alone had the power to say what was a suitable object for religious veneration; it had its own procedures for officially recognizing gods, and anyone who ignored them was in effect challenging the legitimacy of the democratic state. All of this Socrates was up against when he faced the 500 Athenian citizens who were to judge him.

Plato was at the trial; the *Apology* (or 'defence-speech') *of Socrates* which he wrote a few years afterwards was probably his first work. There are reasons to believe that in this work Plato tried harder to represent the real Socrates than he subsequently did elsewhere, though he did not necessarily try to reproduce his exact words. So I shall rely on Plato (as I have done for much of the information about Socrates provided so far). There is no alternative. The Socrates of Plato's *Apology* is the only Socrates there is, or has been for nearly all of the history of philosophy.

From a legal point of view, Socrates' speech is a miserable performance. He begins by saying that he has no skill as a speaker; this is a standard rhetorical first move, but in this case one would have to agree with him, if his aim in speaking were simply to get himself acquitted. Almost everything he says to rebut the official charges is either irrelevant or else unpersuasive. For example, on the subject of religion he confines himself to mocking his accuser. He gets him to contradict himself by provoking him into saying that Socrates is a complete atheist who believes in no gods at all. But if that were so, Socrates points out, how could he also be guilty of introducing new gods? To the charge that he has corrupted the young, Socrates makes the unconvincingly convoluted reply that he cannot intentionally have done any such thing, since this would have been against his own interests. To corrupt someone is to harm him, he says, and if you harm someone then that person will try to harm you back. So clearly he would not have risked that. This argument will have persuaded nobody.

Socrates knew that his judges were already prejudiced against him by the slanders of Aristophanes, and set out to correct these false impressions. He is not, he says, a man who teaches for money, like the professional 'Sophists' with whom Aristophanes has confused him. This seems to have been true enough: he did not charge a fee. But he did sing for his supper. He accepted hospitality in a tacit bargain for his edifying conversation, and apparently did no other sort of work. So the way he earned his living was not really different from that of the Sophists – not that either way of life would be regarded as inherently suspicious today. He also tried to dismiss the slander that he taught people how to win arguments by trickery when they were in the wrong. Far from it, he protested, for he did not know enough to teach anybody anything.

This is the main theme of the *Apology*, which is more of a general defence of his way of life than a rebuttal of the official charges. The nub of this defence is Socrates' claim that he has positively benefited the Athenians by subjecting them to his philosophical cross-examinations, but that they have failed to realize this and merely been angered by it, which is why he has ended up on trial for his life.

Socrates says that he is fulfilling the wishes of the gods when he goes about and argues with people. A friend of his once went to the oracle at Delphi and asked if there was any man wiser than Socrates. No, came back the answer, which threw Socrates into a frightful confusion – or so he says. For he always held that he was not wise at all. 'After puzzling about it for some time, I set myself at last with considerable reluctance to check the truth of it.' He did so by interrogating all sorts of people who had a reputation for wisdom or specialized knowledge. But he was always disappointed, because it seemed that there was nobody whose alleged wisdom could stand up to his questioning. He was always able to refute the efforts of others to establish some thesis of theirs, usually by highlighting some unwelcome and unexpected consequences of their views. He also questioned poets, but they could not even elucidate their poems to his satisfaction. After one such encounter:

> I reflected as I walked away, Well, I am certainly wiser than this man. It is only too likely that neither of us has any knowledge to boast of, but he thinks that he knows something which he does not know, whereas I am quite conscious of my ignorance. At any rate it seems that I am wiser than he is to this small extent, that I do not think that I know what I do not know.

Then it dawned on him what the oracle must have meant:

> whenever I succeed in disproving another person's claim to wisdom in a given subject, the bystanders assume that I know everything about that subject myself. But the truth of the matter, gentleman, is pretty certainly this,

that real wisdom is the property of God, and this oracle is his way of telling us that human wisdom has little or no value. It seems to me that he is not referring to Socrates, but has merely taken my name as an example, as if he would say to us, The wisest of you men is he who has realized, like Socrates, that in respect of wisdom, he is really worthless.

In other words, the superior wisdom of Socrates lies in the fact that he alone is aware of how little he knows. Of course, there is a little more to Socrates' wisdom than just that, as he is made to admit elsewhere in Plato's dialogues. Although, he claims, 'the arguments never come out of me; they always come from the person I am talking with', he acknowledges that he is 'at a slight advantage in having the skill to get some account of the matter from another's wisdom and entertain it with fair treatment'. He aptly describes himself as an intellectual midwife, whose questioning delivers the thoughts of others into the light of day. But this skill in elucidation and debate, which he obviously has in abundance, is not a form of real wisdom so far as Socrates is concerned. Real wisdom is perfect knowledge about ethical subjects, about how to live. When Socrates claims ignorance, he means ignorance about the foundations of morality; he is not asserting any general sort of scepticism about everyday matters of fact. His concern is solely with ethical reflection, and he cannot with a clear conscience abandon his mission to encourage it in others:

If I say that this would be disobedience to God, and that is why I cannot 'mind my own business', you will not believe that I am serious. If on the other hand I tell you that to let no day pass without discussing goodness and all other subjects about which you hear me talking and examining both myself and others is really the very best thing that a man can do, and that life without this sort of examination is not worth living, you will be even less inclined to believe me. Nevertheless that is how it is.

His pious references to the wisdom of God (sometimes he speaks of a single God, sometimes of the gods) are apt to disguise how unconventional his attitude to divinity was. When he says that only God has wisdom, he seems to mean this figuratively, just as one might shrug and say, 'God knows!'. For consider how he sets about interpreting 'God's' words and trying to tease out hints of 'His' wisdom. The Delphic oracle was as authentic a voice of God as any available: yet Socrates did not just accept what it says but instead set out 'to check the truth of it'. He says elsewhere that 'it has always been my nature never to accept advice from any of my friends unless reflection shows that it is the best course that reason offers; he seems to have adopted exactly the same approach to the advice of God. Presented with the divine pronouncement that no man is wiser than Socrates, he refuses to take this at face value until he has satisfied himself that a true meaning can be found for it.

He seems to be speaking in a roundabout way when he refers to his mission as divine, because the Delphic oracle did not explicitly tell him to go forth and philosophize. He does at one point say that his mission to argue and question was undertaken 'in obedience to God's commands given in oracles and dreams and in every other way that any divine dispensation has ever impressed a duty upon man'. But when he continues by saying that this is a true statement 'and easy to verify', his verification consists merely in arguing that his mission is a morally good thing. He does not give any evidence that God told him to do it. He probably came closest to the heart of the matter when he said, 'I want you to think of my adventures as a sort of pilgrimage undertaken to establish the truth of the oracle once for all.' It was his conscience and intelligence which told him to interrogate those who believed themselves to be wise. He could claim that this 'helps the cause of God' because such activities do help to confirm the Delphic pronouncement that nobody is wiser than Socrates. But the talk of God is largely a gloss, which serves to mark Socrates' high moral purpose and to win the approval of his hearers. His basic motive for philosophizing was simply that it seemed to him the right thing to do.

Socrates says he is influenced in his actions by what he calls his *daimonion*, a guardian spirit or voice which has been with him since childhood. This seems to have been the unorthodox divinity or 'new gods' referred to in the charges against him. Once again the advice of the *daimonion* is treated as advice to be reasoned with before it is endorsed, like the counsel of friends or the words of the Delphic oracle. The voice of the *daimonion* is pretty clearly what we would call the voice of cautious conscience. He says that 'when it comes it always dissuades me from what I am proposing to do, and never urges me on'.

The guardian spirit warned him off any involvement in politics, he says, because if he had made a public figure of himself, he would have been killed long before he could have done much good. That is why he chose to minister to the people privately:

> I spend all my time going about trying to persuade you, young and old, to make your first and chief concern not for your bodies nor for your possessions, but for the highest welfare of your souls, proclaiming as I go, wealth does not bring goodness, but goodness brings wealth and every other blessing, both to the individual and to the state.

This persuasion seems to have been rather strident at times. He implies that the Athenians should be 'ashamed that you give your attention to acquiring as much money as possible, and similarly with reputation and honour, and give no attention or thought to truth and understanding and the perfection of your soul'. He must have particularly annoyed them when he said, during his trial, that he thought he was doing the Athenians 'the greatest possible service' in showing them the errors of their ways. This was at a stage of the proceedings when he had already been voted guilty and was required to argue for a suitable penalty, to counter the prosecution's proposal that he be put to death. Typically, he treats this responsibility with irony. What he actually deserves for doing the Athenians such a service, he says, is not a punishment but a reward. He suggests free meals for life at the expense of the state. Such an honour was usually reserved for victors at the Olympic games and suchlike; he has earned it even more than they have, he says, because 'these people give you the semblance of success, but I give you the reality'. He ends this part of the speech by suggesting a fine instead, at the instigation of Plato and other friends who offer to pay it for him. But the Athenians had already lost their patience. They voted for the death penalty by a larger majority than that by which they had found him guilty. This means that some of them, having previously found him innocent, were so enraged by his cheek that they either changed their minds or else decided to get rid of him anyway.

One story has it that as Socrates was leaving the court, a devoted but dim admirer called Apollodorus moaned that the hardest thing for him to bear was that Socrates was being put to death unjustly. What? said Socrates, trying to comfort him. Would you rather I was put to death justly?

As for the prospect of death itself, he was already very old and close to death anyway, so he says, and he had had a good and useful life. Besides:

> to be afraid of death is only another form of thinking that one is wise when one is not ... No one knows with regard to death whether it is really the greatest blessing that can happen to a man, but people dread it as though they were certain that it is the greatest evil, and this ignorance, which thinks that it knows what it does not, must surely be ignorance most culpable ... and if I were to claim to be wiser than my neighbour in any respect, it would be in this ... that not possessing any real knowledge of what comes after death, I am also conscious that I do not possess it.

If there were an afterlife, he added, he would get the chance to meet 'heroes of the old days who met their death through an unfair trial, and to compare my fortunes with theirs – it would be rather amusing'.

For all his talk of ignorance, and his insistence that he merely acted as a midwife for the ideas of others, Socrates did have strong beliefs of his own. Unfortunately he never wrote them down. For one of these beliefs was that philosophy is an intimate and collaborative activity; it is a matter for discussions among small groups of people who argue together in order that each might find the truth for himself. The spirit of such a pastime cannot accurately be captured in a lecture or a treatise. That is one reason why Plato and Xenophon (and several of their contemporaries whose works are now lost) chose to present Socrates' teaching in the form of dialogues. Dialogue had been his *métier* and dialogue would be his monument.

There are four main witnesses for the intimate thoughts of Socrates: Plato, Xenophon, Aristophanes and Aristotle. None of these men is quite what a historian might have wished for. Plato has by far the most to say on the subject, but as an objective guide to Socrates he suffers from the disability of having practically worshipped him. He is therefore likely to have exaggerated what he took to be his finest qualities. Also, in the course of some forty years of thinking and teaching, during which Plato's ideas naturally changed quite a lot, he paid Socrates the tribute of using him as a mouthpiece. To Plato, Socrates was pre-eminently wise, so whenever something seemed to Plato to be wise, he put it in the mouth of Socrates. Plato himself – or else a close associate – once described his dialogues as 'the work of a Socrates embellished and modernized'. This is double trouble, because not only does the Socrates in Plato's dialogues often speak for Plato rather than for himself, but he is also made to say rather different things at the various stages of Plato's literary career.

What about the other three witnesses? Xenophon's failings as a source are quite different. He was not (like Plato) too much of a philosopher to act as a guide to Socrates, but rather too little of one. It is no crime to be a retired general turned gentleman-farmer, but such a man is perhaps not the safest custodian of the key to one of the world's great thinkers. Xenophon implausibly uses the figure of Socrates to pass on his own tips about farming and military tactics. He also depicts him as a boringly conventional goody-goody: 'All his private conduct was lawful and helpful: to public authority he rendered such scrupulous obedience in all that the laws required, both in civil life and in military service, that he was a pattern of good discipline to all.' A leading scholar of ancient philosophy has understandably referred to Xenophon as 'that stuffy old prig'. In fairness to Xenophon it must be said that anyone who admired an eccentric like Socrates as much as he did cannot have been all that stuffy. But Xenophon was certainly no Socrates himself, and he may often have failed to grasp both the strangeness of his character and what he was getting at. If Xenophon tried too hard to make Socrates respectable and a sound chap, then the playwright Aristophanes tried too hard to do the opposite. His Socrates is a slapstick fool who is intrigued by such questions as from which end a gnat breaks wind. Aristotle's disability in describing Socrates is simply stated: he was born fifteen years too late.

Yet it is Aristotle who holds a vital clue. Although he never heard Socrates' opinions at first hand, he studied for some twenty years in Plato's Academy and had plenty of opportunity to hear Plato's views from Plato himself. He was therefore in a position to disentangle the thinking of the two men. To a considerable extent, Aristotle's testimony lets one subtract Plato from his own dialogues and see the Socratic remainder. Aristotle was also much less in awe of Socrates than Plato was, and therefore managed to take a more dispassionate approach to his teachings.

The fact that the four main sources for Socrates were so different turns out to be something of a boon. It means that the features which are common to their various accounts are all the more likely to be authentic. And the more we know about each of the four and what he was up to, the easier it is to discount his bias and see the true Socrates loitering behind. By following up such clues, modern scholars have pieced together much of the philosophy of the man who literally argued himself to death.

It is simplest to consider the views of Socrates in relation to those of Plato. The approximate dating of Plato's dialogues, plus some information about his life, make it possible to retrace his steps on an intellectual journey that started in the company of Socrates but eventually left him far behind. At first Plato largely limited himself to re-creating the conversations of his revered teacher. Gradually, Pythagorean and other mystical glosses were put on Socrates' ideas as Plato came increasingly under the influence of Italian Pythagoreans. And eventually Plato reached a point where he invoked the name of Socrates to expound on all sorts of subjects.

The important discussions of the real Socrates were exclusively concerned with how one ought to live. They were mostly about the virtues, of which there were conventionally held to be five: courage, moderation, piety, wisdom and justice. His mission was to urge people to care for their souls by trying to understand and acquire these qualities. This task was enough to keep Socrates busy, but Plato was much more ambitious on his master's behalf. He wrote many dialogues that do not focus on morality at all but which usually still have Socrates as the main speaker. For example, Plato's *Republic* starts out as a discussion of justice but ends up touching on practically everything that interested Plato.

Even when the real Socrates made a point of saying that he did not have a clue, Plato often plunged ahead and credited him with firm opinions. For instance, Socrates thought that what happens after death is an open question. But in the *Phaedo*, which purports to give Socrates' last words before he drank hemlock in prison, Plato makes him produce a whole barrage of proofs for the immortality of the soul.

Plato seems to have had few doubts about what would happen after death. He thought that the soul was separable from the body, that it existed before birth and that it would definitely continue to exist after death. Under Pythagorean influence, he held that while it was tied to a physical body during life it led a defiled and inferior existence from which it needed to be 'purified' and 'freed from the shackles of the body'. According to Plato in this dialogue, what the good man can hope to enjoy after death is reunification, or at least communion, with those incorporeal higher forms of existence that are conventionally called 'the divine'. The philosopher, in particular, should regard the whole of his life as a preparation for the blissful release of death. As we have seen, Socrates lived a shambling, poor and unconventional life that was certainly unworldly. But Plato was positively other-worldly, which is a rather different thing (and actually he led a mostly comfortable existence until escaping the shackles of his amply fed body).

Socrates pursued the virtues because he felt morally obliged to, here and now. Earthly life imposed its own duties, brought its own blessings and was not simply a preparation for something else. Plato's motives were less straightforward because he had at least one eye fixed on something beyond. One belief about virtue that the two men held in common is that the pursuit of goodness is not only a matter of acting in certain ways but also an intellectual project. Yet they saw this project differently. Socrates believed that coming to understand the virtues was a necessary precondition for possessing them. A man could not be truly virtuous unless he knew what virtue was, and the only way he might be able to get this knowledge was by examining accounts of the particular virtues. That is why Socrates went around questioning people and arguing with them. Plato believed in this argumentative search too, but he also interpreted it as something almost mystical. While Socrates saw the search for definitions as a means to an end, namely the exercise of virtue, Plato saw the search as an end in itself. To look for a definition was, for Plato, to seek the ideal, eternal, unchanging Form of whatever was under discussion; the contemplation of such Forms was itself the highest good. That is what he thought Socrates' questioning really amounted to and what it ought to aim at.

For Plato, philosophy was the ladder to this elevated

world of the Forms, but not everyone could climb it. Its higher rungs were reserved for those who were especially talented in dialectical argument, an élite, like the initiates of cult religions, or the followers of Pythagoras who had been privy to the master's secrets. Socrates had a more egalitarian approach to knowledge and virtue. The unexamined life, as he famously said in his defence-speech, is not worth living, and this is not a fate to which he meant to condemn all but a chosen few. Anybody could examine his own life and ideas and thus lead a worthwhile existence. Socrates would happily question and argue with anybody, cobbler or king, and for him this was all that philosophy was. He would have had little use for Plato's Forms or the rare skills needed to find them.

One thing which led Plato to the mysterious Forms was his fascination with mathematics, again a Pythagorean matter and again a point of difference between him and Socrates. Above its gates, Plato's Academy was said to have had the words 'No one ignorant of geometry admitted here'; Aristotle later complained that for Plato's followers, 'mathematics has come to be the whole of philosophy' – a petulant exaggeration, but a pointed one. What struck Plato about the objects dealt with in mathematics, such as numbers and triangles, is that they are ideal, eternal, unchanging and pleasingly independent of earthly, visible things. Plainly one cannot see or touch the number four: it therefore exists in a different sort of realm, according to Plato. And the lines, triangles and other sorts of objects that figure in mathematical proofs cannot be identified with anything physical either. Particular physical lines and triangles are nothing more than approximations to ideal mathematical ones. A perfect line, for example, would have no thickness; but any visible line, or rim of a physical object, always will. Given the impressiveness of mathematics, Plato reasoned, other sorts of knowledge ought to copy it and be about ideal and incorporeal objects too. These objects of knowledge were the Forms.

In one of his dialogues, Plato used a geometrical example to argue that knowledge of the Forms, which for him meant all the important sorts of knowledge, is acquired before birth. The truths of pure reason, such as those of mathematics, are not discovered afresh but are painstakingly recollected from a previous existence in which the soul was disembodied and could encounter the Forms directly. Thus one does not strictly speaking learn these truths at all: one works to remember them. When a soul is born into a body, the knowledge which it previously enjoyed slips from memory: as Wordsworth wrote in his *Intimations of Immortality*, 'our birth is but a sleep and a forgetting'. Wordsworth was not particularly thinking about geometry, but he liked the general idea. To illustrate this theory, Plato makes 'Socrates' elicit some apparent knowledge of geometry from an uneducated slave-boy. This is supposed both to confirm the Platonic idea that some knowledge is recollected from an earlier existence and to show why the teaching of Socrates is indeed, as Socrates had claimed, really like midwifery.

The problem which 'Socrates' sets the slave is that of determining the sides of a square of a given area. He starts by drawing a square whose sides are two feet long, and whose area is thus four square feet, and asks how long the sides would have to be if its area were instead eight square feet. At first the slave ignorantly reasons that the sides would have to be twice as long as those of the original square, i.e., four feet. By drawing another diagram, 'Socrates' soon shows him that this must be wrong, since the area of such a square would be not eight but sixteen square feet. The slave is surprised to learn that he does not know as much as he thought he did. 'Socrates' notes that at this point, 'we have helped him to some extent toward finding the right answer, for now not only is he ignorant of it but he will be quite glad to look for it.' Next, with the aid of further diagrams and by asking the right questions about them, Socrates gradually leads the slave to work out the answer for himself: the sides of a triangle with twice the area of the original one would have to be the same length as a diagonal drawn across the original square – which, in effect, boils down to the famous theorem of Pythagoras. Bingo: since Socrates never actually told him this, the slave must have 'known' it already.

This little episode does not really prove Plato's theory of recollection, as Plato himself acknowledged. But the story does illustrate a distinctly Socratic thesis about knowledge and how it can be imparted. Socrates' questions to the slave are indeed leading ones (and the diagrams help, too), yet it is nevertheless true that the slave comes to see the answer for himself. He has not simply been told it as one might be told how many feet there are in a yard or what the capital of Greece is. He has come to appreciate something through his own intellectual faculties. So Socrates can modestly make his usual claim that he has not handed over any knowledge himself but has just acted as a midwife to bring it out of somebody else. And there is another thing: as

Socrates points out, in order for the slave to know this piece of mathematics properly, it is not quite enough for him to work through the example just once:

> At present these opinions [of the slave's], being newly aroused, have a dreamlike quality. But if the same questions are put to him on many occasions and in different ways, you can see that in the end he will have a knowledge on the subject as accurate as anybody's ...
>   This knowledge will not come from teaching but from questioning. He will recover it for himself.

Repeated doses of Socratic questioning are called for. In other words, what the slave needs is exactly the sort of treatment that the real Socrates offered the largely ungrateful Athenians. As he says in the *Apology*, if anyone claims to know about goodness, 'I shall question him and examine him and test him.' Thus, in his fanciful story of assisted recollection, Plato has given us a striking illustration of the sort of thing Socrates was doing when he claimed to help other people deliver their own opinions. It is as if Socrates were drawing out and firming up some knowledge that was already there.

This is all very well for Plato's example of his beloved triangles and squares. It is not hard to believe that a skilled questioner can bring a pupil to appreciate a mathematical truth without explicitly stating this truth for him – anyone who has had a good teacher will recognize this experience. But what about matters of justice and the other virtues, which is what the real Socrates was interested in? Ethics is messier than mathematics; it does not, for one thing, seem to have any proofs to offer. So presumably the business of learning about virtue will be quite different from the business of learning about mathematics.

Socrates knew this. He had no illusions about being able conclusively to prove any ethical doctrines. Quite the contrary, in fact, for he was forever insisting on his own uncertainty and the tentativeness of his enquiries. For example, before starting a defence of one thesis, he admits that, 'Sometimes, however, I am of the opposite opinion, for I am all abroad in my ideas about this matter, a condition obviously occasioned by ignorance.' No doubt he is wrong to maintain this thesis now, he says to his interlocutor, but let us follow the argument wherever it leads and perhaps you will be able to put me right. When Socrates says earlier on in this dialogue that, 'I am full of defects, and always getting things wrong in some way or other', he is partly just being modest. But he was quite clear that he had no mathematical-style proofs about virtue.

Does he ever get anywhere, then? Does he really succeed in delivering any knowledge about virtue? In one sense, yes. He does, albeit indirectly, lay out several pronounced and rather extraordinary views about virtue, which all slot together to form a theory of human life. As for whether he succeeds in convincing his hearers of this theory, the answer is generally no. But he does not really aim to do that anyway because he is not absolutely sure that the theory is right and, besides, people must find their own way to the truth about such matters. What he aims to do is to put opinions about virtue to the test, and this applies both to his own opinions and to those of the people he is talking to. The test is to be trial by dialectical ordeal: definitions or accounts of various matters are to be queried and thereby elucidated, and whatever seems to survive such questioning is provisionally to be accepted. The results yielded by this approach fall short of true wisdom in various ways, but it is nevertheless the best approach available. Such enquiry does lead to a sort of knowledge, so Socrates' bare-faced denials that he knows anything are partly ironic.

Most of the authentically Socratic investigations in Plato's dialogues wind up without settling on a final conclusion. Socrates ambitiously sets off to find out what, say, justice is; he argues away for a while; and then usually has to go home apparently empty handed. But he is not really empty handed. The discussions usually succeed at least in showing up something important along the way. For example, in one early Platonic dialogue, Socrates quizzes a man called Euthyphro on the nature of piety or holiness. Although Socrates does not manage to establish exactly what piety is, he does manage to show something interesting about what it is not.

The two men meet outside the law courts, where Euthyphro is about to prosecute his own father for unintentionally (though perhaps culpably) causing the death of a slave who had himself murdered another slave. Socrates is surprised that Euthyphro should want to pursue such a case. Euthyphro insists that although his family think it impious for a son to prosecute his father as a murderer, he knows what he is about. His family are ignorant about what is holy, whereas he has 'an accurate knowledge of all that'. He therefore has no doubts about the rightness of his action. Socrates wonders at Euthyphro's confident wisdom and asks him to share it and tell him what holiness is. At first Euthyphro says that it is what the gods love. But

Socrates gets him to see that since the gods are commonly represented as having fierce disagreements, they presumably do not always love or approve the same things. This means that whether or not a god approves something cannot be the criterion of whether or not it is holy: one god might approve it and another not, in which case one would be none the wiser as to its holiness. So Socrates and Euthyphro amend the proposed definition and say that the holy is what all the gods agree in approving. But now a question occurs to Socrates: 'Is what is holy holy because the gods approve it, or do they approve it because it is holy?'

This is an excellent question, so good in fact that at first Euthyphro does not understand it. It comes down to this: would absolutely anything that the gods approved of count as holy, just because they approved of it, or are they bound to approve only of certain things, namely those which would count as holy whether they approved of them or not? Unfortunately Plato did not have the vocabulary to make this distinction absolutely clear. So when Socrates tries to explain it, his account gets tangled in irrelevant grammatical matters and is not altogether compelling. Yet Socrates does seem to have uncovered a dilemma about the relationship between religion and morality. If we ask the same sort of question about what is morally good instead of about what is holy, we can see that we are faced with a revealing choice: either goodness cannot be explained simply by reference to what the gods want, or else it is an empty tautology to say that the gods are good – in which case the praise of the gods would simply be a matter of power-worship. As Leibniz put it, at the start of the eighteenth century (by which time the gods had long ago dwindled to one God):

> Those who believe that God has established good and evil by an arbitrary decree ... deprive God of the designation *good*: for what cause could one have to praise him for what he does, if in doing something quite different he would have done equally well?

The Socrates in Plato's dialogue did not develop the argument that far. But he does appear to have seen that moral values cannot simply be derived from considerations about what the gods want, since to do so would rob the gods (or God) of any distinctively moral authority. Euthyphro apparently accepts the point, though later he wavers and hurries into court before he can be pinned down. Thus Socrates does succeed in making useful progress even though he does not finally settle the matter at hand.

Yet there is still something unconvincing about what Socrates says he is up to in arguments like this. Can his questioning, or indeed any sort of intellectual enterprise, really have the sort of practical benefits he claims? Even though he never professes to establish the whole truth about virtue, and although we can agree that he nevertheless manages to make some intellectual headway, it is hard to see how his interrogations can have the power with which he seems to credit them. The problem lies in his belief that discussing the virtues can lead one actually to become a better person. This is no casual aside: it is this very idea which Socrates invokes to justify subjecting people to his trying examinations. It is all for their own good, he thinks, not only because such discussions are worthwhile in themselves but mainly because having them is the only path to personal virtue. This sounds implausible, to say the least. Surely it is one thing to come to know that a principle of action is right and quite another to behave in accordance with it. Could not someone find out all sorts of things about virtue by talking to Socrates but still go off and be wicked? As we have seen, Critias, Charmides and maybe Alcibiades seem to have done just that.

Aristotle frequently attacked Socrates along these lines: 'We must not limit our enquiry to knowing what it [virtue] is, but extend it to how it is to be produced.' He accused Socrates of failing to distinguish between practical questions and theoretical ones:

> he thought all the virtues to be kinds of knowledge, so that to know justice and to be just came simultaneously ... Therefore he enquired what virtue is, not how or from what it arises. This approach is correct with regard to theoretical knowledge, for there is no other part of astronomy or physics or geometry except knowing and contemplating the nature of things which are the subjects of those sciences ... But the aim of the practical sciences is different ... For we do not wish to know what bravery is but to be brave, nor what justice is but to be just, just as we wish to be in health rather than to know what health is ...

Socrates had a sort of answer to this. He could have replied along the following lines: 'You are not being fair to me. The reason why Critias, Charmides and some other troublesome pupils failed to be virtuous is simply that they had not yet learned enough about virtue. If only we had got further in our discussions, these people would indeed have become just. Thus while I agree that we not only want to know what virtue is but want to be virtuous ourselves, my point is that if we really did know what it was, virtue would follow of its own accord. As I keep saying, I do not yet know what it is; so I cannot yet produce it in myself, let alone in others. That is precisely why we must keep on looking for it.'

The main point of this reply is fair enough. We cannot say that Socrates' claim about what his methods could achieve has been refuted: it has never yet been put to the test, because he has not yet found out what virtue is. But even so, why should anyone believe him when he says that full knowledge of virtue, if we ever managed to get it, would itself produce virtuous behaviour? It sounds an implausible hypothesis when we consider how weak-willed, selfish and short-sighted people often are. People frequently think that something is morally wrong and yet do it anyway. Why should we think they would be any different if only they knew more?

Aristotle reckoned that Socrates suffered from an over-simplified picture of human psychology: 'He is doing away with the irrational part of the soul, and is thereby doing away also both with passion and character.' Socrates saw human action and emotion in largely rational or intellectual terms; he ignored impulses and wilful irrationality. 'No one, he said, acts against what he believes best – people act so only by reason of ignorance.' This explains the exaggerated importance that Socrates attached to enquiries about virtue. If the only reason why people fail to do whatever is best is that they are ignorant, then the cure for immorality would indeed be more knowledge.

On this subject, Plato seems for once to have been more down to earth and realistic than Socrates. He recognized an 'irrational part of the soul' and saw it as often in conflict with the rational part. (In his more Pythagorean moments, he described this as a conflict between soul and body.) Producing virtue was thus for Plato not just a matter of imparting knowledge but of encouraging certain behaviour. In the utopian state described in his *Republic*, this involved careful training and discipline of the young and close attention to their early environment – even to the sort of music they listened to and the sort of stories they were allowed to hear.

Socrates himself evidently had no need of such training. He was by all accounts supremely disciplined and a master of rational self-control. Maybe that was the problem. Perhaps it explains why he seems to have had such impossibly high expectations for others and to have supposed that if only they really knew what justice was they would immediately become just themselves. It has been said of Socrates that 'in the strength of his character lay the weakness of his philosophy'. This is a neat formulation, but the ideas of Socrates had rather more coherence than it suggests. Besides, it must be said that his implausibly rationalistic account of psychology was not the only problem anyway. Even if some wise person were as disciplined as he was, and had somehow been born with the irrational part of his soul missing, it is hard to see how this would automatically make such a person morally good. Could not someone be as rational as Socrates, as wise as he sought to be, but also as bad as Milton's Satan, who knowingly embraced evil with the words, 'Evil, be thou my Good'? Not according to Socrates, who held (said Aristotle) that 'No one would choose evil knowing it to be such.' Not only did Socrates conveniently ignore impulsiveness and irrationality, he apparently declared that wilful immortality was simply impossible. He seems never to have met a fallen man, let alone a fallen angel.

Was he then just naive? Nietzsche wrote of the 'divine naiveté and sureness of the Socratic way of life', but what he seems to have had in mind is the clear-eyed focus of Socrates' vision, not any merely foolish innocence. Nietzsche thought long and hard about Socrates' habit of expressing himself in apparently naive propositions, and concluded that it was in fact 'wisdom full of pranks'. Nietzsche realized that it is important to bear in mind the circumstances in which Socrates conducted his discussions. Most of the paradoxical views that can be attributed to Socrates are based on things which he said to someone, or which he agreed to, for a distinctive purpose and in a distinctive context. He sought to teach – while denying that he taught at all – by teasing, cajoling and provoking. He tried to uncover the truth about things by playfully trying out various ideas on his hearers. And intellectual pranks were no small part of it. 'This was Socrates' Muse,' wrote Galen, a doctor and philosopher of the second century AD: 'to mingle seriousness with a portion of lightheartedness.'

One cannot excuse all the implausibilities in his views by saying that he did not really mean them. This might salvage an appearance of mundane common sense for

Socrates, but only at the cost of discarding almost everything he said. One can, though, often interpret Socrates better by bearing his unusual educational project in mind. I shall now piece together the theory of human life that lies behind Socrates' apparently naive and implausible pronouncements. What emerges is a set of ideas that have proved to be, at the very least, extremely fruitful, not only in edifying some of his immediate hearers but also in stimulating a great deal of subsequent moral philosophy.

Socrates' theory starts and ends with the soul; in the *Apology*, he says that the most important thing in life is to look to its welfare. The soul, he says elsewhere, is that which is 'mutilated by wrong actions and benefited by right ones'. He does not mean the actions of others, but those of oneself. To do good is to benefit one's own soul and to do wrong is to harm it. Since the soul's welfare is paramount, no other sort of harm is so important. Nothing that other people can do to you can harm you enough to cancel out the benefit you bestow on yourself by acting rightly. It follows that bad people ultimately harm only themselves: 'Nothing can harm a good man either in life or after death.'

Socrates therefore has no fear of the court which is trying him. He will not stoop to dishonourable behaviour in order to win acquittal, for 'the difficulty is not so much to escape death; the real difficulty is to escape from doing wrong, which is far more fleet of foot'. One reason why it is hard to stop evil catching up with you is that if someone tries to do you wrong, it is often tempting to try to get your own back on them. But since it is always wrong to do evil – which would harm your soul whatever your excuse for doing it might be – Socrates points out that one must never return evil for evil. In other words, one must turn the other cheek.

This conflicts with old Greek moral conventions, according to which it is acceptable to harm one's enemies, though not one's friends and especially not one's family. The rigorous ethics of Socrates removes such distinctions between people and enjoins a universal morality instead. One striking thing about it is that it does so by appealing to self-interest, not to the sort of altruistic feelings that are usually thought of as the main motive for moral behaviour. Doing good is a matter of looking after the part of yourself which matters most, namely your soul. This is not like ordinary selfishness, though, because the only way to achieve this sort of benefit for yourself is by acting justly and practising the other virtues too. It cannot be gained by greedily putting your own interests above those of other people, but only by putting moral self-improvement above any other motive. Neither does this unusual ethics rest on any hope of heavenly reward or fear of its opposite. The benefits of virtue are reaped more or less immediately, for 'to live well means the same thing as to live honourably' and 'the just [man] is happy and the unjust miserable'. In Socrates' view, happiness and virtue are linked, which is why it is in people's own interests to be moral.

This is particularly hard to swallow. For one unfair fact of life is that the wicked do sometimes seem to prosper, which rather darkens Socrates' sunny landscape. But to Socrates' mind, the successful care of the soul brings all sorts of good things that may not immediately be apparent. He argues that there are unexpected connections between some of the good things in life, and that happiness turns out to be a more complicated matter than one might at first think. It might seem that wicked people can enjoy all sorts of pleasures, but in fact there are some that they cannot enjoy, and these are important enough to cast doubt on the idea that such people can truly be said to be happy at all. Intellectual pleasures allegedly come into this class, and there are all sorts of other satisfactions which cannot be obtained without the exercise of the virtues. To take a simple example: unless you practice the virtue of moderation, you will not enjoy good health, and will probably deprive yourself of many future pleasures for the sake of a few present ones. So without exercising the virtues a man cannot be all that happy after all.

It turns out that among the aspects of the good life which are subtly and surprisingly linked are the virtues themselves. Socrates argues that they come as a package-deal or not at all. His arguments typically proceed by trying to show that some particular virtue cannot work properly unless another is present as well. Courage, for instance, requires wisdom. It is no good being daring if you are foolish, for such would-be courage will degenerate into mere rashness. And all the other virtues are intertwined in similar ways. One of them, namely the virtue of wisdom, plays a special part. For without some degree of wisdom, people will be too bad at seeing the consequences of actions to be able to tell what is right and what is wrong, which is the fundamental prerequisite for virtuous living. Without wisdom they will be unable to be truly happy either, because every benefit that has the potential to make one happy also has the potential to be misused and thus to do the opposite. One therefore needs wisdom both to reap the benefits of good things and to be virtuous.

For Socrates, the connection between virtue and wisdom was so close that he seems in some sense to have identified the two. They certainly seemed to run into one another. According to Socrates, if someone has any of the other virtues, he must have wisdom as well – because otherwise he would not have managed to be virtuous. And if he has wisdom, he must have all of the virtues – because, being wise, he will realize that he cannot be happy without practising all the other virtues too. As we have seen, Socrates thought that moral behaviour benefits the soul and that a person who acts wickedly is doing himself a spiritual mischief. If this is true, then anyone who is genuinely wise will realize this fact. Anyone who realizes it – and who values his own soul, as any wise person surely must – will therefore try to avoid doing wrong. This train of thought explains why Socrates held that nobody does evil knowingly, for if someone does wrong, the only plausible explanation for his doing so is that he does not realize that his actions will harm his soul. He is, in effect, acting out of ignorance. All in all, these sorts of considerations supported Socrates' idea that if his discussions helped people towards wisdom, he would thereby be helping them towards virtue too.

In one of Plato's dialogues, Socrates encapsulates much of his theory in the course of summing up a discussion with Callicles, a young aristocrat who was about to enter public life:

So there is every necessity, Callicles, that the sound-

minded and temperate man, being, as we have demonstrated, just and brave and pious, must be completely
good, and the good man must do well and finely
whatever he does, and he who does well must be happy
and blessed, while the evil man who does ill must be
wretched.

Did Socrates really manage to demonstrate all of that? His
hearers frequently shied at the logical jumps he effortlessly
made himself. So much seemed questionable, particularly
what he said about happiness. Aristotle was typically
forthright in his objections on this point: 'Those who say
that the victim on the rack or the man who falls into great
misfortunes is happy if he is good, are, whether they mean
to or not, talking nonsense.' At one point one of Socrates'
hearers understandably remarked, in no doubt baffled
tones, that 'if you are serious and what you say is true, then
surely the life of us mortals must be turned upside down'.

That is precisely what Socrates aimed to do: to reshape
people's moral ideas. Clearly this was not going to be easy.
In order to succeed in doing it by debate, the discussions
would have to be rather different from purely theoretical
ones, for 'it is no ordinary matter that we are discussing, but
how we ought to live'. A degree of exaggereration and
simplification would sometimes be needed if the ethical
point at hand was to be made forcefully. For example,
when Socrates said that nothing can harm a good man, he
did not mean to deny that various undesirable things can
happen to the virtuous. He was trying to persuade his
hearers to regard such misfortunes as less important than
the misfortune of spoiling your own soul. When he said

that the evil man is wretched, he did not mean that such a man could not occasionally enjoy a good night out. He was exhorting his hearers to appreciate the satisfactions of virtue, in the broadest sense of virtue, and perhaps to pity the man who could not enjoy them. And when he said that goodness brings wealth and every other blessing, he did not mean that if you behave yourself, you will get rich quick. In this context – in which he was more concerned to deny that wealth will automatically bring goodness than to persuade anyone of exactly the reverse – he was holding up a picture of the best sort of human life, in which all good things are pursued and enjoyed to the full, thanks to the exercise of practical wisdom and the other virtues.

This is indeed no ordinary set of dogmas; in fact, they are not dogmas at all. What I have called Socrates' theory of human life is not something which he explicitly expounded as such. These ideas are the ones on which he depended in his questioning of others, or which had apparently withstood trial by dialectical ordeal. The final goal, which perhaps would never be reached, was to achieve a sort of expert knowledge like the expert knowledge of skilled craftsmen, though not about shoemaking or metalwork but about the ultimate craft of living well.

What Socrates came out with in discussions should often be seen as nothing more definite than faltering steps on this road to expert moral knowledge. Sometimes the road twisted as he coaxed and prodded with irony, or tossed in an argument that seemed likely to propel his fellow-travellers in an interesting direction (or at least to make them stop and think). The result, as Nietzsche said, was wisdom full of pranks. And because it was a specifically moral sort of wisdom or knowledge that Socrates was trying to arrive at, his arguments are tinged with exhortation, idealism and appeals to the moral sentiments as well as to logic and common sense. That is why, considered in the abstract and as attempts at pure logic, they seem to have many implausible gaps of the sort Aristotle noticed.

Socrates does not just paint an inspiring picture of the ideal life. His style of talk makes an intimate marriage between exhortation and logic, which is why it stands as a contribution to argumentative philosophy rather than to preaching. Everything he says is presented in the context of an argument: reasons are demanded, inferences are examined, definitions are refined, consequences are deduced, hypotheses are rejected. This is the only approach serious enough to do justice to the matter of how one should live. Responsible exhortation must, for Socrates, be embedded in reasoned argument. A bare summary of his provisional conclusions, such as I have given here, cannot convey the strength of this marriage of idealism and down-to-earth logic. Such a summary inevitably reduces his thoughts to a shoal of beached propositions gasping out of their element. His thoughts flourished in the swim of discussion, and can be seen alive nowadays only in the setting of Plato's early dialogues.

Socrates was not an easy guru to follow, not least because a guru was one thing that he resolutely refused to be. Still, it is hardly surprising that after his death several of his friends wanted to carry on the good work somehow. Since it was, and is, no simple matter to say exactly what the good work amounted to, it should be equally unsurprising that these would-be successors of Socrates ended up championing very different causes. The greatest of his heirs was Plato. The rest were a mixed bunch. But three of them seem to have had a significant influence in one way or another.

Two of the men who were with Socrates when he died – Antisthenes of Athens, and Euclides of nearby Megara – went on to become founders or father figures of schools of thought whose traces could still be seen hundreds of years later. The school founded by a third companion of Socrates, Aristippus of Cyrene in Libya (*c.*435–*c.*355 BC), has not lived on in the same way, which was no great loss. What Aristippus and his followers made of the teachings of Socrates is of interest mainly as an instance of how easily Socrates' followers could exaggerate and twist what they had learned.

The Cyrenaics who followed Aristippus were devoted to pleasure, but in a curiously philosophical way. Impressed by the rational self-control of Socrates, Aristippus turned his own self-discipline to the single-minded pursuit of gratification. While Socrates saw no reason not to enjoy the good things in life – provided, of course, that this did not interfere with his search for virtue – Aristippus saw little reason to do anything else. After Socrates died, Aristippus became a sort of licensed court jester to Dionysius I, the tyrannical ruler of Syracuse in Sicily, who is reputed to have died in a drinking bout to celebrate winning the prize in a drama contest.

The basis of Aristippus' pursuit of enjoyment, riotous or otherwise, was apparently sincere and partly Socratic. Like most moralists, Socrates held that one must beware of becoming a slave to one's desires. Aristippus agreed. But his rather novel interpretation of this was to exert authority over his desires by getting them to work overtime for him. This made him happy; and what, after all, could be wrong with happiness? Had not Socrates dangled the promise of happiness as an incentive to virtue? There could not be much wrong with it, then.

Socrates had a somewhat highfaluting conception of happiness as a state of spiritual satisfaction obtained by noble living. Here Aristippus begged to differ. According to him, the form of happiness one should aim for was one's own physical pleasure. He regarded such pleasure as the only workable criterion of what is good and bad generally. He apparently held that it is impossible to have certain knowledge of anything but one's own sensations, a philosophical idea that had several defenders at the time. So pleasurable sensations, which were undoubtedly a good thing in some sense even if nothing else was, may have seemed the logical thing for a philosopher to concentrate on in an uncertain world.

The pursuit of pleasure was thus a serious business. The philosopher's job was to engineer his desires and his circumstances in such a way as to maximize his pleasurable sensations, and to preach the wisdom of this way of life to others (who naturally ought to pay for such valuable advice). It took the self-discipline of a Socrates to do this difficult job properly, or so Aristippus seems to have thought, and it was important not to be distracted by other pursuits that might divert one from the only practical and intelligible quest in life, namely pleasure. Mathematics and science, for example, were no help and so should be ignored. Here once more the example of Socrates could be invoked, after a fashion, for did he not relentlessly pursue the matter of how to live, at the expense of all other questions?

Socrates would have enjoyed showing Aristippus and other Cyrenaics where they had gone wrong. He would have wanted to know, for instance, what had happened to justice and the other virtues he had championed. He would also have rejected the ideas of the Cynics, though they were much more interesting. Like the Cyrenaics, Antisthenes (c.445–c.360 BC) and the later Cynics hijacked some of what they had got from Socrates and blew it out of proportion. 'A Socrates gone mad' is how Plato is supposed to have described the Cynic Diogenes, a follower of Antisthenes. But the Cynics still managed to keep more of their Socratic inheritance than did Aristippus, and indeed their main doctrine was the exact opposite of Cyrenaic indulgence.

Like Aristippus, Antisthenes thought that a Socratic strength of mind was needed for the pursuit of happiness. There the similarity with Aristippus ended. Antisthenes held that happiness was to be found not in satisfying desires, as the Cyrenaics maintained, but in losing them. He was impressed by Socrates' indifference to wealth and comfort, and turned this into an ascetic philosophy that positively embraced poverty. Socrates, after all, had said that nothing could harm a good man. Antisthenes drew the conclusion that so long as one was good, nothing else in life mattered at all. This certainly goes beyond Socrates, who never denied that wealth or possessions were, in their proper place, a better thing to have than to lack. His apparent indifference to them was largely a by-product of the demanding search for virtue and a healthy soul, not to mention mere absent-mindedness.

While Socrates was quite prepared to ignore ordinary ways and values when his principles demanded it, Antisthenes appeared to pursue unconventionality for its own sake. If something was neither virtuous nor wicked, then it did not make the slightest difference whether one did it or not. As can be imagined, this was a powerful recipe for eccentricity. Freed of the desire for possessions, and liberated from conventional behaviour, the wise man could wander around declaiming against society's foolish ways and generally making a spectacle of himself. He would console himself with the knowledge that conventional values are worthless and quite different from the natural values of the genuinely good life. Unfortunately, it was never made clear what natural values and true virtue actually involved. Antisthenes was much better at loudly saying what they were not.

Diogenes of Sinope, on the Black Sea (c.400–c.325 BC) came to Athens and was taken by the ideas of Antisthenes. But he thought that Antisthenes had failed to live up to his own teachings, which would not have been surprising. Diogenes made up for this magnificently, especially in eccentricity and unconventional living. One of the best-known tales about early philosophers says that Diogenes lived in an earthenware tub; another says that he set a fashion among the Cynics for public masturbation. True or not, the scores of stories about his wacky words and deeds show what a disconcerting impression he made. He revelled in the nickname of 'the dog' (kyon), which is how the Cynics, or 'dog-men', got their name. It was given to him because he sought the uncomplicated, instinctive and shameless life of an animal – animals being the true exponents of 'natural' values. He had a sharp tongue and was quick to savage those he disagreed with, which may also have contributed to his nickname. He was particularly hostile to Plato and liked to play practical jokes on him. He apparently turned up at one of Plato's lectures brandishing a plucked chicken in order to heckle him contemptuously on a point of definition – a low-life echo of Socrates' 'wisdom full of pranks'.

Diogenes' disturbing renunciation of conventional life evidently did not go so far as to make a hermit of this 'Socrates gone mad'. Life was too busy for that. There were people to be persuaded, examples to be set, there was preaching to be done and practical advice to be given. His activities seem to have made him quite popular. When his tub was destroyed, the citizens of Athens are said to have clubbed together and bought him a new one. His sincerity and the simplicity of his life seem to have been respectfully admired from a safe distance, although his teachings were far too radical to attract more than a small number of committed followers or to have any direct political effect. He taught that happiness consisted in satisfying only the most basic needs and in disciplining oneself not to want any more. Everything else was to be renounced – riches, comfort, ordinary family life – because none of it made one a morally better person. All the restrictive trappings of civilization in the city-state, from taboos against incest or eating human flesh to the institution of marriage, social-class barriers and traditional religion, were to be overcome for the same reason. The ideal society would be a loose community of spartan, self-sufficient, rational beings who indulged in any and every form of relationship to which all parties consented, unbound by conventional prohibitions.

Much of what Diogenes said was meant to shock; he probably did not make a regular habit of breaking all the taboos he condemned. But he did want to jolt people into examining their lives. Over the years, and especially in the first two centuries of the Christian era, Cynicism attracted all sorts of wandering hippies and free-loving, back-packing beggars, who were keener on general denunciation and on ridiculing society than on philosophy or doing good. Such people, and the satirical and sarcastic literature that was influenced by the movement, gave rise to the modern meaning of 'cynical'. But the earliest Cynics, Bohemian though they were, earnestly saw themselves as moral teachers and seem to have performed a useful service. Crates of Thebes (c.365–c.285 BC), for example, gave away his sizeable fortune to become a pupil of Diogenes. He apparently made house calls as a sort of therapist or pastor, offering a service of moral guidance that was not available to ordinary people from any other source – certainly not from the formal schools of philosophical research set up by Plato and Aristotle. Hipparchia, the sister of a pupil of Crates, was desperate to join Crates in his unconventional life, but had to threaten her well-off parents with suicide before they would let her go. They eventually consented, and she 'travelled around with her husband and had intercourse publicly and went out to dinners'.

Euclides, the last of the followers of Socrates to be considered here, was so devoted to the master that when

Athens banned the citizens of Megara from entering the city, he is said to have dressed up in women's clothes and slunk in under cover of darkness to be with him. Euclides shared not only Socrates' interest in the nature of moral goodness but also his passion for argument. While Socrates often seemed prepared to follow a promising line of reasoning wherever it led to, Euclides was interested in logical arguments for their own sake, especially paradoxical ones. One opponent spoke of 'wrangling Euclides, who inspired the Megarians with a frenzied love of controversy'.

Frenzied or not, the intellectual curiosity of the Megarians led them to come up with some of the most enduring riddles about logic and language. Eubulides, a pupil of Euclides, is credited with several, including the most famous one, commonly known as the Liar. This is the paradox presented by someone who says, 'This statement is false.' The problem is what to say about such a statement; arguments about its truth tend to go round in a dizzying circle. For example, if it is false, then the speaker spoke truly because that is what he said it was. On the other hand, if he spoke truly, then it must be false because what he said is that it was false. Thus if it is false, it follows that it is true; and if it is true, it follows that it is false. This riddle is easier to make fun of than it is to solve. It has a remarkable ability to bounce back in the face of any proposed solution. One can sympathize with the poet Philetas of Cos, who is said to have worried about it so much that he wasted away, becoming so thin that he had to put lead weights in his shoes to stop himself blowing over. The epitaph on his gravestone read:

O Stranger: Philetas of Cos am I,
'Twas the Liar who made me die,
And the bad nights caused thereby.

It may be hard to see the puzzle itself as profound, but attempts to get to the bottom of it certainly have been. The Liar has stimulated a great deal of work on the nature of truth and linguistic meaning, by mathematical logicians and by linguists who look at the formal structure of languages. It seems, however, to have caused no further casualties. One eventual by-product of an interest in the sort of 'self-reference' involved in the paradox – the paradoxical statement is curiously about itself – was Gödel's Theorem, one of the most significant results of modern mathematics, which shows that there are certain limits to mathematical proof.

The pupils and successors of Euclides turned Megara into a real-life version of the farcically exaggerated 'logic factory' portrayed in Aristophanes' play about Socrates. The fact that to some sceptics their work seemed like mere 'wrangling' and controversy for its own sake, which no doubt some of it was, recalls the reception that Socrates' incessant arguments about virtue got from some of the less intellectual citizens of Athens. One reason why Euclides would have felt it was his task as a philosopher both to hold forth about moral goodness and to get involved in abstruse logical questions was his admiration for Socrates' view that knowledge is the path to virtue. Socrates may not himself have discussed logic, but Euclides probably felt that doing so was one way to continue the search for wisdom. In particular, if one understood the process of argument, then this would presumably help one to carry on the good work of Socratic examination.

All these schools of philosophy that flowed from Socrates shared his idea that wisdom brings virtue and virtue brings happiness. They evidently differed over what they took happiness to involve – indulgent pleasure in the case of the Cyrenaics, ascetic discipline in the case of the Cynics. But they agreed that philosophical reflection of some sort was the way to find it, and that such an occupation amounted to the good life. The ethical views of these philosophers were all rather individualistic (to an extreme, in the case of Diogenes) and one can see how the unusual example of Socrates' life could have led to this. But in the case of the Cynics, at least, there was a clear break with Socrates over the ties of social obligation and about loyalty to the values of the city-state. The Cynics stressed a contrast between the life of virtue and the life enjoined by the city in which one happens to be born or live. In one sense Socrates did this too, but in another sense he did not. He certainly would have accepted that the individual must follow his own conscience, not the city's dictates when those dictates are unjust. But he sought to better the life of the city, not to relinquish it altogether. He urged the Athenians to live justly together and to improve their laws and behaviour where necessary, not to abandon the whole enterprise of civilization and lose respect for the law.

Socrates made it clear that although you must disobey the laws if they are unjust, you must nevertheless submit to punishment if caught, which is exactly what he himself did when he was condemned. Some friends gave him the chance to escape prison and flee Athens before execution; one of Plato's early dialogues, the *Crito*, deals with this episode and gives Socrates' reasons for rejecting the offer. As well as feeling a moral obligation to the legitimate authority of the city and the due process of law, Socrates loved Athens and did not relish life anywhere else. Some of the things he is made to say in Plato's dialogues suggest that he had misgivings about democracy as a form of government; this has led to him being sometimes described as anti-democratic. But it was really Plato who had those misgivings, as he did eventually about all the forms of government he came across. Socrates himself showed every sign of deep loyalty to the constitution of Athens. He often praised the city and its institutions, and seems never to have left it except on its military service. On the question of whether he approved its type of democracy, Socrates voted with his feet – or rather, showed his preference by failing to do so. There were many other states with non-democratic governments to which he could have emigrated. Perhaps most embarrassingly for those of his opponents in his own time who would have liked to cast him as an enemy of democracy, it was well known that he had risked death under the anti-democratic Tyrants by refusing to take part in the arrest of an innocent man.

Socrates was, if anything, too democratic for the Athenians. It was this aspect of his character and teaching which led to the exaggerated individualism of some of his imitators. His attitude to religion and morality can be seen as ultra-democratic. Nothing is to be taken for granted, especially not if it is handed down by an authority which puts itself above the moral reasoning of the people, be that putative authority in the form of Zeus or of a human tyrant. Every man must work out for himself what is good and right, and nobody can escape the obligation of examining himself and his life. The result of such discussions between citizens should ideally be a just society with just laws, arrived at through such collective self-examination. In the Socratic dream of democracy, individual conviction would lead to collective agreement – not about everything, presumably, but at least about the outlines of how to live.

Socrates was no politician. He felt he could play his part only by debating with individuals, one by one or in small groups: 'I know how to produce one witness to the truth of what I say, the man with whom I am debating, but the others I ignore. I know how to secure one man's vote, but with the many I will not even enter into discussion.'

Over the years, the votes for Socrates have steadily accumulated as Plato's dialogues have carried his debating, or a semblance of it, far beyond fifth-century Athens and its dinner parties. There are now at any rate few who would disagree with one thing that Socrates told his judges: 'If you put me to death, you will not easily find anyone to take my place.'

SOURCES

Abbreviations used in these notes:

CDP *The Collected Dialogues of Plato*, E. Hamilton and H.
     Cairns (eds) (Princeton University Press, 1961)
CWA *The Collected Works of Aristotle*, J. Barnes (ed.) (Princeton
     University Press, 1984)
LCL Loeb Classical Library
LOP *Lives of the Philosophers*, Diogenes Laertius, translated by
     R. D. Hicks (Harvard University Press, 1972)

p. 3 You are mistaken ... Plato, *Apology*, 28b (CDP, p. 14)

p. 3–4 started wrestling ... Plato, *Symposium*, 220c (CDP,
        p. 571)

p. 4 fell into a fit ... ibid., 174d, 175b (CDP, pp. 529–30)

p. 4 I have never lived ... Plato, *Apology*, 36b (CDP, p. 21)

p. 5 anyone who is close ... Plato, *Laches*, 187e (CDP, p. 131)

p. 5 Marsyas: Plato, *Symposium*, 215b (CDP, p. 566)

p. 5–6 speaking for myself ... ibid., 215d (CDP, p. 567)

p. 6 I've been bitten ... ibid., 218a (CDP, p. 569)

p. 7–8 The first step, then ... Xenophon, *The Banquet*, V
        (transl. adapted from E. C. Marchant and O. J. Todd,
        Xenophon, LCL edn, 1923, Vol. 4, p. 599)

p. 14 After puzzling about it ... Plato, *Apology*, 21b (CDP, p. 7)

p. 14 I reflected as I walked away ... ibid., 21d (CDP, p. 7)

p. 14–15 whenever I succeed ... ibid., 23a (CDP, p. 9)

p. 15 the arguments never ... Plato, *Theaetetus*, 161a (CDP, p. 866)

p. 15–16 If I say that this ... Plato, *Apology*, 37e (CDP, p. 23)

p. 16 it has always been ... Plato, *Crito*, 46b (CDP, p. 31)

p. 16 in obedience to God's commands ... Plato, *Apology*, 33c (CDP, p. 19)

p. 17 I want you to think ... ibid., 22a (CDP, p. 8)

p. 17 when it comes ... ibid., 31d (CDP, p. 17)

p. 18 I spend all my time ... ibid., 30a (CDP, p. 16)

p. 18 ashamed that you give ... ibid., 29e (CDP, p. 16)

p. 18 these people give you ... ibid., 36e (CDP, p. 22)

p. 19 Apollodorus: Xenophon, *Socrates' Defence*, 28

p. 19 to be afraid of death ... Plato, *Apology*, 29a (CDP, p. 15)

p. 19 heroes of the old days, ibid., 41b (CDP, p. 25)

p. 20 the work of ... Plato, *2nd Letter*, 314c (CDP, p. 1,567)

p. 21 All his private conduct ... Xenophon, *Memoirs of Socrates*, IV (transl. E. C. Marchant, LCL edn, p. 309)

p. 21 old prig ... Jonathan Barnes, *The Presocratic Philosophers* (Routledge, 1982), p.448

p. 22 modern scholars: particularly Gregory Vlastos, *Socrates: Ironist and Moral Philosopher* (Cambridge, 1991); *Socratic Studies* (Cambridge, 1994)

p. 23 purified, (etc.): Plato, *Phaedo*, 67c–d (CDP, p. 50)

p. 25 mathematics has come to be ... Aristotle, *Metaphysics*, 992a32 (CWA, p. 1568)

p.26 our birth is but a sleep ... Wordsworth, *Intimations of Immortality* V, (1807)

p.27 we have helped him ... Plato, *Meno*, 84b (CDP, p. 368)

p. 28 At present these opinions ... ibid., 85c (CDP, p. 370)

p. 28 I shall question him ... Plato, *Apology*, 29e (CDP, p. 16)

p. 29 sometimes, however ... Plato, *Lesser Hippias*, 372d (CDP, p. 209)

p. 29 I am full of defects ... ibid., 372b (CDP, p. 209)

p. 30 an accurate knowledge ... Plato, *Euthyphro*, 5a (CDP, p. 172)

p. 31 is what is holy ... ibid., 10a (CDP, p. 178)

p. 32 Those who believe that God ... Leibniz, *Theodicy* (1710), 176 (transl. E. M. Huggard, Open Court, 1985, p. 236)

p. 33 We must not limit our enquiry ... Aristotle, *Magna Moralia*, 1182a4 (CWA, p. 1868)

p. 33 he thought all the virtues ... ibid., 1216b2 (adapted from CWA, p. 1925)

p. 34 he is doing away with ... ibid., 1182a21 (CWA, p. 1868)

p. 34 No one, he said, acts ... Aristotle, *Nicomachean Ethics*, 1145b27 (CWA, p. 1810)

p. 35 in the strength of his character ... K. Joel, in W. K. C. Guthrie, *Socrates* (Cambridge, 1971), p. 138

p. 36 Milton: *Paradise Lost*, IV. 110

p. 36 no one would choose evil ... Aristotle, *Magna Moralia*, 1200b26 (CWA, p. 1900)

p. 36 divine naiveté ... Nietzsche, *The Birth of Tragedy* (1872), 13 (transl. W. Kaufmann, Random House, 1967, p. 88)

p. 36 wisdom full of pranks: Nietzsche, *Der Wanderer und sein Schatten* (1880), 86

p. 36 This was Socrates' ... Galen, *On the Use of the Parts of the Body*, I.9

p. 37 mutilated by ... Plato, *Crito*, 47e (CDP, p. 33)

p. 37 nothing can harm ... Plato, *Apology*, 41d (CDP, p. 25)

p. 37 the difficulty is not ... ibid., 39b (CDP, p.24)

p. 38 to live well means ... Plato, *Crito*, 48b (CDP, p. 33)

p. 38 the just is happy ... Plato, *Republic*, 354a (CDP, p. 604)

p.40 –41 So there is every ... Plato, *Gorgias*, 507b (CDP, p. 289)

p. 41 Those who say that the victim ... Aristotle, *Nicomachean Ethics*, 1153b19 (CWA, p. 1823)

p. 41 if you are serious ... Plato, *Gorgias*, 481c (CDP, p. 265)

p. 41 it is no ordinary matter ... Plato, *Republic*, 352d

p. 46 A Socrates gone mad: Diogenes Laertius, *Lives of the Philosophers*, VI.54 (LOP, Vol. 2, p. 55)

p. 49 travelled around with her husband ... *Lives of the Philosophers*, VI.96 (as transl. J. M. Rist in *Stoic Philosophy*, Cambridge, 1969, p. 61)

p. 50 wrangling Euclides ... Timon of Phlius, in Diogenes Laertius, op. cit., II.107 (LOP, Vol.1, p. 237)

p. 51 O Stranger ... Athenaeus, *Deipnosophistai*, IX.410E (transl. St George Stock in *Stoicism*, London, 1908, p. 36)

p. 51 Gödel's Theorem: see *Gödel's Proof*, E. Nagel and J. R. Newman (London, 1959)

p. 54 I know how to produce ... Plato, *Gorgias*, 474a (CDP, p. 256)

p. 54 If you put me to death ... Plato, *Apology*, 30e (CDP, p. 16)

OXFORD MEDICAL PUBLICATIONS

Oxford Specialist Handbook of
Old Age Psychiatry

Oxford Specialist handbooks published and forthcoming

General Oxford Specialist Handbooks
A Resuscitation Room Guide
Addiction Medicine
Perioperative Medicine, second edition
Post-Operative Complications, second edition

Oxford Specialist Handbooks in Anaesthesia
Cardiac Anaesthesia
Neuroanaesthesia
Obstetric Anaesthesia
Paediatric Anaesthesia

Oxford Specialist Handbooks in Cardiology
Adult Congenital Heart Disease
Cardiac Catheterization and Coronary Intervention
Echocardiography
Fetal Cardiology
Heart Failure
Hypertension
Nuclear Cardiology
Pacemakers and ICDs

Oxford Specialist Handbooks in End of Life Care
End of Life Care in Nephrology
End of Life in the Intensive Care Unit

Oxford Specialist Handbooks in Neurology
Epilepsy
Parkinson's Disease and Other Movement Disorders
Stroke Medicine

Oxford Specialist Handbooks in Paediatrics
Paediatric Endocrinology and Diabetes
Paediatric Dermatology
Paediatric Gastroenterology, Hepatology, and Nutrition
Paediatric Haematology and Oncology
Paediatric Nephrology
Paediatric Neurology
Paediatric Radiology
Paediatric Respiratory Medicine

Oxford Specialist Handbooks in Psychiatry
Child and Adolescent Psychiatry
Old Age Psychiatry

Oxford Specialist Handbooks in Radiology
Interventional Radiology
Musculoskeletal Imaging

Oxford Specialist Handbooks in Surgery
Cardiothoracic Surgery
Hand Surgery
Hepato-pancreatobiliary Surgery
Oral Maxillo Facial Surgery
Neurosurgery
Operative Surgery, second edition
Otolaryngology and Head and Neck Surgery
Plastic and Reconstructive Surgery
Surgical Oncology
Urological Surgery
Vascular Surgery

Oxford Specialist Handbook of
Old Age Psychiatry

Dr Bart Sheehan

Associate Clinical Professor in Old Age Psychiatry
University of Warwick
Coventry, UK

Dr Salman Karim

Consultant/Honorary Lecturer in Old Age Psychiatry
Greater Manchester West Mental Health Foundation Trust/
University of Manchester, UK

Professor Alistair Burns

South Manchester University Hospitals NHS Trust
Wythenshaw, UK

OXFORD
UNIVERSITY PRESS

OXFORD
UNIVERSITY PRESS

Great Clarendon Street, Oxford OX2 6DP

Oxford University Press is a department of the University of Oxford.
It furthers the University's objective of excellence in research, scholarship,
and education by publishing worldwide in

Oxford New York

Auckland Cape Town Dar es Salaam Hong Kong Karachi
Kuala Lumpur Madrid Melbourne Mexico City Nairobi
New Delhi Shanghai Taipei Toronto

With offices in

Argentina Austria Brazil Chile Czech Republic France Greece
Guatemala Hungary Italy Japan Poland Portugal Singapore
South Korea Switzerland Thailand Turkey Ukraine Vietnam

Oxford is a registered trade mark of Oxford University Press
in the UK and in certain other countries

Published in the United States
by Oxford University Press Inc., New York

British Library Cataloguing in Publication Data
Data available

Library of Congress Cataloging in Publication Data
Oxford handbook of emergencies in clinical surgery

Typeset by Cepha Imaging Private Ltd., Bangalore, India
Printed in Italy
on acid-free paper by Legoprint S.p.A
Asia Pacific offset

ISBN 978–0–19–921652–9

10 9 8 7 6 5 4 3 2 1

Foreword

The publication of the Oxford Specialist Handbook of Old Age Psychiatry offers an opportunity to reflect on the history of the field, the advances to which many contributed and the challenges that still stand in front of us.

One can justifiably claim that modern Old Age Psychiatry was born in the United Kingdom in the 1950s. Following the Hippocratic school tradition, pioneer British investigators identified the major psychiatric syndromes of late life after astute clinical observations. Martin Roth, Raymond Levy, John Copeland, Elaine Murphy, Robin Jacoby, Felix Post and many others relied on studies of the clinical presentation and course of illness to distinguish depression from dementia, delirium, and psychotic disorders of late life. They identified their comorbid conditions, and began to form meaningful theories on their pathogenesis and etiology.

There has been an explosion of progress since that time. Molecular mechanisms of brain cell degeneration and degradation have been identified. Apoptosis, while it prevents carcinogenesis by eliminating cells with damaged DNA, it was shown to be the cause of programmed cell suicide in the central nervous system. The discovery that reactive oxygen species promote apoptosis has led to treatment trials of antioxidants with some success.

In Alzheimer's disease, genetic advances and recombinant DNA studies identified some of its pathological mechanisms and cleared the way for drug discovery. Several genes predisposing to Alzheimer's disease are now known and the common pathway leading to the formation of amyloid and tau protein has been identified. Knock-in technology enabled the development of animal models for Alzheimer's disease that can serve in developing drugs aimed at specific molecular targets.

In late-life depression, attention to comorbid cognitive abnormalities began to clarify its pathogenetic mechanisms. Executive dysfunction is common in depression of old adults. Depressed elders with executive dysfunction have a clinical presentation resembling medial frontal lobe syndrome, poor or slow short-term response to antidepressants, and chronic or relapsing long-term course. These observations initiated imaging studies that began to clarify the structural and functional neuroanatomy of geriatric depression and provided the theoretical background for targeted treatment studies.

Scientific progress in Psychiatry of Old Age has attracted the "best and the brightest" students of the human mind and the most devoted clinicians and advocates. More than 400 specialists posts exits in the United Kingdom and more than 3000 Board certified geriatric psychiatrists exist in the United States. Many clinical and research training programs have been created in the English speaking world and elsewhere. Moreover, training in psychiatry of old age is a required as part of the general psychiatry specialty training in most countries.

Despite the excitement and scientific progress, major challenges are in front of us. There are problems in the scientific, the clinical, and the manpower domain.

Despite major strides in understanding the pathogenesis of the major psychiatric syndromes of late life, the available treatments help only a fraction of patients. In Alzheimer's disease, although we have more drugs, our patients derive only limited benefits. This view is dramatized by the National Institute of Health and Clinical Excellence (NICE) report, which suggests that use of anti-Alzheimer's drugs in mild and severe dementia is not cost effective. A number of approaches to slowing progression of Alzheimer's disease have failed either because of intolerance or because of increased risk of complications. These include vaccination, vitamin E, estrogens, and non-steroidal anti-inflammatory agents.

The new antipsychotic drugs are moderately effective in agitated demented patients with psychotic symptoms. However, they increase mortality and cerebrovascular accidents. Although these effects are weak, they limit the available clinical options and may increase institutionalization.

Many antidepressant drugs have been developed. The main advantage of the new antidepressants is their safety and tolerability. While new antidepressants are tolerated by many elderly patients, their efficacy is comparable to that of classical antidepressants. A well designed study of old-old depressed patients showed no advantage of a serotonin reuptake inhibitor over placebo, except in cases with severe depression.

The demographic imperative of the rapidly aging population demands more efficacious and safe treatments but also a functional system of care delivery. Primary care physicians are the main care providers of older adults with psychiatric disorders. The current generation of elders perceives psychiatric illness as stigmatizing. As a consequence they underreport their symptoms, avoid referral to mental health professionals, and resist treatment offered by generalists. The busy pace of the primary care office work imposes a barrier to the treatment of older adults reluctant to accept mental health care. The PROSPECTR Study showed that about 50% of depressed older primary care patients received any antidepressant treatment even when their physicians are informed of their diagnosis.

Despite the enormous needs for care, the Medicare insurance system of the US offers low reimbursement rate to the point that exclusive practice of geriatric psychiatry is unsustainable. Many graduates of American fellowship programs abandon the practice of geriatric psychiatry soon after graduation or accept very few elderly patients.

A barrier to continuous education in psychiatry of old age is the increasing gap between clinical training and the proliferation of new investigative techniques and findings. Few clinicians can read and understand fully papers published in Archives of General Psychiatry and other eminent psychiatric journals. As a consequence, clinicians rely on lower quality publications summarizing new research findings and offering recommendations for care. However, much is lost in the translation.

The Oxford Specialist Handbook of Old Age Psychiatry summarizes the safe and reliable knowledge of our field in a clear and concise way. It outlines the progress made and points out to our challenges. Most importantly, it outlines how to use the accumulated knowledge and wisdom of our field in the service of our patients.

George S. Alexopoulos, M.D.
Professor of Psychiatry
Director
Weill-Cornell Institute of Geriatric Psychiatry
New York

Contents

Preface *ix*
Detailed contents *xi*
Symbols and abbreviations *xvi*

1	Introduction	**1**
2	Dementia	**15**
3	Delirium	**75**
4	Mood disorders	**95**
5	Anxiety and behaviour disorders	**125**
6	Paranoid illness and schizophrenia	**143**
7	Services	**155**
8	Ethical and legal issues	**167**
9	Prescribing issues in older people	**193**

Index *211*

Preface

There is increasing recognition of the mental health needs of older people, among the public, social care staff, in all medical settings, and in all countries. In the UK, the specialty of old age psychiatry is now recognized as a discipline with a distinct career path and specialty status and has several hundred practitioners. It grew out of a need to care for people with chronic organic illnesses but quickly metamorphosed into a specialty looking after all mental health problems among people aged over 65 years.

Age-defined services may come under threat in a time where age discrimination is a hot topic. What will remain, of course, is a need for a holistic and sensitive approach to the care of people with dementia, expertise with comorbid physical and mental health problems, and appreciation of the distinct psychological and psychiatric issues for people reaching and passing the age of retirement.

The authors, all UK old age psychiatrists, have tried to capture the uniqueness of caring for older people and use the successful template of the Oxford Handbook series. We aim to provide a 'way in' to the specialist approach in this area, and we hope to provide a stimulus to further enquiry in this exciting area of practice.

We are grateful to Barbara Dignan and Helen Tomlinson in Manchester for work on drafts of the book.

BS	Coventry
SK, AB	Manchester

Detailed contents

1 Introduction

History of a specialty 2

Overview of mental disorder among older people in
    different settings 3

Tips on assessing older people with psychiatric disorder: 1 4

Tips on assessing older people with psychiatric disorder: 2,
    Physical examination 6

Demographics of ageing 8

Epidemiology of mental disorders in old age 10

Normal ageing 12

2 Dementia

Introduction 16

The manifestation of dementia 17

Diagnosis and differential diagnosis 18

Differential diagnosis of dementia: depression 20

Differential diagnosis of dementia: decline in memory with normal
    ageing 22

Differential diagnosis of dementia: other issues 24

Rarer causes of dementia 25

Signs and symptoms of dementia 26

History 27

Mental state examination in dementia 28

Physical examination and investigation 30

Imaging in dementia 32

Functional imaging in dementia 33

Epidemiology of dementia 34

Alzheimer's disease (AD) 35

Criteria for diagnosis of AD 36

Vascular dementia (VaD) 38

Criteria for diagnosis of VaD 40

Lewy body dementia (DLB) 42

Neuropathology in AD 44

Genetics of AD 46

Neurochemistry 47

Neuropathology in non-Alzheimer dementias 48

Fronto-temporal dementia (FTD) 49

Assessment scales 50

Risk factors for dementia 52

Management of dementia: an overview 54

The cholinergic system and cholinesterase inhibitors (CHEIs) 56

Specific treatments available for AD—the CHEIs 57

Antidementia drug prescribing—the practicalities 59

Memantine for AD 60

Other treatments for AD 61

Cautionary tales in dementia treatment 62

Drug treatment in non-Alzheimer dementias 63

NICE and dementia 64

Management of behavioural and psychological symptoms of dementia
    (BPSD): 1, Approaches 66

Management of BPSD: 2, Medication choice 68

Are antipsychotics dangerous in dementia? 70

Carers of people with dementia 72

3 Delirium

Definition and description 76

Activity levels in delirium 78

Case example of delirium 80

Common causes of delirium 82

Distinguishing delirium from other mental illnesses: 1, Dementia 84

Distinguishing delirium from other mental illnesses: 2, Psychosis 85

Managing the delirious patient in general hospital—principles 86

Management of delirium in a general hospital—key tips 88

Managing the delirious patient in a care home 90

Pharmacological management of delirium 92

Non-pharmacological management of delirium 94

4 Mood disorders

Mood disorders—an overview 96

Diagnosing depression 97

Depression—epidemiology 98

Special presentations of depression in older people: 1,
   Pseudodementia 99

Special presentations of depression in older people: 2,
   Hypochondriasis 100

Special presentations of depression in older people: 3,
   Severe retardation 101

Suicide in older people 102

Managing an older person after an overdose 104

Aetiology of depression in older people: 1, Biological factors 106

Aetiology of depression in older people: 2, Psychological
   and social factors 108

Management of depression among older people—drug
   treatment 109

Drug treatment of depression—alternatives to SSRIs 110

Drug treatment—second line 112

ECT 114

Psychological treatment of depression 115

Managing the recently bereaved 116

Managing depression in frail older people 117

Depression rating scales 118

GDS-15 119

Mania and bipolar illness 120

Managing mania and bipolar illness 121

Drugs for mania 122

5 Anxiety and behaviour disorders

Anxiety presentations 126

The main anxiety disorders 128

Somatoform disorders and somatization 130

Drug treatments for anxiety disorders 132

Non-drug treatment for anxiety disorders 133

Alcohol in older people 134

Alcohol and cognitive impairment 135

Management of alcohol misuse among older people 136

Benzodiazepines 138

Managing insomnia in older people *139*

Sexuality in older age *140*

Squalor/neglect *142*

6 Paranoid illness and schizophrenia

Clinical presentations—background *144*

Clinical presentations—late-onset paranoid illness *146*

Aetiology *147*

Management principles *148*

Antipsychotic prescribing *150*

Graduates *152*

7 Services

Services—overview *156*

Specialist services—young-onset dementia (YOD) *158*

Specialist services—old age liaison psychiatry *160*

Specialist services—day hospitals *161*

Specialist services—memory clinics *162*

Care homes *164*

8 Ethical and legal issues

Elder abuse *168*

Types of abuse *169*

Approach to possible cases of abuse *170*

Crime and older people *171*

Capacity/competence—general principles *172*

Tips for those assessing capacity *174*

Capacity to make a will *176*

Capacity to make health care decisions *178*

Capacity to make social care decisions *180*

Financial capacity *182*

The Mental Capacity Act (2005) *184*

Mental health legislation *186*

Mental Health Act—in-patient issues *187*

Mental Health Act—community issues *188*

End-of-life issues *190*

9 Prescribing issues in older people

Pharmacokinetics *194*

Pharmacodynamics *195*

Polypharmacy *196*

Aggression in the elderly *198*

Assessing aggressive patients *199*

Specific management of aggression *200*

Sleep disorders/insomnia *202*

Prescribing for insomnia *204*

Psychosis in Parkinson's disease *206*

Post-stroke depression *207*

Post-stroke mania *208*

Other post-stroke disorders *209*

Index *211*

Abbreviations

1°	primary
2°	secondary
AA	Alcoholics Anonymous
AB	amyloid beta (or B amyloid)
ABC	antecedent behaviour consequence
ACA	anterior cerebral artery
AD	Alzheimer's disease
ADAS	Alzheimer's disease assessment scale
ADDTC	Alzheimer's Disease Diagnostic and Treatment Centers
ADL	activity of daily living
A&E	accident and emergency
AMT	Abbreviated Mental Test
ApoE	apolipoprotein E
APP	amyloid precursor protein
B-ADL	Bristol Activities of Daily Living Scale
BMI	body mass index
BP	blood pressure
BPSD	behavioural and psychological symptoms of dementia
CAM	Confusion Assessment Method
CAMCOG	Cambridge Cognitive Examination
CBT	cognitive behaviour therapy
CES-D	Centre for Epidemiological Studies Depression Scale
CHEI	cholinesterase inhibitor
CI	confidence interval
CJD	Creutzfeld–Jakob disease
CNS	central nervous system
CPN	community psychiatric nurse
CRP	C-reactive protein
CT	computed tomography
CVA	cerebrovascular accident
CVD	cerebrovascular disease
CVS	cardiovascular system
DLB	dementia with Lewy bodies
DSM	Diagnostic and Statistical Manual
DWML	deep white matter lesion
ECG	electrocardiogram

ECT	electroconvulsive therapy
EEG	electroencephalogram
ESR	erythrocyte sedimentation rate
FBC	full blood count
FTD	fronto-temporal dementia
GAD	generalized anxiety disorder
GDS	Geriatric Depression Scale
GI	gastrointestinal
GP	general practitioner
HDL	high-density lipoprotein
HDRS	Hamilton Depression Rating Scale
HIV	human immunodeficiency virus
HMPAO	hexamethylpropyleneamine oxime
HRT	hormone replacement therapy
5-HT	5-hydroxytryptamine (serotonin)
Hz	hertz
ICD	International Classification of Diseases
IM	intramuscular
IMCA	independent mental capacity advocate
IQ	intelligence quotient
IU	international units
IV	intravenous
LDL	low-density lipoprotein
LFT	liver function test
LPA	lasting power of attorney
MADRS	Montgomery and Asberg Depression Rating Scale
MAOI	monoamine oxidase inhibitor
MCA	Mental Capacity Act
MCI	mild cognitive impairment
mg	milligram
MI	myocardial infarction
mL	millilitre
mmol	millimol
MMSE	Mini Mental State Examination
MRI	magnetic resonance imaging
MSU	mid-stream urine
NFT	neurofibrillary tangle
NHS	National Health Service
NICE	National Institute for Health and Clinical Excellence

NINCDS-ADRDA	National Institute of Neurological and Communicative Disorders and Stroke–Alzheimer's Disease and Related Disorders Association
NINCDS-AIREN	National Institute of Neurological and Communicative Disorders and Stroke–Association International pour la Recherché et l'Enseignement en Neurosciences
NMDA	N-methyl-d-aspartic acid
NPI	Neuropsychiatric Inventory
NSAID	non-steroidal anti-inflammatory drug
OCD	obsessive–compulsive disorder
PCA	posterior cerebral artery
PEG	percutaneous endoscopic gastrostomy
PET	positron emission tomography
PHQ-9	Patient Health Questionnaire–9
POW	prisoner of war
PS	presenilin
PTSD	post-traumatic stress disorder
QALY	quality-adjusted life year
RCT	randomized controlled trial
REM	rapid eye movement
SNRI	serotonin noradrenaline reuptake inhibitor
SPECT	single photon emission computed tomography
SPET	single photon emission tomography
SSRI	selective serotonin reuptake inhibitor
TFT	thyroid function test
THA	tetrahydroaminoacridine
T3	tri-iodothyronine
TIA	transient ischaemic attack
U&E	urea and electrolytes
UTI	urinary tract infection
VaD	vascular dementia
WHIMS	Womens Health Initiative Memory Study
YOD	young-onset dementia

Chapter 1

Introduction

History of a specialty 2
Overview of mental disorder among older people in different
    settings 3
Tips on assessing older people with psychiatric disorder: 1 4
Tips on assessing older people with psychiatric disorder: 2,
    Physical examination 6
Demographics of ageing 8
Epidemiology of mental disorders in old age 10
Normal ageing 12

History of a specialty

Old age psychiatry is a relatively young discipline which grew out of the appreciation (before it became a popular mantra) of the numbers of older people, the distinctive and rich psychopathology of their illnesses and the need to provide bespoke services. Clinical pioneers in the UK such as Felix Post, Tom Arie, Gary Blessed, Klaus Bergmann and David Jolley complemented academics such as Martin Roth, David Kay, Raymond Levy, John Copeland, Elaine Murphy and Robin Jacoby in forming a drive towards the creation of a unique set of circumstances which, coupled with political will in the late 1980s, formed the specialty of old age psychiatry. Advances in the understanding of the dementias and the basic biology of AD (by Bernard Tomlinson and Elaine Perry), gave a scientific boost to the major organic disorders which, until then, had been the focus of service descriptions and clinical characterizations

It is easy to forget that the basic clinical categorization of the major mental disorders in older people only began to be appreciated in the 1950s with straightforward longitudinal studies by Roth and colleagues which tracked the natural history of older people admitted to hospital and eloquently demonstrated by a simple categorization their differing outcomes.

Thus the modern classification of disease was born emphasizing the chronicity of the dementias, the good recovery of the people with depression, and the high mortality rate for delirium.

Old age psychiatry is in robust health in the UK, with over 400 specialist posts in the field and an active training programme, and with an identity and cohesion linked to this critical mass the specialty is booming. However, the threat to all age-related services in the modern NHS leads to a reconsideration of the nature of the specialty—is it all things to all men (and women) over a certain pre-defined age or should it concentrate on organic disorders, the roots from which it grew?

The real excitement in old age psychiatry revolves around the therapeutic advances and basic understanding of the dementias. At no time since the creation of the specialty has there been such a wide array of drug and non-drug approaches to treatment and interest from basic scientists about uncovering not only the basic mechanisms of the major disorders but also seeing how that can be followed through to successful treatments.

This handbook reflects the current state of knowledge in old age psychiatry and will serve as a basis for the challenges which our specialty, in common with many others, faces in the future.

Overview of mental disorder among older people in different settings

Perspectives on which older people have a mental disorder have changed greatly with time. In the 1950s, mental illness among older people would have conjured up images of long-stay wards with dormitory arrangements in the old asylums. Increased interest in epidemiological research, in part driven by an ageing population, has delineated the prevalence of psychiatric disorders in different settings. Old age psychiatrists and community mental health teams tend to see equal numbers of new cases of dementia and functional psychiatric illness. In-patient bed provision is typically about equally occupied by dementia and functional cases. Dementia, by its progressive nature, tends to accrete and the caseloads of community teams will typically have far more long-term patients with dementia. Provision of long-stay care for people with dementia in the UK initially moved from hospital care to local authority care homes but now is almost exclusively provided in privately run residential and nursing homes. Dementia is usual in residents of residential and nursing home, even those in non-specialist elderly frail care homes. About 200 000–250 000 people with dementia now live in care homes in the UK. Depression is common in this setting, with prevalence estimates between 20% and 40%, but this may resolve, especially with appropriate treatment.

In primary care, where most care is delivered, the situation is different. Over 90% of older people consult with their GP each year, allowing unique case-finding opportunities. An average GP will have about 35 cases of dementia on his or her caseload at any time (not all identified), roughly similar to the numbers with declared rheumatoid arthritis or epilepsy. Five to ten new cases of possible or probable dementia may be identified and referred by a GP in a year.

Many cases of psychiatric illness never declare to services. Table 1.1 gives the approximate known prevalence of psychiatric disorders in various settings. It can be assumed that these figures are similar across developed countries. European studies of the prevalence of depression and dementia in the community confirm this. In the developing world, the population is ageing much more rapidly than has ever been seen in the West. Early epidemiological work shows that the prevalence of dementia, and the social consequences of it, are similar among older people in developing countries. Services are rudimentary or non-existent in such countries, leaving people with dementia even more dependent on their families than in developed countries.

Table 1.1 Prevalence of common psychiatric disorders among older people by setting

	Dementia	Depression	Delirium
General hospital admissions	20%	20%	15%
Residential/nursing homes	50–60%	20–40%	5%
Primary care older attendees	5–10%	10–20%	unknown
Community	5–10%	10–15%	unknown

Tips on assessing an older person with psychiatric disorder: 1

General

Take time

Assessment of older people with psychiatric disorder may take some time. Collateral history may be required, while deafness or frailty will prolong assessments. Patients may well have multiple medical, social, and psychiatric problems, increasing assessment time. Patience and planning of assessment times will be needed.

Collateral history

In any psychiatric assessment, a collateral history is desirable. Among older people with cognitive impairment is essential. In practice, most older people are happy to allow this. A breach of confidentiality is justified if information is required to help maintain the person's safety. Family members, social and health-care staff, or care home staff are invaluable sources of information. Key questions may include: 'How long has she been forgetful?', 'Has she been repeating herself more?', 'Has she locked herself out?', 'Has she left the gas on?', 'Has she been more irritable or resistant?'. Attention may need to be paid to inclusion of the older person in the assessment, rather than just interviewing the informant.

Reduce distractions

Noisy hospital wards are among the worst places to take a history and assess a patient with dementia. Reducing outside noise, minimizing sensory impairments (putting in teeth/hearing aids/spectacles), going to a quiet room, switching off televisions will all be helpful.

Repetition

For those who are frail, deaf, or cognitively impaired, repetition may be needed. This may help to maintain dignity or establish facts. Sometimes it is strategic; for example, in deciding on capacity issues: an older person may forget the detail of what was discussed but may on two separate occasions show clear evidence of capacity so the decision is valid even if forgotten in between

Mental state examination

The structure of mental state examination among older people is the same as with younger people. The emphases within each component are different and are outlined below.

Appearance and behaviour

- Are there signs of recent weight loss? Is there resting tremor? Is there agitation (more common in depression in old age). Does the person show distractibility/poor attention span (common in dementia)? Do they defer to a carer (common in cognitive impairment)?

Speech

- Are they dysarthric (common in Parkinson's disease, motor neuron disease, after stroke, but also in the edentulous)? Are they dysphasic (very common after stroke or as part of a wider picture of impairment in dementia)?

Affect

- Are they markedly low (severe, psychotic depression is more common in old age and often accompanied by agitation and/or retardation)?

Thoughts

- Is there insight into the extent of cognitive impairment and social care needed (frequently deficient in dementia)? Does the person have particular mood congruent delusions (very common in old age depression—especially nihilistic and hypochondriacal delusions)?

Perceptions

- Are there visual hallucinations (characteristic of DLB)? Do they appear distracted by illusions/hallucinations (common in delirium)?

Cognition

- The ability to make a meaningful assessment of cognitive state is essential when assessing older people. Sometimes this is translated as ability to use the MMSE, but other instruments may be more appropriate. For example, the Abbreviated Mental Test score has good sensitivity to change and is often used to demonstrate fluctuating impairment in delirious patients on general hospital wards. The CAMCOG gives a more detailed assessment of cognitive impairment than the MMSE, allowing domains of memory, orientation, speech, abstract thinking, attention/calculation, and visuospatial skills to be mapped. It is sometimes mistakenly thought that a poor score on a cognitive test means a diagnosis of dementia—it does not. At best these instruments are used as screening instruments for significant impairment and as a baseline which may be useful in plotting progress, for example in borderline cases or people on anti-dementia drugs.

Tips on assessing an older person with psychiatric disorder: 2, Physical examination

Some consideration of the patient's physical state should always be made. The prevalence of comorbid physical illness is very high among older psychiatric patients, and physical disorder may be directly relevant to the assessment. For example, if older people with cognitive impairment are hypertensive, have atrial fibrillation, and show localized neurological signs like dysphasia or hemiplegia, the likelihood of VaD is higher. If a patient with dementia reports hallucinations and shows cogwheel rigidity, then DLB is more likely. If an older person with severe depression shows evidence of malnutrition and dehydration then urgent admission for ECT may be required.

The list below should be tailored to the individual case being assessed; not every psychiatric assessment needs all these examinations. The ability to do a comprehensive psychiatric assessment should be accompanied by the skill to do each of these examinations when needed.

System[1]

General examination
- Hygiene: Any signs of recent weight loss? Alert? Do they look generally ill?

Systemic disease
- Any jaundice (examine sclerae). Any anaemia? Lymph glands enlarged? Any thyroid signs?

Skin/nails
- Are there any bruises (sign of falls/abuse)? Is skin turgor normal (may be dehydrated)? Any pressure sores (especially bed-bound people)?

Cardiovascular
- Check blood pressure. Is there any postural drop (consider checking this if the patient has been falling/dizzy)? Check pulse. Is there atrial fibrillation? Is the pulse weak and thready (if dehydrated)?

Respiratory
- Is the patient cyanosed? Is the respiratory rate increased (below 16/min is normal)? Are there any clear signs of infection, e.g. localized dullness/crepitations?

Abdomen
- Is there any organomegaly? Is there evidence of faecal loading? A rectal examination is essential if the person is constipated.

Central nervous system
- Is there any obvious sign of visual loss, especially visual field loss? Is downward gaze grossly impaired (found in some disorders causing parkinsonism)? Alcoholics with Wernicke's encephalopathy may show grossly impaired eye movements.

- In the limbs, is there any clear hemiplegia? Check for reduced power, abnormal reflexes, and change in tone in limbs on either side. Is there cogwheel rigidity? Are gait and balance normal (gait ataxia is characteristic of normal pressure hydrocephalus)?

Musculo-skeletal
- Are any joints red/hot/swollen/painful? Is there clear deformity, e.g. ulnar deviation in fingers in rheumatoid arthritis. What restrictions in function do joint problems cause?

1 Bowker LK, Price JD, Smith SC (eds) (2006). Clinical assessment of older people. In: *Oxford Handbook of Geriatric Medicine*. Oxford, Oxford University Press, pp. 70–73.

Demographics of ageing

The last century witnessed an unprecedented increase in the average human lifespan. The estimated total world population of older people was about 200 million in 1950 and is expected to rise to 1.9 billion by 2050—a nine-fold increase in 100 years. Currently, about 6% of the world's population comprises those aged 65 years or above. There is wide variation across the world in the proportions of older people.

The developing world

The developing world has a bigger proportion of children in the population (nearly 50% in some countries). The estimated current figures suggest that people above the age of 65 comprise about 5% of the population in Latin America and Southeast Asia and 3% in most of Africa. In the developing world, only 20.5% of the population will comprise older people in 2050 (compared with 32.5% for the developed world). Due to its huge total population, this means there will be 1.6 billion older people in the developed world by 2050, or over 80% of the world's elderly population.

North America

In North America, the population of older people was 35.0 million in 2000 (12.4% of the total population). By 2030, these figures are expected to rise to about 70 million (or twice the number in 2000).

Europe

Projected figures in Europe suggest that the number of prevalent dementia cases will rise from 7.1 million to about 16.2 million over the next five decades.

United Kingdom

In the UK over the last 35 years, the population aged over 65 grew by 31%, from 7.4 to 9.7 million, whilst the population aged under 16 declined by 19%, from 14.2 to 11.5 million. The largest percentage growth in population in the year to mid-2006 was at ages 85 and over (5.9%). The number of people aged 85 and over grew by 69 000 in the year to 2006, reaching a record 1.2 million. The proportion of people aged over 65 is projected to increase from 16% in 2004 to 23% by 2031.

The ageing world

The reasons for this explosion in the older population in the world in general, and in the developed world in particular are many, and are not just a result of increasing life expectancy. Other factors including the declining fertility rate, declining child mortality, education, and economic development play a big part. The ageing population of the world presents major challenges for society and for health services. Health services will have to adapt to new demands of an ageing population as well as to associated costs.

Mental health in an ageing world

Mental health issues are extremely important, as mental disorders, notably dementia and depression, are common in old age. Mental ill-health can profoundly affect the quality of a person's old age and has a significant impact upon the use of health and social services.

Challenges in the developed world

Even in a developed country like the UK, with established mental health services for older people, repeated reports have shown that the mental health issues of older people remain poorly understood, highly stigmatized, and are not given the priority necessary in policy, practice, and research—despite official reports since at least 2000 highlighting discrimination and calling for action.

Two-thirds of older people with depression never even discuss it with their GPs, and of the third that do discuss it, only half are diagnosed and treated. This means that of those with depression only 15%, or one in seven, are diagnosed and receive any kind of treatment. Even when they are diagnosed, older people are less likely to be offered treatment, and depression is sometimes still regarded as an inherent symptom of growing older. With the rising numbers of older people there will be an estimated 3.5 million older people with symptoms of depression by 2050.

In the UK there are currently 700 000 people with dementia. Dementia affects one in five people aged over 80 and one in 20 aged over 65. In less than 20 years there will be nearly a million people in the UK with dementia, and this will rise to 1.7 million by 2050. The overall cost of dementia is £7 billion a year, and this will treble in 30 years.

Challenges in the developing world

In the developing world an ageing of the population which is unprecedented in human history is now occurring. This is certain to place huge demands on social structures which will have to cope with increasing numbers of frail and unwell older people. In particular, assumptions that families will look after older relatives may be untenable. There is already evidence that mental health issues are of low priority in poorer countries with small health and social care budgets which are allocated across competing demands. Unrecognized and untreated mental illness may become a fate for many of those growing older in the developing world.

Epidemiology of mental disorders in old age

The epidemiology of mental disorders in old age is a rapidly evolving area. Most epidemiological research in this area has been conducted in Europe and North America. An overview of the prevalence of common mental disorders in old age will be given in this chapter.

Dementia

The prevalence of dementia increases with age. Most studies have shown a prevalence of 0.8% in the 65–70 year age group which increases exponentially to 28.5% in the 90+ age group. The prevalence of dementia is about equal for older men and women and is probably about equal across national boundaries.

Depression

Depression is common in old age and is considered the most treatable/reversible mental health disorder in old age. Studies conducted worldwide suggest an average rate of all depressive syndromes of 13%. Major depression is a powerful and independent risk factor for suicide in older people, with the suicide rate almost twice as high as in younger people. In the European Union, the death rate from suicide per 100 000 populations in people above the age of 65 is 18.8 compared with 9.2 for people below 65 years age.

There is, however, a general consensus that a number of methodological difficulties might have resulted in an underestimation of depression problems in epidemiological studies. The main confounders include exclusion of institutionalized individuals from sampling, diagnosis of dementia, and poor recognition of atypical depression when using DSM or ICD criteria.

Anxiety disorders

There is a paucity of epidemiological research on other psychiatric disorders including anxiety, substance misuse, psychosis, and somatoform disorders in old age. Although these conditions are common in adult age groups, decreasing rates of anxiety disorders and substance misuse have been reported in older age. As the elderly population grows, even currently less common conditions are likely to become more prominent at a population level.

A number of methodological difficulties might account for decreasing rates of anxiety in older people. Firstly the current diagnostic assessment methods focusing on somatic symptoms of anxiety may not adequately differentiate between anxiety and symptoms of medical illness that are more common in the elderly. Secondly the assessment instruments are likely to miss comorbidity with other psychiatric disorders.

Drug abuse

Alcohol and drug abuse are consistently found to be less common among older people. This may be partly explained by premature deaths among substance abusers, by cohort effects (people in their 20s in the 1950s in the UK drank under half the amount of alcohol of their modern equivalents), and personal/societal distaste for substance use in older age.

Psychosis

Psychotic syndromes in later life appear to increase with age if a broader definition is used, but there is a paucity of epidemiological research on specific syndromes such as late-onset schizophrenia and delusional disorders. Psychotic symptoms in other disorders like depression and dementia are much more frequent than true paranoid illness in late life. It is also clear that the devastating effects of schizophrenia among younger people are rarely found among older people newly developing the condition.

Normal ageing

There is no satisfactory definition of the normal ageing process. It can be defined as a cumulative process of adverse changes in physiological, psychological, and social functions that characterize average older people.

Normal ageing as a social concept refers to an accepted range of variation in health, appearance, and performance of adults at different stages of their lives. It is also a scientific concept referring to research findings in gerontology that can be useful in identifying variations from the normal ageing pattern. It is, however, always difficult to make a distinction between normal and pathological ageing.

Biological theories of ageing

According to biological theories the ageing process can be divided into primary and secondary ageing. *Primary ageing* refers to those declines in function that are genetically controlled and *secondary ageing* consists of random changes resulting from acquired disease and trauma. These theories suggest that if the hostile events related to secondary ageing could be prevented, life would be extended, but because of primary ageing decline and death are inevitable.

Deliberate biological programming

Studies on the ageing processes of human cells have shown that mitotic cells can divide a finite number of times and then die. Individual cells have a memory for the number of duplications, which is probably encoded in the genetic material. In other words, there exists a system of programmed cell death, thus making survival beyond a certain time limit impossible.

The ageing clock

This theory is based on the observation of biological clocks in both humans and animals. It suggests that ageing is a process that converts fit adults into frail adults with a progressively increased risk of illness, injury, and death. It refutes the concept of an absolute genetic control on the lifespan of an individual and suggests that living in favourable environments with positive living habits is the biggest influence on lifespan.

Accumulation theories

Other theories suggest that an accumulation of harmful substances such as free radicals and lipofuscin (an insoluble pigmented compound derived from incomplete degradation of normal cellular materials) with time result in an ageing process, eventually leading to death.

Psychological theories of ageing

These can be broadly divided into cognitive and personality theories.

Cognitive theories

The cognitive theory is based on studies of cognitive changes associated with age. In general, adults with higher intelligence and education tend to show minimum decline in their performances with increasing age, while a significant decline is observed in adults with lower intelligence and education. Older adults in general tend to perform less well in new and novel situations. The decline in cognitive skills is neither inevitable nor universal and some skills may improve or may be acquired with age.

Personality theories

Erikson's famous eight-stage theory of ego development suggested that the elderly person might either find ego integrity through satisfaction with his or her past life or despair and disgust over past failures. More recent workers have proposed an anti-stage theory of ageing, where personality, development, and adjustment are affected by historical events throughout the life.

Most studies have reported relative stability of personality traits from adulthood into late life. When personality changes occur, they appear to be related to losses, particularly those involving health and social support systems. Some studies have reported sex differences in personality in older age, men tending to become more affiliative and nurturing and women tending to become more individualistic and more aggressive as they become older.

Further reading

Busse EW (2002). General theories of aging. In: *Principles and practice of geriatric psychiatry*, 2nd edn (ed. JRM Copeland, MT Abou-Saleh and DG Blazer), pp. 19–22. Chichester, John Wiley.

Chapter 2

Dementia

Introduction 16
The manifestation of dementia 17
Diagnosis and differential diagnosis 18
Differential diagnosis of dementia: depression 20
Differential diagnosis of dementia: decline in memory with normal ageing 22
Differential diagnosis of dementia: other issues 24
Rarer causes of dementia 25
Signs and symptoms of dementia 26
History 27
Mental state examination in dementia 28
Physical examination and investigation 30
Imaging in dementia 32
Functional imaging in dementia 33
Epidemiology of dementia 34
Alzheimer's disease (AD) 35
Criteria for diagnosis of AD 36
Vascular dementia (VaD) 38
Criteria for diagnosis of VaD 40
Lewy body dementia (DLB) 42
Neuropathology in AD 44
Genetics of AD 46
Neurochemistry 47
Neuropathology in non-Alzheimer dementias 48
Fronto-temporal dementia (FTD) 49
Assessment scales 50
Risk factors for dementia 52
Management of dementia: an overview 54
The cholinergic system and cholinesterase inhibitors (CHEIs) 56
Specific treatments available for AD—the CHEIs 57
Antidementia drug prescribing—the practicalities 59
Memantine for AD 60
Other treatments for AD 61
Cautionary tales in dementia treatment 62
Drug treatment in non-Alzheimer dementias 63
NICE and dementia 64
Management of behavioural and psychological symptoms of dementia (BPSD): 1, Approaches 66
Management of BPSD: 2, Medication choice 68
Are antipsychotics dangerous in dementia? 70
Carers of people with dementia 72

Introduction

- Dementia describes a clinical syndrome which has three manifestations—neuropsychological, neuropsychiatric, and ADLs. A traditional definition of dementia is useful to bear in mind (e.g. an acquired global impairment of higher mental functions without impairment of consciousness). This distinguishes it from learning disability (i.e. it is acquired), emphasizes the global nature of the symptoms (as opposed to an isolated amnesia), and distinguishes it from delirium (which is characterized by clouding of consciousness).
- The expression of the syndrome of dementia, therefore, can be conveniently described in these three main areas, with an emphasis on one or more of the clinical features indicating the cause (e.g. slow onset of cognitive loss in AD compared with VaD, florid psychiatric symptoms in DLB).
- As a syndrome, the term dementia is similar to describing 'liver failure' or 'heart failure'. Recently, some commentators have suggested that we should return to the older concept of 'brain failure' rather than dementia, as it more accurately defines the clinical syndrome, but the overwhelming negative connotations of 'brain failure' make this unlikely in practice.

The syndrome of dementia

- **Neuropsychological deficits**
  - Amnesia, aphasia, agnosia, apraxia
- **Neuropsychiatric features**
  - Behavioural and psychological symptoms (BPSD)
  - Psychiatric symptoms
  - Behavioural disturbances
- **Activities of daily living**
  - Instrumental
  - Basic

The manifestation of dementia

The manifestation of the clinical syndrome of dementia can be divided into three parts:

- First, a neuropsychological element consisting of: amnesia (loss of memory); aphasia (either a receptive aphasia or expressive aphasia, the latter being more apparent in conversation, and nominal aphasia tested by direct questioning of naming of objects); apraxia (the inability to carry out tasks despite intact sensory and motor nervous systems, manifest in dementia most usually by an inability to dress, often shown by putting on a shirt or coat back to front, or the inability to use a knife and fork correctly); and agnosia (the inability to recognize things such as one's own mirror reflection or a family member—remember this is different from forgetting someone's name).

- Second, a neuropsychiatric component with symptoms such as psychiatric disturbances and behavioural disorders (also known as behavioural and psychological symptoms of dementia, BPSD) which are present in a substantial proportion of patients. The commonest are (approximate frequencies in brackets): depression (up to 66% at some point during their dementia); paranoid ideation (30%); misidentifications (usually based on agnosia, 20%); hallucinations (most commonly auditory, suspect an intercurrent delirium or DLB (dementia with Lewy bodies) if persistent visual hallucinations are present, 15%); aggression (20%); wandering (20%). An alternative way of describing these features appears in Fig. 2.1.

- Third, deficits in activities of daily living. Towards the later stages of dementia these are manifest by obvious problems in dressing, eating, and going to the toilet. In the early stages they may be manifest by a failure to wash or dress to a person's usual standard; in people living alone, neglect of diet can lead to weight loss, and neglect of household tasks may lead to comments about cleanliness of the house.

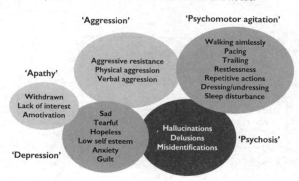

Fig. 2.1 Neuropsychiatric syndromes in dementia.
Source: Adaped from McShane R. *Int Psychogeriatr 2000*; 12 (Supp1): 147–153.

Diagnosis and differential diagnosis

The diagnosis of dementia is a two-stage process. First, the diagnosis of dementia, as a clinical syndrome, and second, the elucidation of the aetiology of the dementia. The main differential diagnoses of dementia and its aetiology are summarized in Figs 2.2 and 2.3.

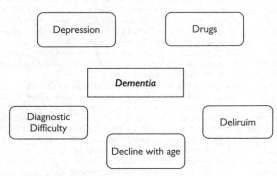

Fig. 2.2 Differential diagnosis.

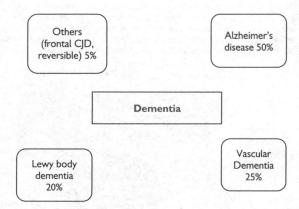

Fig. 2.3 Aetiology.

Differential diagnosis of dementia: depression

Depression

The symptoms of depression can be similar to those of dementia and the term pseudodementia has been used to describe people in whom the presenting symptoms are highly suggestive of a dementia but whose primary diagnosis, after investigation and treatment, is depression (Table 2.1). Patients with depression and no evidence of dementia may also present with self-neglect and loss of interest and may perform poorly on tests of cognitive function, often giving depressive 'don't know' answers to questions rather than providing an incorrect answer. The diagnosis of depression can usually be reached if patients are questioned about their mood, and symptoms such as diurnal mood variation, poor appetite, early morning wakening, poor concentration, anergia, negative thoughts about the future and their own self-worth. Crying (or at least the feeling that a person wants to cry but is unable to do so) is a sensitive measure of depressed mood. Older people may not complain of low mood but will admit to experiencing a loss of pleasure (anhedonia) and to giving up their interests over and above what might be normally expected for an older person. Failure to enjoy the presence of grandchildren is a sensitive indicator of significant depression.

Table 2.1 Pseudodementia and dementia

	Pseudodementia	Dementia (AD)
History	Onset can be dated accurately	Onset vague
	Rapid progression of symptoms	Symptoms slowly progressive
	Symptoms of short duration	Symptoms of long duration
	Previous or family history of depression common	Previous or family history of depression rare
	Family very aware of disabilities early on	Family usually unaware of disability
Symptomatology	Patients complain of memory loss	Patients rarely complain of memory loss
	Patients emphasize disability	Patients hide disability
	Symptoms often worse in the morning	Confusion worse in the evening
Examination	Patients convey distress	Labile mood
	Affective change usual	Affective change less common
	'Don't know' answers to questions	Questions tend to be answered incorrectly
	Variability in performance	Performance consistently poor
	Memory gaps usually apparent	Specific memory gaps rare
	Patients make little effort to perform tasks	Patients try hard
	General physical examination and investigations usually normal in both cases	
Investigations		
CT	Usually little evidence of atrophy	Cerebral atrophy and ventricular enlargements
EEG	Usually normal	Pronounced slow activity
SPET	Blood flow patterns usually normal	Parietotemporal and frontal abnormalities often seen
Prognosis	Good	Poor
Treatment	Antidepressants in all cases	Antidepressants if affective disorder severe
	ECT if necessary	ECT not recommended

Source: Reproduced from Burns, Downs, Kampers, *Current Dementia*, Current Medicine Group, 2003. With kind permission.

Differential diagnosis of dementia: decline in memory with normal ageing

There are a number of terms to describe the normal decline of memory and executive functions which occurs with age and the implications this has for the individual. Age-associated memory decline and age-related cognitive decline are examples but MCI (mild cognitive impairment) is the term which has stuck and is the most widely used. It describes the clinical situation where a person complains of memory problems which is corroborated by others, where there is objective evidence of cognitive dysfunction but no evidence of dementia. The diagnostic criteria have been formalized by Petersen and colleagues[1] thus:

- Cognitive complaint, usually memory.
- Normal general cognitive function, i.e. cognitive screening test in normal range for age (e.g. MMSE).
- 1.5 standard deviations below age-appropriate norms on memory tests or memory component of other cognitive tests (tests determined by clinician judgement).
- ADLs not significantly affected.
- Not meeting DSM dementia criteria, i.e. impairments not sufficient to impair professional and social activities.

There is good evidence that people satisfying criteria for MCI have a 10–15-fold increased risk of developing Alzheimer's disease at follow-up compared with the normal population. There do not appear to be any good predictive factors of who will go on to develop dementia, but the presence of more severe objective evidence of cognitive loss does indicate a higher chance of developing the disorder. Currently there are no specific treatments for MCI other than treating any comorbid conditions, including depression, and following people up with repeat neuropsychological tests. Often, people in whom there is a family history of dementia are more sensitized to the early symptoms.

The important aspect of MCI is that individuals are 10–15 times more likely to develop dementia than people without MCI. There are several subtypes of MCI described—amnestic MCI is the commonest—and the risk is of the development of AD. People with MCI who have more than one domain (e.g. memory) affected may go on to develop VaD. There is no evidence that any intervention reduces the risk of a person with MCI developing dementia; recent trials of the effect of CHEIs in preventing progression to AD have been resoundingly negative.

The concept of MCI has recently been extended to include non amnestic MCI, referring to people who complain about cognition, are not demented, but who show impairment on testing on a non-memory domain of cognition. See Fig. 2.4.

1 Petersen RC, Smith GE, Waring SC, Ivnik RJ, Tangalos EG, Kokmen E. Mild cognitive impairment: clinical characterization and outcome. *Arch Neurology* 56(3): 303–308.

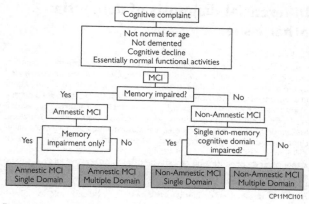

Fig. 2.4 Mild cognitive impairment (MCI).
Source: Reproduced from Petersen, RC and Morris, JC (2005). *Arch Neurol* **62**: 1160–1193.

Differential diagnosis of dementia: other issues

Delirium

One of the most important differential diagnoses of dementia is delirium (also called colloquially a confusional state). Delirium can be recognized by the presence of marked fluctuations in the clinical picture of the patient (a change over a day may cause relatives and even staff to suppose a degree of control is being exercised by the patient) and is characteristically associated with impaired concentration, poor attention, overarousal, changes in behaviour, fearful affect, and perceptual abnormalities such as visual hallucinations. Clouding of consciousness was previously the hallmark by which delirium was diagnosed but it is a difficult sign to detect and disorders of attention and concentration tend to be used as proxy measures. It can be difficult to differentiate between delirium and a dementia characterized by fluctuating cognitive performance such as VaD or DLB. A clear history of abrupt onset, drug or illness precipitants, and quick resolution of the syndrome will usually decide the matter.

Drugs

A number of drugs can give rise to symptoms of dementia. A proper drug history can usually pick up drugs which have been prescribed and which can adversely affect cognitive function. Drugs which cause anticholinergic side-effects are particularly commonly given to older people and the confusion can exacerbate cognitive impairment. Benzodiazepines may oversedate older people and diminish cognitive performance. Antiparkinsonian treatments may cause profound cognitive impairment and features of delirium and/or psychosis.

Diagnostic difficulty

The cornerstone of an accurate diagnosis of dementia is a history from a reliable informant and if there is none available there is always doubt. People with severe sensory impairment (visual and/or hearing) can provide a challenge because of communication difficulties and (although seen much less often now) individuals who have been institutionalized for many years can have behaviours which can be hard to characterize. Specialist expertise in the diagnosis of dementia in individuals with learning disability is often needed; a particular given the greater life expectancy among people with learning disability, especially Down's syndrome (most older Down's syndrome patients manifest changes consistent with AD).

Rarer causes of dementia[1]

Rarer causes of dementia include Huntington's disease, neurosyphilis, normal pressure hydrocephalus, hypothyroidism, vitamin B_{12} deficiency, head trauma, alcohol-related dementias, Creutzfeldt–Jakob disease and progressive supranuclear palsy.

Cortical dementias
- AD.
- Frontal lobe degeneration (fronto-temporal dementia, Pick's disease).

Subcortical dementias
- Extrapyramidal syndrome:
  - Parkinson's disease
  - Huntington's disease
  - Progressive supranuclear palsy
  - Wilson's disease
  - Spinocerebellar degenerations
  - Idiopathic and basal ganglia calcification
- Hydrocephalus.
- Dementia syndrome in depression.
- White matter diseases:
  - Multiple sclerosis
  - HIV encephalopathy

VaDs
- Lacunar state.
- Binswanger's disease.

Dementias with combined cortical and subcortical dysfunction
- Multi-infarct dementias.

Infectious diseases
- Slow virus dementias and general paralysis.

Toxic and metabolic encephalopathies
- Systemic illnesses.
- Endocrinopathies.
- Deficiency states.
- Drug intoxications.
- Heavy metal exposure.
- Industrial dementias.

Miscellaneous dementia syndromes
- Post-traumatic.
- Post-anoxic.
- Neoplastic.

[1] From Cummings JL and Benson DF (1992). *Dementia: a Clinical Approach*, 2nd edn. London, Butterworth Heinemann.

Signs and symptoms of dementia

People with the symptoms of dementia may present to specialist services for help at various stages of their illness—in the past, this was usually when the symptoms were of moderate severity and had started to impair day-to-day activities. The advent of memory clinics and the overall increase in the publicity surrounding dementia and AD has undoubtedly prompted people to come forward earlier for investigation and treatment, and early diagnosis and access to treatment is now an identified priority. By the moderate and severe stages the patient will be usually unable to give an accurate history, and indeed may deny any difficulties. A collateral history should be obtained from anyone available, preferably a family member. Although the symptoms may appear to have had a sudden onset, perhaps coinciding with the death of a spouse or a move from a familiar neighbourhood, such an impression may have merely brought the condition to the notice of others. Support of the patient by a spouse or other caregiver can minimize problems that become evident to others only after a bereavement. A good history from a son or daughter usually describes the true nature of the sequence of events. Failing cognitive function can be minimized by adherence to rigid routines that are disrupted when the patient moves away from familiar surroundings.

The overall course of AD is usually steadily and smoothly progressive with death following usually within 5–7 years when the onset is in later life. Figure 2.5 shows the changes that occur during the course of dementia. Theoretically, there may be an initiating factor, such as a genetic predisposition to the illness, followed by a promoting event such as a head injury at some point before the onset of the first symptoms. Often, in retrospect, emotional changes can be one of the first noticeable alterations. Problems with cognitive function supervene shortly after with deterioration following an S-shaped decline (relatively fast deterioration in the middle stages), with problems in ADLs and then deterioration in behaviour (this is obviously an oversimplification of a more complex process).

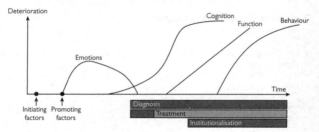

Fig. 2.5 The natural history of dementia.

History

- The single most helpful investigation is obtaining a history from the patient together with information from informants, from whom it is particularly important to obtain a history of the temporal sequence of events since the onset of the problems. These will include members of the patient's family and close friends and other professionals involved with the patient. The GP is obviously a valuable source of information about the patient's family history, past medical and personal history, pre-morbid personality, social circumstances, and dynamics of family relationships.
- Discussion with an informant will usually establish the onset and duration of the presenting problem. Difficulties with memory and changes in personality are usual. Problems encountered with hobbies such as following a complicated knitting pattern or playing bridge may be the first change noted. Difficulties may have become apparent after a sudden alteration in circumstances such as the death of a spouse. The course of the illness is also of importance in distinguishing between VaD and AD. A detailed account of the difficulties that patients experience in their ADLs is important with due deference paid to preserved abilities.
- Evidence of memory impairment can be obtained from the patient telling the same story or asking the same questions during the interview as well as from specific questions about whether the patient forgets, unless reminded, family anniversaries or important appointments. Reports of episodes where patients become lost are also important. Language difficulties may be apparent during the interview but are often elicited only on direct questioning. Evidence of dyspraxia can be obtained by judging the patient's ability to use a knife and fork and to dress. Changes in personal habits or interactions with family or friends may indicate a change in personality. Evidence of hallucinations or delusions can also be obtained from family members who may describe the situation when the patient appears to talk to someone when there is no one there, to see things when no one else can, or to have odd ideas, for example accusing others of stealing from him or her or of not being who they claim.
- Medical history may be of aetiological importance, such as a family history of dementia or vascular risk factors such as hypertension, diabetes, ischaemic heart disease, or CVD.

Mental state examination in dementia

The discipline of adhering to the traditional headings in the mental state examination is important in a logical assessment. Bear in mind that it can be as important how a person says something as exactly what they say. This can often be apparent when a relative interrupts to correct what is in reality a minor point of fact.

Appearance and behaviour

- Disinhibited or inappropriate behaviour is often apparent and worthy of note, and guarded or irritable behaviour may indicate paranoid ideas or personality change. Clouding of consciousness is an important clinical sign in differentiating between a delirium and a dementia but a devil to detect unless a person obviously has wandering attention and even drowsiness. Never forget to make a visual physical assessment, and the easy recognition of pallor, jaundice, or even finger clubbing is invariably helpful as well as reinforcing the medical training of the assessor. Overt signs of depression, such as agitation or retardation, may be apparent at interview. The 'omega' sign (folding of the skin between the eyebrows into that shape) indicates agitation.

Speech

- Evidence of dysphasia or dysarthria can be obvious. Other abnormalities include perseveration (when the patient continues to give the answer to the previous question in response to new questions), pallilalia (when the last word of an answer is repeated with increasing frequency), logoclonia (when the last syllable is repeated), and logorrhoea (a meaningless outpouring of words). The patient may echo the examiner's speech (echolalia) or actions (echopraxia). These signs are rarely seen but never forgotten. In dementia, speech may more often be fluent but somewhat banal, indicating paucity of content.

Mood

- Mood disturbances are often found in association with dementia and can be the presenting feature. Objective evidence of agitation, anxiety, irritability, or low mood should be noted. Subjective symptoms of depression are less likely to be forthcoming but should be sought.

Thought content

- The content of thought is often impoverished in dementia but careful questioning may reveal the presence of delusions or depressive ideas and the patient may elaborate on psychotic experiences. Delusional misidentifications are particularly striking where a person reports having two of something, such as a spouse or home.

Perceptions

- Some patients may be hallucinating at interview but as psychotic symptoms are common in dementia they should be inquired about in all patients by a non-directive question such as 'Does your imagination play tricks on you?'.

Cognition

- Traditionally, this was assessed using a number of unstructured questions covering the main domains of orientation to time and place (and often person, indicating the recognition of other people), attention (counting back from 20 to 1, or months of the year backwards), short- and long-term memory (immediate recall of a name and address, the commonest being, John Brown, 42 Church Street, Bedford, and autobiographical details such as the name of the person's first school), language (naming objects), and praxis (drawing a three-dimensional cube).
- However, standardized tests of memory such as the MMSE or the Mental Test score (or more commonly the AMT score) are now more commonly used. Their advantages are that they can be repeated to show change over time and give a quantified and recognized measure of cognitive function. The disadvantage is that they have encouraged a formulaic approach to the assessment of cognition and so there is often a lack of appreciation as to the skills required to carry out a proper assessment of cognition. Further details of assessment instruments are provided later.

Physical examination and investigation

Physical examination includes a search for the signs of conditions known to cause dementia. Blood pressure should be measured. Assessment of vision and hearing is important, as exacerbating factors. A neurological examination will detect focal neurological signs that are more commonly found in VaDs and will detect the presence of primitive reflexes that are found in dementia.

Further investigations should be carried out for everyone in whom a dementia is suspected. In the past, tests were directed towards what were considered 'reversible' or 'potentially reversible' dementias, and it was standard teaching to test for vitamin B_{12} and folate and thyroid dysfunction in case one missed a treatable, i.e. reversible, dementia. Now, these investigations should be directed as much to identifying comorbid conditions which need and merit treatment in their own right, i.e. a person with VaD who has a lowish vitamin B_{12} level should have that treated not so much in the expectation that the dementia will be reversed but that a comorbidity will be treated in the same way that it would be if found in a person free from dementia.

Debate inevitably surrounds which screening tests are necessary, the argument being that the low yield makes them superfluous. A standard screen will usually include a full blood count, (alcohol-related dementia), ESR (or CRP, inflammatory disease), vitamin B_{12} and folate (vitamin B_{12} and folate deficiency), U&E (metabolic disorders), calcium and phosphates (parathyroid disorder), syphilis serology (general paresis of the insane), HIV testing where appropriate (acquired immune deficiency syndrome dementia), chest X-ray and ECG as indicated by abnormalities on clinical examination. Lumbar puncture is indicated if there is any evidence of encephalitis.

Potentially reversible causes of dementia are found in around 10% of people investigated, but only a fraction of these completely reverse with treatment of a comorbid condition although more will partially respond to treatment. The commonest causes are: drugs, depression, metabolic causes: thyroid disease, vitamin B_{12} deficiency, calcium disturbance, liver disease, normal pressure hydrocephalus, subdural haematoma, and neoplasm.

Dementia screen

- **Always:**
  - Full blood count
  - U&E
  - Thyroid function tests
  - Liver function tests
  - Vitamin B_{12}
  - Folate
  - ESR or CRP
  - Blood glucose
- **Sometimes (when clinically indicated; some tests, e.g. syphilis serology, not supported as routine in NICE guidance):**
  - Syphilis serology
  - HIV testing
  - Calcium screen
  - Chest X-ray
  - ECG

Imaging in dementia

There are two main types of structural imaging which are used routinely in practice—CT and MRI. It is generally accepted practice that some form of structural imaging should be carried out in any person in whom a dementia is suspected. CT is probably still the most commonly used technique, its primary role being to exclude the possibility of structural brain lesions such as tumours (primary or secondary), cerebral infarctions, subdural or extradural haematomas, cerebral abscess, and normal pressure hydrocephalus. In addition, lobar cerebral atrophy can be identified, which may indicate the presence of a focal syndrome such as a frontal lobe dementia and CVD, not resulting in a cerebral infarction, can be seen. Both these findings can have treatment implications. Skilled neuroradiologists can identify characteristic changes on CT and MRI which increase the sensitivity and specificity of diagnosis of AD, especially thinning of the medial temporal lobe structures and hippocampi.

MRI does not use ionizing radiation but is a more arduous procedure than CT, taking longer to scan, and the apparatus is more claustrophobic and noisy than CT. Resolution is better and white matter is particularly easy to visualize. The properties of CT and MRI are summarized in Table 2.2.

The indications for MRI are similar to CT and surround the need to exclude intracranial pathology, and quantify regional atrophy and document the presence of CVD. Generally speaking, MRI provides better pictures of intracranial structures especially cerebral white matter. MRI cannot be carried out when a patient has a cardiac pacemaker or intracranial aneurysm clips. The noise and confinement of the scanner is poorly tolerated in approximately 5% of subjects.

Table 2.2 Comparison between MRI and CT

MRI	CT
Higher spatial and anatomical resolution.	Shorter scan times
Superior soft tissue definition and contrast	Widely available
Imaging in multiple planes—therefore superior views of middle and posterior fossa, pituitary, brainstem and spinal cord	Lower cost
Uses non-ionizing radiation.	Better tolerated
Wide application for quantitative analysis	Good for bone abnormalities
Greater sensitivity to detect white matter pathology and lesions causing epilepsy	Better for lesions with little or no water content (e.g. meningiomas) and detection of acute intracerebral haemorrhage

Functional imaging in dementia

- SPET (or SPECT, if the word 'computed' is used to qualify tomography) involves the administration of compounds that are distributed in the brain according to cerebral blood flow; in this way, a relative measure of cerebral activity can be assessed in different brain regions. Most commonly, SPECT investigations measure blood flow, e.g. perfusion HMPAO SPECT, which has been recommended in NICE guidance (2006) as an investigation to help distinguish AD, VaD, and frontotemporal dementia. SPECT imaging can be useful as an adjunct to the diagnosis of dementia. Characteristic temporo-parietal hypoperfusion is seen in AD, frontal hypoperfusion is diagnostic of dementia of the frontal lobe type, and patchy deficits may indicate VaD.

- In recent years ligands for dopamine transporters have been developed which when used in SPECT imaging (Datscans) are certainly helpful in distinguishing parkinsonian syndromes (including DLB and Parkinson's disease) from other syndromes which can cause tremor (benign essential tremor and AD).

- PET provides a direct measure of cerebral metabolic activity and can be used to assess cerebral metabolism and cerebral receptors. It is still primarily a research tool, although in some centres is used clinically.

- EEG is particularly useful in differentiating dementia from delirium. In normal ageing, the EEG has four predominant wave forms—delta (less than 4Hz,) theta (4–7Hz), alpha (8–13Hz) and beta (14–30Hz). In patients with severe dementia EEG generally reveals significant abnormalities in terms of regular slow-wave activity. Generally, a relatively normal EEG in the presence of severe dementia is indicative of AD, whereas a very abnormal tracing with minimal clinical changes is associated with delirium. As the dementia progresses in AD, there is slowing of the EEG tracing with decreased alpha and beta activity and increased, somewhat symmetrical, delta and theta waves.

Epidemiology of dementia

There are currently an estimated 700 000 people in the UK with dementia. The global prevalence has been estimated recently as 25 million. Hofman et al.[1] have summarized the prevalence of dementia in Europe. Women tend to outnumber men from the age of 75 onwards.

Age range (years)	Prevalence rates (%)
30–59	0.1
60–64	1
65–69	1.4
70–74	4.1
75–79	5.7
80–84	13.0
85–89	21.6
90–94	32.2
95–99	34.7

Costs

It is estimated that in the UK dementia costs £17 billion per annum. It has been well demonstrated that the presence of behavioural problems and the presence of more severe dementia increases the costs significantly.

The Alzheimer's Society has published a report on the implications of AD in the UK. The main headlines are shown in the box.

Dementia statistics (UK)

- 683 597 people with dementia in the UK
- 1 person in 88
- 940 110 by 2021
- 38% increase over the next 15 years
- 154% over the next 45 years
- Costs: £17 billion per year

(data from Dementia UK, 2007, ⊟http://www.alzheimers.org.uk/)

1 Hofman R, Rocca W, Brayne C et al. (1991). The prevalence of dementia in Europe: a collaborative study of 1980–1990 findings. Eurodem Prevalence Research Group. *Int J Epidemiol* **20**: 736–48.

Alzheimer's disease (AD)

Alois Alzheimer (1864–1915) was a psychiatrist and pathologist who combined his clinical practice with pathological examination of brains. He was a true innovator and described a number of unique microscopic stains and detailed several aspects of brain anatomy. In 1907, he published his description of a patient, Auguste D, who presented with symptoms of memory loss and paranoid delusions. She died after 4½ years, and at post-mortem Alzheimer found the characteristic cerebral atrophy, senile plaques and neurofibrillary tangles seen in AD.

Signs and symptoms of AD

- Common early symptoms of AD are memory impairment and disorientation in time and place. In one-third of patients, a psychiatric problem is the presenting complaint. Memory impairment particularly affects short-term memory, and the significance of such a change is sometimes not fully appreciated by families and others (including professionals), being dismissed as a 'normal' age-related change. Changes in personality may, retrospectively, be regarded as one of the earliest signs of dementia and are well documented in the later stages. Many types of personality change are seen, including increased rigidity, increased egocentricity, impairment of regard for the feelings of others, coarsening of affect, impairment of emotional control, hilarity in inappropriate situations, diminished emotional responsiveness, sexual misdemeanour, hobbies relinquished, diminished initiative or growing apathy, and purposeless hyperactivity. Impairment of judgement is an important symptom that may put the patient at risk and cause concern to families.

- In addition to the changes in personality and judgement the symptoms of AD can be summarized as the 'five As': amnesia (memory loss), aphasia (language disturbance), apraxia (inability to perform motor actions), agnosia (failure to recognize persons and objects), and associated symptoms. The associated symptoms are collectively described as non-cognitive or neuropsychiatric or by the acronym BPSD. Psychological symptoms include disorders of mood (depression and elation), disorders of thought content (delusions and paranoid ideas), and disorders of perception (hallucinations, misidentification). Behavioural disturbances include aggression, wandering, hoarding, sexual disinhibition, and eating disturbances. It is often the appearance of BPSD that caregivers find so difficult to cope with and that results in referral to specialist services.

- The gold standard for the diagnosis of AD are the NINCDS–ADRDA criteria. These describe the criteria for the clinical diagnosis of AD for the purposes of research. A number of studies have demonstrated the validity and reliability of these criteria in accurately predicting the presence of AD at post-mortem in around 90% of patients.

Criteria for diagnosis of AD[1]

I: The criteria for the clinical diagnosis of *probable* AD include:

- Dementia established by clinical examination and documented by the MMSE, Blessed dementia scale, or similar examination and confirmed by neuropsychological tests.
- Deficits in two or more areas of cognition.
- Progressive worsening memory and other cognitive functions.
- No disturbance of consciousness.
- Onset between the ages of 40 and 90, most often after age 65; and absence of systemic disorders or other brain diseases that in and of themselves could account for the progressive deficits in memory and cognition.

II: The diagnosis of *probable* AD is supported by:

- Progressive deterioration of specific cognitive functions such as language (aphasia), motor skills (apraxia), and perception (agnosia).
- Impaired ADLs and altered patterns of behaviour.
- Family history of similar disorders, particularly if confirmed neuropathologically.
- Laboratory results of:
  - Normal lumbar puncture as evaluated by standard techniques
  - Normal pattern or non-specific changes in EEG, such as increased slow-wave activity
  - Evidence of cerebral atrophy on CT with progression documented by serial observation.

III: Other clinical features consistent with the diagnosis of *probable* AD, after exclusion of causes of dementia other than AD include:

- Plateaus in the cause of progression of the illness.
- Associated symptoms of depression, insomnia, incontinence, delusions, illusions, hallucinations, catastrophic verbal, emotional or physical outbursts, sexual disorders, and weight loss.
- Other neurological abnormalities in some patients, especially with more advanced disease and including motor signs, such as increased muscle tone, myoclonus or gait disorder.
- Seizures in advanced disease.
- CT normal for age.

IV: Features that make the diagnosis of *probable* AD uncertain or unlikely include:

- Sudden, apoplectic onset.
- Focal neurological findings such as hemiparesis, sensory loss, visual field deficits, and incoordination early in the course of the illness.
- Seizures or gait disturbances at the onset or very early in the course of the illness.

1 Reproduced from Burns, Downs, Kampers, *Current Dementia*, Current Medicine Group, 2003. With kind permission.

V: Clinical diagnosis of *probable* AD:

- May be made on the basis of the dementia syndrome, in the absence of other neurological, psychiatric, or systemic disorder sufficient to cause dementia, and in the presence of variation in the onset, in the presentation or in clinical cause.
- May be made in the presence of a second systemic or brain disorder sufficient to produce dementia, which is not considered to be the cause of the dementia.
- Should be used in research studies when a single, gradually progressive severe cognitive deficit is identified in the absence of other identifiable causes.

VI: Criteria for diagnosis of *definite* AD are:

- The clinical criteria for probable AD and histopathological evidence obtained from a biopsy or autopsy.

VII: Classification of AD for research purpose should specify features that may differentiate subtypes of the disorder, such as:

- Familial occurrence.
- Onset before age of 65.
- Presence of trisomy-21.
- Coexistence of other relevant conditions, such as Parkinson's disease.

Vascular dementia (VaD)

Differentiation between AD and VaD in elderly people can be difficult during life and an accurate diagnosis often depends on a reliable informant supplying a collateral history. Classically the onset of a VaD is sudden and follows a clearly definable cerebrovascular accident. The course is usually described as a stepwise progression with episodes of clouding of consciousness and subsequently a fluctuating level of cognitive impairment. Apoplectiform features punctuate the progress of the disorder and are due to episodes of infarction. Commonly they consist of abrupt episodes of hemiparesis, sensory change, dysphasia, or visual disturbances. At first they can be transient and followed by gradual restitution of function but later on permanent neurological deficits appear. When the onset is more gradual, non-cognitive changes are said to pre-date the impairments of memory and intellect. There is greater mood lability and a greater tendency toward depression and anxiety than is commonly seen in AD. Very occasionally lacunar infarcts can be associated with gradual mental deterioration without focal signs. Other early features include somatic symptoms such as headache, dizziness, tinnitus, and syncope, which may be the main complaints for some time prior to diagnosis. The patchy nature of the psychological deficits in contrast to the global impairment of AD is said to distinguish between the two types of dementia with relative preservation of personality and insight in the VaDs.

The key features that distinguish between AD and VaD were described by Hachinski et al.[1] and made into a checklist from which a score (the Hachinski score) is derived. The original score was based on features of VaD in a textbook of psychiatry and studies of the cerebral blood flow in patients with dementia. The initial study group were relatively young and more mildly affected by their illness than are patients seen in most old age psychiatry services. A bimodal distribution of scores was found and suggested that patients with a score below 4 had a dementia of the Alzheimer's type and those having a score of 7 or above a VaD. Patients scoring between 4 and 7 were thought to have a mixed picture. These key features are shown in the box below. More recently the validity of using the Hachinski score to differentiate between VaDs and other types of dementias has been questioned. The Hachinski score has been criticized as not being sufficiently sensitive. Moreover, higher scores on the Hachinski do not reliably make a diagnosis of VaD more likely and the checklist does not take into account results from neuroradiological examinations. Infarctions are common in older people, including those with AD, and thus a mixed picture is common.

The Hachinski ischemic score

- Abrupt onset
- Stepwise progression
- Fluctuating course
- Normal confusion
- Relative presentation of personality
- Depression
- Somatic complaints
- Emotional incontinence
- History of hypertension
- History of strokes
- Evidence of associated atherosclerosis
- Focal neurological symptoms
- Focal neurological signs

1 Hachinski VC, Iliff LD, Zilhka E et al. (1975). Cerebral blood flow in dementia. Arch Neurol 32(9): 632–637.

Criteria for diagnosis of VaD

In DSM-IV, the key features of VaD include the presence of focal neuro-logical signs and symptoms (e.g. exaggeration of deep tendon reflexes, extensor plantar response, pseudobulbar palsy, gait abnormalities, weak-ness of an extremity) or laboratory evidence indicative of CVD (e.g. mul-tiple infarctions involving cortex and underlying white matter) that are aetiologically related to the disturbance. Two other influential sets of diag-nostic criteria have been published for the presence of VaD. The ADDTC criteria require evidence of two or more strokes by history, neurolog-ical signs, and/or neuroimaging or a single stroke with a clear temporal relationship to the onset of dementia and evidence of at least one infarct outside the cerebellum on brain imaging. The NINCDS–AIREN criteria (see I–VI below)[1] require evidence of CVD on both examination and on brain imaging and a relationship between the onset of dementia and CVD as evidenced by (a) dementia occurring within 3 months of a stroke or (b) abrupt deterioration in cognitive function or fluctuating stepwise course.

In general, the clinical features that have been found to be most accurate in differentiating vascular and Alzheimer-type dementia include neurological signs and symptoms, a history of strokes, hypertension, and abrupt onset.

I: The criteria for the clinical diagnosis of VaD include all the following:

- **Dementia** defined by cognitive decline from a previously higher level of functioning and manifested by impairment of memory and of two of more cognitive domains (orientation, attention, language, visuospatial functions, executive functions, motor control and praxis), preferably established by clinical examination and documented by neuropsychological testing; deficits should be severe enough to interfere with activities of daily living not due to physical effects of stroke alone.

Exclusion criteria: cases with disturbance of consciousness, delirium, psychosis, severe aphasia, or major sensorimotor impairment precluding neuropsychological testing. Also excluded are systemic disorders or other brain diseases (such as AD) that in and of themselves could account for deficits in memory and cognition.

- **CVD** defined by the presence of focal signs on neurological examination, such as hemiparesis, lower facial weakness, Babinski sign, sensory deficit, hemianopia, and dysarthria consistent with stroke (with or without history of stroke), and evidence of relevant CVD by brain imaging (CT or MRI) including multiple large vessel infarcts or a single strategically placed infarct (angular gyrus, thalamus, basal forebrain or posterior cerebral artery (PCA) or anterior cerebral artery (ACA) territories), as well as multiple basal ganglia and white matter lacunes or extensive periventricular white matter lesions, or combinations thereof.
- **A relationship between the above two disorders** manifested or inferred by the presence of one or more of the following:
  - (i) onset of dementia within 3 months following a recognized stroke
  - (ii) abrupt deterioration in cognitive functions; or fluctuating, stepwise progression of cognitive deficits.

1 Reproduced from Burns, Downs, Kampers, *Current Dementia*, Current Medicine Group, 2003. With kind permission.

II: Clinical features consistent with the diagnosis of *probable* VaD include the following:

- Early presence of a gait disturbance (small-step gait or *marche a petit pas*, or magnetic apraxic–ataxic or parkinsonian gait).
- History of unsteadiness and frequent, unprovoked falls.
- Early urinary frequency, urgency, and other urinary symptoms not explained by urinary disease.
- Pseudobulbar palsy.
- Personality and mood changes, abulia, depression, emotional incontinence, and other subcortical deficits including psychomotor retardation and abnormal executive function.

III: Features that make the diagnosis of VaD *uncertain* or *unlikely* include:

- Early onset of memory deficit and progressive worsening of memory and other cognitive functions, such as language (transcortical sensory aphasia), motor skills (apraxia), and perception (agnosia), in the absence of corresponding focal lesions on brain imaging.
- Absence of focal neurological signs, other than cognitive disturbances.
- Absence of cerebrovascular lesions on brain CT or MRI.

IV: Clinical diagnosis of *possible* VaD may be made:

- In the presence of dementia (Section I) with focal neurological signs in patients in whom brain imaging studies confirm definite CVD are missing; or
- In the absence of clear temporal relationship between dementia and stroke; or
- In patients with subtle onset and variable course (plateau or improvement) of cognitive deficits and evidence of relevant CVD.

V: Criteria for diagnosis of *definite* VaD are:

- Clinical criteria for *probable* VaD.
- Histopathological evidence of CVD obtained from biopsy or autopsy.
- Absence of neurofibrillary tangles and neuritic plaques exceeding those expected for age.
- Absence of other clinical or pathological disorder capable of producing dementia.

VI: Classification of VaD for research purposes

- This may be made on the basis of clinical, radiological, and neuropathological features, for subcategories or defined conditions such as cortical VaD, subcortical VaD, behavioural disturbances, and thalamic dementia.
- The term 'AD with CVD' should be reserved to classify patients fulfilling the clinical criteria for possible AD and who also present clinical or brain imaging evidence of relevant CVD.
- Traditionally, these patients have been included with VaD in epidemiological studies. The term 'mixed dementia', used hitherto, should be avoided.

Lewy body dementia (DLB)

- DLB is characterized by a fluctuating course with distressing psychotic symptoms and marked behavioural disturbance interspersed with periods of lucidity where the degree of cognitive impairment seems relatively minor in relation to the severity of the behavioural disturbance. The diagnosis of DLB is made based on the consensus criteria described by McKeith's Newcastle group and subject to later experimental confirmation in prospective post-mortem studies (see box). This group is in large part responsible for the realization that DLB is the third most common cause of dementia and can be readily identified in life using these clinical criteria.

- The consensus criteria for DLB consists of the following features. The cardinal feature is the presence of *progressive cognitive decline* which interferes with normal social or occupational function. Deficits on tests of attention and frontal/subcortical skills and visuospatial ability may be prominent and memory impairment may not necessarily occur in the early stages but may be evident with progression. The core features of DLB are *fluctuation of cognition* with pronounced variations in attention and alertness; spontaneous motor features of *parkinsonism*; recurrent *visual hallucinations* which are typically well-formed and detailed. Features supportive of the diagnosis are repeated falls, syncope, transient loss of consciousness, neuroleptic sensitivity, systematized delusions, and hallucinations (other than visual).

- The psychiatric symptoms may be the presenting feature or may appear in the context of long-standing Parkinson's disease. Sleep disturbance, autonomic lability, and marked sensitivity to neuroleptic drugs are also characteristic of the illness. At times it can be difficult to differentiate between a VaD and DLB and as with AD and VaDs a mixed picture is not uncommon.

Revised criteria for the clinical diagnosis of dementia with Lewy bodies (DLB)[1]

1. **Central feature** (essential for a diagnosis of possible or probable DLB)
   - Dementia defined as progressive cognitive decline of sufficient magnitude to interfere with normal social or occupational function.
   - Prominent or persistent memory impairment may not necessarily occur in the early stages but is usually evident with progression.
   - Deficits on tests of attention, executive function, and visuospatial ability may be especially prominent.
2. **Core features** (two core features are sufficient for a diagnosis of probable DLB, one for possible DLB)
   - Fluctuating cognition with pronounced variations in attention and alertness.
   - Recurrent visual hallucinations that are typically well formed and detailed.
   - Spontaneous features of parkinsonism.
3. **Suggestive features** (If one or more of these is present in the presence of one or more core features, a diagnosis of probable DLB can be made. In the absence of any core features, one or more suggestive

features is sufficient for possible DLB. Probable DLB should not be diagnosed on the basis of suggestive features alone.)
- REM sleep behaviour disorder.
- Severe neuroleptic sensitivity.
- Low dopamine transporter uptake in basal ganglia demonstrated by SPECT or PET imaging.

4. **Supportive features** (commonly present but not proven to have diagnostic specificity)
- Repeated falls and syncope.
- Transient, unexplained loss of consciousness.
- Severe autonomic dysfunction, e.g., orthostatic hypotension, urinary incontinence.
- Hallucinations in other modalities.
- Systematized delusions.
- Depression.
- Relative preservation of medial temporal lobe structures on CT/MRI scan.
- Generalized low uptake on SPECT/PET perfusion scan with reduced occipital activity.
- Abnormal (low uptake) MIBG myocardial scintigraphy.
- Prominent slow wave activity on EEG with temporal lobe transient sharp waves.

5. **A diagnosis of DLB is *less likely***
- In the presence of cerebrovascular disease evident as focal neurologic signs or on brain imaging.
- In the presence of any other physical illness or brain disorder sufficient to account in part or in total for the clinical picture.
- If parkinsonism only appears for the first time at a stage of severe dementia.

6. **Temporal sequence of symptoms**
DLB should be diagnosed when dementia occurs before or concurrently with parkinsonism (if it is present). The term Parkinson disease dementia (PDD) should be used to describe dementia that occurs in the context of well-established Parkinson disease. In a practice setting the term that is most appropriate to the clinical situation should be used and generic terms such as LB disease are often helpful. In research studies in which distinction needs to be made between DLB and PDD, the existing 1-year rule between the onset of dementia and parkinsonism DLB continues to be recommended. Adoption of other time periods will simply confound data pooling or comparison between studies. In other research settings that may include clinico-pathologic studies and clinical trials, both clinical phenotypes may be considered collectively under categories such as LB disease or alpha-synucleinopathy.

1 Reproduced from McKeith IG, Dickson DW, Lowe J et al. (2005). Diagnosis and management of dementia with Lewy bodies: third report of the DLB consortium. *Neurology* **65 (12)**: 1863–72, with permission from Lippincott, Williams & Wilkins.

Neuropathology in AD

The definitive diagnosis of AD requires neuropathological examination. The most obvious finding on the naked eye examination is generalized atrophy of the cerebral hemispheres but in particular the medial temporal lobes and hippocampal regions (Fig. 2.6). Throughout the microscopic pathology the most distinctive and widespread are senile (neuritic) plaques and neurofibrillary tangles (Fig. 2.7). Plaques are best seen with silver stain or immunocytochemistry using antibodies to β-amyloid peptide. These are extracellular plaques and consist of a dense core surrounded by less dense material. These neuritic plaques may well be the successor of diffuse plaques which consist of deposits of fibrillary material without any evidence of a central core of amyloid. Neurofibrillary tangles (NFTs) are abnormal structures inside neurones and are well seen with silver stains or using immunocytochemical stains of antibodies against their principal component, hyperphosphorylated tau. They are smaller than plaques and most contain a nucleus, although some tangles are clearly extracellular and appear to be the result of neuronal death (a 'ghost' tangle).

The main component of the plaque is a peptide (AB) which is derived from the amyloid precursor protein (APP). The AB peptide, popularly known as amyloid, is a 40–42 amino acid product which is formed from the abnormal metabolism of the much larger (120 amino acid) APP. This breakdown appears to be caused by secretase enzymes; single genes for these secretase enzymes may by mutation be sufficient to cause familial cases of early onset AD. Though rare, such cases have allowed a joined-up understanding of the cascade of events which allows metabolic perturbations to result in the clinical expression of commonly found AD.

Normal brain   Alzheimer's disease

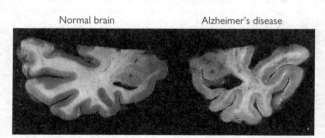

Fig. 2.6 Normal brain compared with Alzheimer brain showing widespread atrophy. Source: Reproduced from *Neurobiology of Alzheimer's Disease* 3rd edn, eds Dawdarn, D and Allen, S (2007), OUP.

Senile plaques   Neurofibrillary tangles

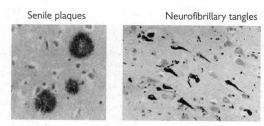

Fig. 2.7 Senile plaques and NFTs.
Source: Reproduced from *Neurobiology of Alzheimer's Disease* 3rd edn, eds Dawdarn, D and Allen, S (2007), OUP.

Genetics of AD

The contribution of molecular genetics to the understanding of AD has exploded over the last 20 years.

- The main component of the plaque is the peptide AB which is derived from APP. A number of mutations were found in the gene encoding for APP in the early to mid-1980s, the first familial gene to be found in AD, in particular in chromosome 21 which fitted neatly with the observation that Down's syndrome (caused by trisomy 21 in the majority of people) is often associated with AD. Several more *APP* mutations have been described.
- Another group of genetic abnormalities are the presenilin mutations. These are transmembrane proteins and the genes *PS1* (linked to chromosome 14) and *PS2* (linked to chromosome 1) have been described, the former appearing to be a dominant, early onset familial chain for AD. The normal biological roles of APP and the presenilin proteins remain unclear.
- Apolipoprotein E (*APOE*) is linked to chromosome 19 and is a polymorphic gene that exists in three alleles—e2, e3, and e4—containing different amino acids. e3 is the most common allele followed by e4 and e2. Any individual has any two of these three resulting in either being homozygous (e2/e2, e3/e3, e4/e4) or heterozygous (e2/e3, e2/e4, e3/e4) in phenotype. The presence of either one or two of the e4 alleles has been associated with the development of cardiovascular disease and a number of studies have documented the greatly increased risk of AD in people with one or two e4 alleles. ApoE is a lipid transport molecule and is a liver-synthesized very low density lipoprotein. Figures vary between studies, but in people with familial AD compared with controls, 20% and 2%, respectively had e4/e4, 57% and 21%, respectively, had e3/e4 and 20% and 57%, respectively, had e3/e3. There is some evidence to show that e4 may be specifically related to the formation of NFTs and amyloid.

Can relatives have tests to show their risks of AD?

This question is sometimes asked by relatives but is also often clearly in the back of their minds. In practice, in those rare families in whom there is a clear autosomal dominant pedigree with early onset (fifth or sixth decade), then genetic testing may reveal a characteristic mutation which makes development of the condition inevitable. Clinical geneticists often handle the implications of testing with such families. Understandably, some might choose not to know. Much more common is being asked by the middle-aged children of older people with dementia whether there is any way of checking their risk. *APOE* e4 genotyping is the main candidate; it has thus far been concluded that the rate of false positives and false negatives is too high to be used in clinical practice.

Neurochemistry

Acetyl choline

This neurotransmitter is involved in vital cholinergic pathways projecting from the basal forebrain and brainstem to the cerebral cortex. Functionally, these circuits are involved in normal perception, learning, attention, cognition, and judgement. Early loss of cholinergic neurons in the basal forebrain nucleus basalis of Meynert has been established for decades. Substantial loss of the enzyme cholinacetyl transferase has been demonstrated pre- and post-mortem, while loss of nicotinic receptors in the brains of AD patients has been reported. Importantly, the magnitude of cholinergic dysfunction is proportional to both neuropathological changes in AD and to the degree of cognitive impairment. Finally, the best evidence-based treatments for AD are the CHEIs which act by restoring cholinergic function.

Noradrenaline

Noradrenergic neurons project to the amygdala, thalamus, and cortex from brainstem nuclei. The noradrenergic system is probably important for alertness, memory, and attention. Though damage to noradrenergic nuclei has been shown in AD (especially to the locus coeruleus), its clinical significance is unclear.

Serotonin

Serotonin (or 5-hydroxytryptamine, 5-HT) is especially important in the regulation of appetite and emotions and may be important for memory. AD patients do not have structural deficits in serotonergic circuits until late in the condition, though some abnormalities of 5-HT receptor density and function have been reported. It has been postulated that this may be important for mood changes in dementia.

Other neurotransmitters

Glutamate is an excitatory neurotransmitter which acts diffusely, including through the NMDA receptor. Glutamatergic neurons degenerate early in AD. Neuronal cell death in many conditions is mediated by the effects of glutamate at the NMDA receptor, while the NMDA antagonist memantine has benefits in later dementia, especially in AD.

Gaba is an inhibitory neurotransmitter. Consistent gabaergic functional abnormalities have not been demonstrated in AD and no gabaergic therapies have been developed.

Neuropathology in non-Alzheimer dementias

Neuropathology of VaD

In VaD, the original descriptions of pathology revolved around large cerebral infarctions resulting in cognitive and functional impairment, either by sheer volume loss or by strategic positioning. It is increasingly accepted that more progressive accumulation of vascular change can cause damage without evidence of discrete infarction. Large infarctions usually affect the cerebral cortex and underlying white matter, usually in watershed areas (areas at the end of the blood supply territory of different arteries) and are sometimes associated with lacunes. Microinfarcts are lesions usually less than 2mm in diameter. White matter changes have been described extensively in dementia and were considered rare before the development of methods to image the brain but are now considered central to the understanding of cerebral VaD. The term Binswanger's disease and leukoaraiosis have been used to describe white matter abnormalities best seen on MRI and these are universal in people with VaD and very common in people with AD.

Neuropathology in DLB

The pathology of DLB consists of Lewy bodies in the neocortex. The Lewy body was described a century ago; refinements in staining and increased interest have focused attention on this piece of pathology. It is an intracellular neuronal inclusion body consisting in large part of aggregated, filamentous α-synuclein and other constituents including ubiquitin and neurofilaments. In Parkinson's disease, Lewy bodies are typically found in the substantia nigra, locus coeruleus, and in the nucleus basalis of Meynert. In DLB they are found much more diffusely, including in the frontal and temporal cortex, hence the term 'cortical Lewy body disease'.

Fronto-temporal dementia (FTD)

FTD is a term referring to dementias where there is predominant degeneration of the frontal and temporal lobes. Confusion among clinicians about how to diagnose and classify people presenting with clinical features suggests that this pathology is common. The major diagnostic classifications, ICD-10 and DSM-IV, do not include this term, but allow a diagnosis of Pick's disease. Pick's disease is a relatively rare and neuropathologically specific subtype of FTD. A degeneration of the frontal lobes lacking either Alzheimer or Pick pathology is more common and is what is strictly known as frontal lobe dementia. Overall prevalence of FTD among people with dementia has been reported at up to 7.5%, that of Pick's disease is probably under 2%, with the balance made up primarily of 'pure' frontal lobe dementia cases. Clinical distinction between the types in life may be impossible.

Clinical and pathological criteria for FTD have been described (see box). The main features are insidious onset and slow progression, early loss of personal and social awareness, early signs of disinhibition, hyperorality, stereotyped behaviour, distractibility, and emotional changes. Spatial orientation and praxis are relatively preserved. Early and striking speech abnormality, especially an expressive dysphasia, may be seen. FTD is the second most common cause of early (below 65 years) dementia and the youth, strength, and behaviour problems of sufferers present particular problems for carers.

Clinical features of FTD[1]

- Insidious onset and slow progression.
- Early loss of personal and social awareness and insight.
- Early signs of disinhibition.
- Mental rigidity and inflexibility.
- Hyperorality, stereotypes, and perseverative behaviour.
- Unrestrained exploration of objects and the environment.
- Distractibility and impulsivity, depression, and anxiety.
- Hypochondriasis.
- Emotional unconcern.
- Inertia.
- Disorders of speech.
- Preserved abilities of spatial orientation.

1 Reproduced from Burns, Downs, Kampers, *Current Dementia*, Current Medicine Group, 2003. With kind permission.

Assessment scales

It is becoming increasingly common to carry out formal ratings in clinical practice. Some of the more commonly used scales are as follows:

- **The Mini Mental State Examination (MMSE)**: This is the most widely used test of cognitive function. It is scored out of 30, and tests the domains of orientation, language, writing, memory, and praxis.
- **Alzheimer's Disease Assessment Scale (ADAS)**: This is now a standard cognitive scale for drug trials. It assesses a number of cognitive functions including memory, language, and praxis and also has a section devoted to non-cognitive features.
- **Clock-face drawing test**: This is a popular test, particularly in General Practice as it is easy to administer and is less threatening to patients (Fig. 2.8).
- **Clinical Dementia Rating**: The Clinical Dementia Rating is probably the most widely used global scale to give an overall severity rating in dementia, ranging from 0 (none), 0.5 (questionable dementia) through mild and moderate to severe dementia. Each is rated in six domains—memory, orientation, judgement and problem solving, community affairs, home and hobbies, and personal care.
- **Global Deterioration Scale**: The Global Deterioration Scale consists of the description of seven stages of dementia from 1 (normal) to 7 where all verbal ability is lost. The scale has been used extensively and validated with post-mortem findings.
- **Cornell scale for depression in dementia**: This is a 19-item scale which specifically assesses depression in people with dementia in five main domains—mood-related signs, behavioural disturbance, physical signs, cyclic functions, and ideation disturbance. A mixture of informant-rated and observational ratings makes it ideal for assessment in patients with cognitive impairment where information from the patient might not always be available. A score of 8 or above suggests significant depressive symptoms.
- **Neuropsychiatric Inventory (NPI)**: Twelve behavioural areas are assessed in the NPI (delusions, hallucinations, agitation, depression, anxiety, euphoria, apathy, disinhibition, irritability, aberrant motor behaviour, night-time behaviours, and appetite/eating disorders), each of which is rated on a four-point scale of frequency and a three-point scale of severity. Distress in carers is also measured.
- **Bristol Activities of Daily Living Scale (B-ADL scale)**: A 20-item scale rated on severity looking at basic ADLs (e.g. feeding, eating, and toileting) and instrumental ADLs (which refer to the performance of more complex tasks such as shopping, travelling, answering the telephone, and handling finances).

Further reading

Burns A, Lawlor B, Craig S (1999). *Assessment Scales in Old Age Psychiatry*. London, Martin Dunitz.

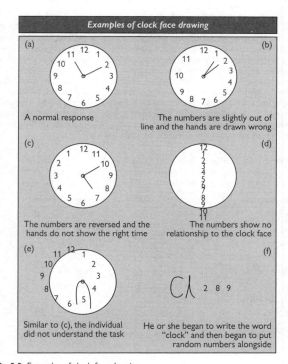

Examples of clock face drawing

(a) A normal response

(b) The numbers are slightly out of line and the hands are drawn wrong

(c) The numbers are reversed and the hands do not show the right time

(d) The numbers show no relationship to the clock face

(e) Similar to (c), the individual did not understand the task

(f) He or she began to write the word "clock" and then began to put random numbers alongside

Fig. 2.8 Examples of clock-face drawing.

Source: Reproduced from Burns, Downs, Kampers, *Current Dementia*, Current Medicine Group, 2003. With kind permission.

Risk factors for dementia

For most presentations of dementia, there are no genetic abnormalities which are proven risk factors for dementia. Early onset genetic types are associated with abnormalities in the amyloid precursor protein (chromosome 21) and also presenilin 1 (chromosome 14) and presenilin 2 (chromosome 1). Late-onset sporadic Alzheimer's disease is associated with the presence of *APOE e4* (chromosome 19). Other relatively well-supported risk factors include raised cholesterol, raised blood pressure, diabetes, history of myocardial infarction as well as the risk factors traditionally associated with dementia in epidemiological studies such as head injury, depression, thyroid disease. See Table 2.3.

Table 2.3 Prediction of dementia: risk factors. Newly developed scoring system based on mid-life vascular and non-vascular characteristics predicts the risk of dementia over 20 years (from Kivipelto *et al.*[1])

Characteristic	Low-risk profile	High-risk profile
Age	<47	>53
Sex	Female	Male
Education	≥10 years	≤6 years
Systolic BP	≤140mmHg	>140mmHg
Total cholesterol	≤6.5mmol/L	>6.5mmol/L
BMI	≤30kg/m2	>30kg/m2
Physical activity	Active	Inactive
APOE e4	No	Yes
Risk of dementia	0.09%	48.93%

1 Kivipelto M, Ngandu T, Laatikainen T, Winblad B, Soininen H, Tuomilehto J (2006). *Lancet Neurol* **5**: 735–41.

Management of dementia: an overview

The management of dementia can be viewed in several ways and Fig. 2.9 summarizes the main treatments available in relation to the major symptoms. Symptomatic treatments are generally directed towards psychiatric symptoms and behavioural problems.

The following antidementia drugs are currently available and licensed for the treatment of AD in the UK:

- CHEIs
  - Donepezil (Aricept®)   5–10mg daily dose
  - Rivastigmine (Exelon®)   6–12mg daily dose
  - Galantamine (Reminyl®)   8–24mg daily dose
- Glutamatergic agent
  - Memantine (Ebixa®)   10–20mg daily dose

The antidementia drugs are used to moderate the course of the illness and different strategies have been described, as outlined in Fig. 2.10, to stabilize the decline (by slowing progression or even arresting it) or to provide symptomatic improvement which eventually wears off.

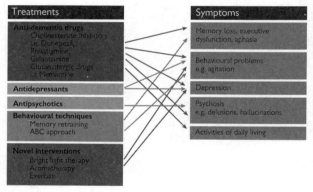

Fig. 2.9 Management of dementia.

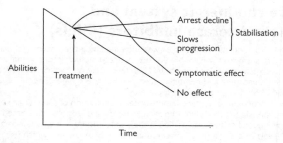

Fig. 2.10 Progress in treatment.

The cholinergic system and cholinesterase inhibitors (CHEIs)

These work on the cholinergic system by inhibiting the enzyme (choline acetyl transferase) which breaks down acetylcholine into choline and acetyl co-enzyme A (see Fig. 2.11). There are also drugs which act directly on the muscarinic and nicotinic receptors, but these have generally been found to be disappointing therapeutically.

Early biochemical studies demonstrated a diminution of cholinergic neurotransmission in the brains of people with AD and led to studies aimed at replacement. Lecithin was trialled in the expectation that it would increase the levels of choline (it is converted in the body to choline, which itself is unpalatable when ingested directly and gives rise to severe gastrointestinal side-effects). Placebo-controlled trials showed some improvements in cognition, but these were not particularly striking. Tacrine [tetrahydroaminoacridine (THA), an anaesthetic agent and powerful cholinesterase inhibitor used sometimes to reverse post-anaesthetic delirium] was shown to be superior to placebo in AD in the mid-1980s. The drug required dosing four times a day and was toxic to the liver, with the majority of people experiencing significant gastrointestinal side-effects. The better-tolerated donepezil, rivastigmine, and galantamine are more acceptable alternatives to tacrine.

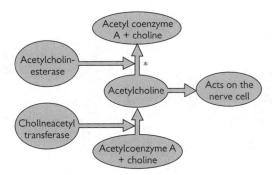

Enzymes involved in the manufacture and breakdown of acetylcholine.

* Blocking this enzyme results in less breakdown of acetylcholine, thus raising the levels available in the brain.

Fig. 2.11 Acetylcholine synthesis in the brain.

Specific treatments available for AD—the CHEIs

- **Donepezil** (Aricept®) was introduced in the UK in 1997 and has had the greatest impact so far on the treatment of AD. Its characteristics include: high oral bioavailability which is unaffected by food; a long plasma half-life of 70 hours permitting once-daily dosing; almost total plasma protein binding; highly selective reversible inhibition of acetylcholine. Pivotal studies all show an improvement in both cognition and clinician-rated improvement with a greater effect of the 10mg dose compared with 5mg. The most common side-effects of donepezil are understandable in terms of the peripheral (as opposed to central nervous system) mechanism of action and are largely gastrointestinal, including nausea, vomiting, diarrhoea, and anorexia. Some patients develop muscle cramps, headache, dizziness, syncope, or flushing. Haematological side-effects include anaemia and thromocytopenia, and cardiac side-effects may be seen including bradyarrythmia and syncope. Other side-effects include headache, insomnia, weakness, drowsiness, fatigue, and agitation.
- **Rivastigmine** (Exelon®) received a licence a year after donepezil. It has an effect both on aceytlcholinesterase and butyrylcholinesterase. It has a short half-life compared with donepezil (2h). Because of its short half-life it needs to be given twice a day, and requires slow titration to minimize the cholinergic side-effects. The trial data suggest a similar side-effect profile to donepezil, including nausea, vomiting, and anorexia. It has just become available as a transdermal patch allowing for a novel once-daily administration. It has an indication for the treatment of Parkinson's-associated dementia.
- **Galantamine** has a dual action as an CHEI and with a modulating effect on nicotinic receptors. It has the expected tolerability problems in keeping with other CHEI, the majority being gastrointestinal. It has a half-life between that of donepezil and rivastigmine.. It can be given once or twice daily and has an optimal dose of between 16mg and 24mg/day. It can be given with food due to its greater than 90% bioavailability. Figure 2.12 shows a comparison of treatment efficacy of the three main drug types. The effect size for the three drugs is essentially similar.

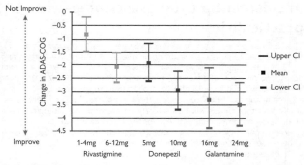

Fig. 2.12 Summary of Cochrane review of AD treatments.
Source: *The Cochrane Library*, Issue 1 2003.

Antidementia drug prescribing—the practicalities

The CHEIs are statistically and clinically superior to placebo in improving cognitive deficits, global ratings of dementia, and ADLs in AD. What is also evident is that higher doses are consistently more effective than lower doses. The duration of effect and long-term safety of the drugs has yet to be fully established, but placebo-controlled trials suggest benefit for 1 year and open-labelled follow-up reports show benefit for longer. There seems little doubt that CHEIs will be the cornerstone of pharmacological treatment of the cognitive deficits in AD for the foreseeable future.

When a patient who has only recently started treatment doesn't appear to be responding to a CHEI there are three options:
• increase the dose
• switch to another CHEI
• withdraw the drug and consider memantine (2006 NICE guidance now strongly recommends against this unless in clinical trials).

A more difficult decision is when to stop a CHEI in a patient who has responded but there is a suspicion, based on either a global impression or deterioration on a rating scale, that the treatment effect is wearing off. NICE guidelines in the UK recommend discontinuation once the MMSE score is below 10, but emphasize that benefits other than cognition should be taken into account in deciding on continuing medication. As CHEIs can provide other benefits it is perhaps wise to consider the possibility of effectiveness in all areas, not just cognition, before discontinuing treatment.

The risks and benefits of stopping must be discussed fully with the patient and carer. If there is doubt about whether a drug is doing more harm than good a trial of withdrawal is appropriate. Clinicians often find that stopping a CHEI in a patient leads to an unexpected deterioration of behaviour (e.g. increased agitation) or cognition, proving the drug was having more of an effect that realized When attempting withdrawal it is important to monitor closely for any deterioration so the medication can be reinstated quickly and the same level of symptomatic effect can be regained.

Memantine for AD

Memantine, a partial glutamate receptor antagonist, is used in the treatment of moderate to severe AD. Glutamate, an excitatory amino acid neurotransmitter, is found diffusely in the cortex and hippocampus, and is excessively available in a number of conditions including AD. Memantine acts to block the effect of glutamate at NMDA receptors. It has been available in Germany for over 20 years for various neurological symptoms and cognitive impairment. Early evidence for a role for memantine in dementia was in VaD and in moderate to severe AD. Evidence in mild to moderate dementia is less convincing than that for CHEIs. It was not included in NICE's 2001 guidance but has been considered in their most recent deliberations and was not recommended because of lack of evidence for cost-effectiveness.

The initial dose is 5mg once a day which should be increased in 5mg increments at intervals of at least 1 week until a maximum dose of 10mg twice a day is reached (although recent studies have shown that a quicker titration regime is well tolerated as is 20mg in a single daily dose). Memantine has 100% bioavailability and its absorption is unaffected by food. Memantine is generally better tolerated than the CHEIs. The most common adverse events of memantine include dizziness, headaches, fatigue, diarrhoea, and gastric pain. In clinical experience the side-effects which are most likely to lead to discontinuation are restlessness and hyperexcitation. There are very few cholinergic side-effects. Currently memantine is predominantly used in the treatment of moderate to severe AD when it is felt that CHEIs are no longer effective. They also have a role as an alternative to CHEIs in the treatment of patients with mild to moderate AD who are either unable to tolerate CHEIs or when CHEIs are contraindicated, e.g. problems with cardiac conduction or severe asthma.

Other treatments for AD

- **Ginkgo biloba** is a herbal medicine and is classified as a dietary supplement; it is therefore widely available without prescription. It has been used for millennia in Chinese medicine. Up to a tenth of people with dementia are on, or have taken, gingko biloba at some point. Possible modes of action include antioxidant action, vasodilation, and inhibition of platelet aggregation. Gingko has few side-effects; a main concern has been its anticoagulant effect and therefore risk of interaction with aspirin. A number of trials have shown benefits on cognitive and other outcomes among people with dementia. Later, better designed trials tend not to confirm such benefits versus placebo so its use cannot be recommended against established treatments like CHEIs.
- **NSAIDs** have been shown to be associated with lower rates of AD in epidemiological studies. Abnormalities in inflammatory pathways, including cytokine modulation of key metabolic abnormalities, including tau phosphorylation and metabolism of APP, have been shown in AD, leading to some optimism about possible treatment benefits. There is now fairly conclusive evidence that NSAIDs are ineffective in the treatment of existing dementia, while protective benefits in at-risk patients have yet to be demonstrated. The story is similar to oestrogens; they can have negative side-effects, especially gastrointestinal bleeding, and so their use is clearly not recommended.
- A trial of selegiline (used in the treatment of Parkinson's disease) and **vitamin E** showed that the latter may help preserve functional abilities in AD. Vitamin E has known antioxidant properties and has been a popular treatment in the USA; subsequent RCTs have failed to justify initial enthusiasm. Of note is evidence that (like the CHEIs) it does not prevent progression from MCI to AD. More recently, meta-analyses of the high-dose regimes (1000–2000IU/day) which have been used in AD have shown that all-cause mortality is raised. The risk among patients at high cardiovascular risk is highest. In the UK, vitamin E can still be bought over the counter. The mixed evidence of efficacy and concern over possible risks mean that it cannot be recommended, though some patients are likely to present on it or enquire about it.

Cautionary tales in dementia treatment

Vaccination

In 1999, a much-hailed study[1] showed that immunization with AB-42 peptide reduced amyloid plaque accumulation in mice with a transgenic model of AD. Excitement increased when it was subsequently shown that psychological performance in memory tests was improved in murine (mouse) models of the disease. This focused attention on the possibility of human vaccination trials. After initial enthusiasm, human trials had to be abandoned when it was found that a significant proportion of participants developed inflammatory changes and a form of aseptic meningitis. Subsequent work has tried to develop amyloid vaccines that do not cause the same problems. The approach is likely to be influential but it is likely to be some years before such a treatment may become available.

Sex hormones

Epidemiological studies have repeatedly shown that sex hormones may have a protective effect against dementia in general and AD in particular. Women are at higher risk than men of AD, and both case–control and prospective epidemiological studies showed that women who had had HRT were at lower risk. This led to speculation that hormone treatments might be of benefit. It was clear from trials that hormones had little or no effect on established cases of dementia. Of greater interest was the possibility that HRT might reduce the risk of incident (new) cases of dementia. The biggest trial, the Women's Health Initiative-memory Study (WHIMS) trial was stopped when it became clear that women who had HRT not only had higher risks of outcomes including certain cancers and cardiovascular conditions, but were also at increased risk of dementia. The dementia risk was probably doubled, and the strategy is unlikely to see the light of day again. The tale emphasizes the need for trials in deciding policy on drug treatment: lesser study designs can lead to policies likely to harm more people than they help.

---

1 Schenk D, Barbour R, Dunn W *et al.* (1999). Immunization with beta-amyloid attenuates Alzheimer's disease-like pathology in the PDAPP mouse. *Nature* **400**: 173–7.

Drug treatment in non-Alzheimer dementias

VaD

The main focus here is primary and secondary prevention by controlling risk events to reduce vascular events. Early identification and treatment of hypertension, which is also a risk factor for AD, has been shown to reduce the risk of dementia among patients who have experienced stroke. Lipid-lowering medications are also important in secondary prevention of stroke and may also protect against dementia. Other factors which are crucial in reducing the risk of VaD are stopping smoking, weight reduction, control of atrial fibrillation with anticoagulation, and nutritional education. The balance of current evidence is such that influential UK guidelines (NICE 2006) currently recommend against the use of statins, vitamin E, HRT, and NSAIDs for the primary prevention of dementia, while secondary prevention by control of identifiable vascular risk factors is supported.

There is a treatment effect of CHEIs in patients with both AD and CVD and there is some evidence of similar benefits in patients with VaD only. Cholinergic structures are vulnerable to ischaemic changes which can lead to significant loss of cholinergic neurotransmission, although rarely to the magnitude seen in AD. Donepezil and galantamine have been shown to have a significant beneficial effect on cognition and global function and estimated effect sizes are similar to those seen in the first trials for AD. CHEIs, however, are still not licensed, and are therefore relatively rarely used, for the treatment of VaD. With recent doubts over the future of CHEI use in AD, this is unlikely to change in the UK in the near future.

Parkinson's disease with dementia

Cholinesterase inhibitors have been shown to benefit patients with DLB and patients with dementia complicating Parkinson's disease. Rivastigmine has been shown in one trial to produce significant improvements in cognition, global ratings of dementia, and behavioural symptoms which were of the same magnitude observed in CHEI trials for AD. CHEIs have not been found to worsen the motor symptoms of Parkinson's disease. Current NICE guidance (2006) for the management of non-motor symptoms in Parkinson's disease[1] is equivocal about use of CHEIs in patients with Parkinson's disease complicated by dementia. These guidelines also recommend the use of clozapine for psychosis in Parkinson's disease, though appropriate monitoring, usually by a blood monitoring service assisting psychiatric services, is certain to be needed. In the NICE 2006 guidelines on the treatment of dementia[2] CHEIs are recommended for treatment of non-cognitive symptoms in DLB.

---

1 NICE (2006). Parkinson's disease: diagnosis and management in primary and secondary care. http://www.nice.org.uk/

2 NICE (2006) Dementia: supporting people with dementia and their carers in health and social care. http://www.nice.org.uk/

NICE AND DEMENTIA **65**

NICE and dementia

NICE (🖳http://www.nice.org.uk/) has focused public and professional attention in the UK on the QALY (estimated costs per QALY). This is an estimated value of the cost of maintaining healthy life for 1 year. This approach has been widely criticized and questioned in relation to AD, as it tends to be biased towards younger people. It is suggested that a cost per QALY of £15 000 is generally regarded as being good value to the NHS, prices approaching £50 000 per QALY are acceptable in special circumstances, but costs over about £35 000–£50 000 are regarded as being too expensive. The anti-Alzheimer drugs, for people in the mild and severe stages, are felt not to be cost-effective.

NICE (2006) guidance for the treatment of AD

- The three CHEIs donepezil, galantamine, and rivastigmine are recommended as options in the management of people with AD of moderate severity only (that is, those with a MMSE score of between 10 and 20 points), and under the following conditions.
- Only specialists in the care of people with dementia (that is, psychiatrists including those specializing in learning disability, neurologists, and physicians specializing in the care of the elderly) should initiate treatment. Carers' views on the patient's condition at baseline should be sought.
- Patients who continue on the drug should be reviewed every 6 months by MMSE score and global, functional, and behavioural assessment. Carers' views on the patient's condition at follow-up should be sought. The drug should only be continued while the patient's MMSE score remains at or above 10 points and their global, functional, and behavioural condition remains at a level where the drug is considered to be having a worthwhile effect. Any review involving MMSE assessment should be undertaken by an appropriate specialist team, unless there are locally agreed protocols for shared care.
- When the decision has been made to prescribe a CHEI it is recommended that therapy should be initiated with a drug with the lowest acquisition cost (taking into account required daily dose and the price per dose once shared care has started). However, an alternative CHEI could be prescribed where it is considered appropriate, having regard to adverse event profile, expectations around concordance, medical comorbidity, possibility of drug interactions, and dosing profiles.
- Memantine is not recommended as a treatment option for people with moderately severe to severe AD except as part of well-designed clinical studies.
- People with mild AD who are currently receiving donepezil, galantamine, or rivastigmine, and people with moderately severe to severe AD currently receiving memantine, whether as routine therapy or as part of a clinical trial, may be continued on therapy (including after the conclusion of a clinical trial) until they, their carers, and/or a specialist consider it appropriate to stop.

Management of behavioural and psychological symptoms of dementia (BPSD): 1, Approaches

- Non-pharmacological treatments can be effective first-line treatments for many people with behavioural problems associated with dementia. There are high rates of prescription of neuroleptic drugs in nursing and residential homes. When drug treatment is required, neuroleptics are generally the treatment of choice and studies suggest a 60% response rate compared with 40% on placebo. Adverse effects of treatment are common, including falls, drowsiness, parkinsonism, akinesia, tardive dyskinesia, cardiac arrhythmias, sensitivity reactions, plus the fact that some neuroleptics *may* accelerate cognitive decline. A recent warning by the Committee on Safety of Medicines has highlighted an increased risk of stroke, TIA, and other cardiovascular adverse events with the neuroleptics risperidone and olanzapine. This has promoted the search for alternatives to neuroleptics. There is good evidence that CHEIs may be effective in the management of behavioural and psychological symptoms—rivastigmine has been shown to be effective in DLB and Cochrane reviews are available on the Cochrane database website (⌨http://www.cochrane.org/) for details of the efficacy of these medications.
- Recently, interest has been kindled in so-called novel treatments for agitation in dementia with approaches such as aromatherapy and bright light therapy. Aromatherapy has been used for a number of years for a variety of health problems, the most common agents being lemon balm or lavender. These can be either give through skin application or by inhalation. Active agents in aromatherapy oils have been identified (the terpines) which cross the blood–brain barrier easily because of their lipid solubility. Bright light therapy has also been trialled for BPSD. The results for bright light therapy are slightly less striking than for aromatherapy but nonetheless there is some evidence to suggest that bright light might have a calming influence over and above any antidepressant effect (the latter being a well-documented effect of bright light).
- Depression occurs commonly in people with dementia, some reports even suggesting it is a universal phenomenon. A significant clinical depression can occur in up to half or two-thirds of patients and is said to be commoner in VaD and DLB. Exercise has been shown to benefit people with depression in AD. There have not been many studies specifically looking at the effect of drugs for the treatment of depression in dementia but those which are available show that the treatment is as effective in the presence of cognitive impairment as in its absence. The SSRIs seem to be the most appropriate agents, with tricyclic antidepressants being relatively contraindicated in view of their negative cardiovascular and anticholinergic side-effects. The box summarizes the management of BPSD.

Management of BPSD[1]

- **Define target symptoms**: speak to someone who knows the patient and can describe their symptoms and behaviours.
- **Establish or reconsider medical diagnoses**: agitation can be a symptom of delirium secondary to physical illness, most commonly occult infection or trauma, dehydration or medication. Always ask yourself is the patient in pain?
- **Establish or reconsider psychiatric diagnoses**: is there are evidence of depression or psychosis?
- **Assess or reverse aggravating symptoms**: are there deficits in hearing or vision or is the environment too dark or noisy?
- **Environment**: has something changed in the circumstances or routine of the patient to account for the symptoms?

1 Profenno, LA, Tariot PN, Ismail MS. Treatments for behavioral and psychological symptoms in Alzheimer's disease and other dementias. In *Dementia* (eds Burns, A, O'Brien, J, Ames, D) London, 3rd edn, 2005, Edward Arnold, pp. 482–98.

Management of BPSD: 2, Medication choice

- Whilst non-pharmacological therapeutic interventions remain the cornerstone approach to the behavioural and psychological symptoms in AD, there are cases where psychotropic medication is required. Medication should be reserved for cases where all other interventions have failed, but clinical experience suggests frequent and early requests to clinicians for prescriptions. The target symptom-based approach is the gold standard and this involves matching the most salient target symptoms to a relevant drug class. The antipsychotics as a group can show benefit for agitation associated with psychotic features and may also show benefit for agitation or aggression not associated with psychotic features.

- It is therefore imperative to always define the true cause of the behaviour and when drug intervention is required, adopt the 'start low and go slow' approach with the chosen antipsychotic and use the simplest dosage regimen possible.

- Neuroleptics are the agents that have been most commonly used for treating behavioural disorders, and they are generally regarded as being moderately effective. It is well documented that they improve anxiety and mood, reduce aggression and agitation, and reduce hostility and uncooperativeness. The primary efficacy is similar for all neuroleptics but the side-effects and induced tolerance of these drugs are variable. They are certainly effective in treating agitation and restlessness; there have been a number of meta-analyses of the literature showing that in patients with AD, neuroleptics are effective in controlling agitation and that about 20% of patients will gain extra benefit from these. More recent studies have concentrated on AD, whereas many earlier studies also included patients with acute confusional states (delirium). There are no absolute rules on dosage—generally one should use a lower dose than one might in a psychotic patient who did not have cognitive impairment. The side-effects are well known and are probably more exaggerated in patients who have dementia—extrapyramidal signs, tardive dyskinesia (in up to 50% of patients), postural hypotension, sedation (due to blockage of histamine receptors), anticholinergic effects, agranulocytosis, liver and cardiac toxicity. Neuroleptics can cause higher mortality and morbidity in patients with DLB. With regard to the specific agents that can be used, there may be little to choose between the main neuroleptics and, as with other drugs, choice is determined often on the basis of familiarity. The main concern has been about the apparent increased risk of cerebrovascular events and of death among patients with dementia prescribed these agents in trials. The risks appear robustly supported and clinicians prescribing antipsychotics in the presence of dementia need to show clear reasons why they believe the risks are outweighed by the benefits.

- A number of non-neuroleptic drugs are also used in the management of patients with dementia. Very limited controlled trial evidence is available to support use of other agents. Some RCT evidence supports the use of the neuroleptics promazine and haloperidol, while there is fairly clear evidence that diazepam (a long-acting benzodiazepine) and lorazepam (a short-acting benzodiazepine) are ineffective (other than as sedatives), though they are frequently prescribed. At least one RCT supports the effectiveness of the anticonvulsant carbamazepine for aggression in people with dementia, while evidence for the effectiveness of valproic acid is equivocal. Antidepressants have been shown to be effective for depression in dementia, but not conclusively to work for non-depressive symptoms.

Further reading

Shah A, Lopes AT (2007). Pharmacological Interventions for BPSD. In: *Therapeutic strategies in dementia* (ed. Ritchie CW, Ames D, Masters CL, Cummings J). Oxford, Clinical Publishing, pp. 203–226.

Are antipsychotics dangerous in dementia?

From the 1980s on, antipsychotics were the mainstay of prescriptions for BPSD. Unlike benzodiazepines, antipsychotics had mounting controlled trial evidence of efficacy for BPSD, including well-designed studies supporting the use of haploperidol, risperidone, and olanzapine. Among those treated with atypical antipsychotics, there appeared to be an advantage of fewer extrapyramidal side-effects. Since the 1990s, there have been concerns about the use of these drugs in dementia. Initial concerns focused on overprescription of these agents, especially among care home residents. In 1997 a prospective study with post-mortem validation[1] suggested that AD patients who had had neuroleptic drugs showed greater pathological and cognitive deterioration. Prescribing fashions change; concern at the time focused on thioridazine.

Since then two arms of evidence have raised concerns. In 2004, the UK Committee for the Safety of Medicines advised all doctors to cease prescribing the atypical antipsychotics risperidone and olanzapine for patients with dementia, due to evidence from controlled trials of increased risk of CVA. There was insufficient evidence to make a confident recommendation about quetiapine. In the USA similar concerns were raised about mortality among patients with dementia prescribed atypical antipsychotics. The debate has broadened; some reports have suggested that risk is equal among older and newer antipsychotics. The evidence of overall increased risk is now widely accepted.

There is, however, little doubt that antipsychotics are among the best supported treatments for BPSD. Confirmation of a possible directly deleterious effect on the progression of the condition has come in later studies of the effect of quetiapine on BPSD in severe institutionalized patients with dementia.[2] Mechanisms of risk are unclear; what is clear is that the risks need to be justified in prescribing these agents for BPSD.

Considerations in prescribing antipsychotic medication for BPSD

- Have non-pharmacological responses to BPSD been considered?
- Have drug treatments other than antipsychotics been tried?
- Is the problem persistent rather than transient?
- What is the cardiovascular risk status of the patient?
- Can cardiovascular risk status be reduced?
- Has the acknowledged risk of cerebrovascular events/fatality been documented and discussed with patient/carers?
- Has a time-limited review of benefits/risks been planned?

---

1 McShane R, Keen J, Gedling K et al. (1997). Do neuroleptic drugs hasten cognitive decline in dementia? Prospective study with necropsy follow up. *BMJ* **314**: 266–70.

2 Ballard C, Margallo-Lana M, Juszczak E et al. (2005). Quetiapine and rivastigmine and cognitive decline in Alzheimer's disease: randomised double blind placebo controlled trial. *BMJ* **330**: 874.

Carers of people with dementia

It is axiomatic to say that caring for a person with dementia is stressful—carers have known that for a long time but it is only relatively recently that the research community has taken this to the next stage

Problems for carers of people with dementia

- Poverty
- Social isolation
- Anxiety
- Insomnia
- Physical illness
- Depression (10–40% of carers of people with dementia reported to have case-level depression)

Factors which predict stress in carers include:
- The personality of the carer.
- Poor previous relationship with person with dementia.
- Wandering, insomnia, aggression, and incontinence.
- Dementia rather than non-dementia diagnosis in patient.
- Social isolation.
- Gender (women appear more at risk).

Interventions for carers of people with dementia are ubiquitous and intervening for the carer cannot, and should not, be distinguished from intervening for the person with dementia. Increased recognition of the morbidity associated with caring for people with dementia has led to increased interest in interventions specifically designed to alleviate carer distress. These are listed below. Evidence for the effectiveness of these interventions is often lacking. What evidence there is may be surprising. Interventions of an educational type have been found to provide little benefit, while respite breaks for carers, though anecdotally important, have not been shown in meta-analytic reviews to have significant benefits. Those interventions best supported by evidence include specific care support, cognitive behavioural support, and group-based carer support.

The NICE (2006) guidance on health and social care of people with dementia and their carers is explicit about what carers of people with dementia should expect

- Health and social care managers should ensure that the rights of carers to receive an assessment of needs, as set out in the Carers and Disabled Children Act 2000 and the Carers (Equal Opportunities) Act 2004, are upheld.
- Carers of people with dementia who experience psychological distress and negative psychological impact should be offered psychological therapy, including cognitive behavioural therapy, conducted by a specialist practitioner.

Interventions for carers of people with dementia

- Group carer support
- Practical assistance—care packages
- Day centre care
- Cognitive behavioural therapy
- Interpersonal therapy
- Information/educational courses
- Antidepressant medication

Delirium

Definition and description 76
Activity levels in delirium 78
Case example of delirium 80
Common causes of delirium 82
Distinguishing delirium from other mental illnesses: 1,
    Dementia 84
Distinguishing delirium from other mental illnesses: 2,
    Psychosis 85
Managing the delirious patient in general hospital—principles 86
Management of delirium in a general hospital—key tips 88
Managing the delirious patient in a care home 90
Pharmacological management of delirium 92
Non-pharmacological management of delirium 94

Definition and description

The concept of delirium dates back to ancient times. The initial descriptions date back 2000 years when Hippocrates described it. Since then there have been repeated attempts at defining this syndrome. The core features of delirium include altered consciousness, global disturbance of cognition, fluctuating course, and perceptual abnormalities. The onset is usually rapid with evidence of an underlying physical cause.

Core clinical features of delirium

- Acute onset
- Fluctuating course
- Inattention
- Disorganized thinking
- Altered level of consciousness
- Cognitive deficits
- Perceptual disturbances
- Psychomotor disturbance
- Altered sleep/wake cycle
- Emotional disturbances

- The *onset* of delirium is acute and the impairment of consciousness characteristically fluctuates, with deterioration in the evening when environmental stimulation is lowered. *Alertness* or arousal to the surrounding environment can either be lowered or increased. Characteristically, in delirium, the alertness fluctuates between falsely increased alertness and a lowered awareness of the surroundings. Other forms of impairment in consciousness, such as impaired attention and difficulty in estimating the passage of time can also be seen. The patient can appear to be distractible and may be unable to perform classical tests of concentration such as serial sevens where the patient counts backwards in sevens from 100, spelling the word 'WORLD' backward, or saying the months of the year or days of the week backward. The interpretation of these assessments should take into account the patient's age and educational background.
- The disturbance of *sleep/wake cycle* is also part of the classical presentation of delirium. The patient usually presents with daytime drowsiness and insomnia at night. Excessive dreaming with persistence of the experience into wakefulness is also common.
- *Speech* and *thinking* are progressively disturbed and the rate of speech is either slowed or speeded up. The capacity to make judgements and to grasp abstract concepts also becomes impaired. Thought processes can appear more incoherent and disorganized as the illness progresses. The patient appears to be unable to differentiate between their own thought processes and their external world and can, at times, present as increasingly preoccupied with their inner thoughts and experiences with very little awareness of their surroundings.

- Disturbance of *memory* is also an important feature. Short-term, immediate, and working memory are commonly affected but long-term memories can also be disturbed. The most common presentation is disorientation in time and place with disorientation in time occurring in the milder stage and then progressing on to disorientation in place. A failure to track time and the intermittent nature of some of the deficits can sometimes result in jumbled up memories of past and present which may at times result in false recall.

Activity levels in delirium

Disturbance of psychomotor *behaviour* is also common. Classically, the patient fluctuates between a lowered state of psychomotor activity and little response to external environment, although inner experiences such as hallucinations or delusions may be present, and the other extreme of psychomotor behaviour presenting as agitation or purposeless behaviour such as groping or picking, which may be associated with complex stereotyped movements. Rarely, psychomotor agitation results in mimicking of a work pattern, which is described as occupational delirium.

More recently, the two fluctuating forms of psychomotor disturbance have been described as hypo- and hyperactive delirium:

- In hyperactive delirium the patient has heightened arousal and can react to surrounding stimuli with verbally and physically aggressive and threatening behaviour. They usually appear restless and wandersome and can sometimes seen pulling repeatedly at clothing—a phenomenon described as 'carphologia'. Abnormalities of *perception* such as visual, auditory, or tactile hallucinations are also common in hyperactive delirium. Other disturbances such as abnormal perception of size of visually perceived objects (micropsia and macropsia) or auditory stimuli (hypo- or hyperacusis) have also been described. Illusions (misinterpretation of external stimuli), usually in visual form, are common along with hallucinations (perceptions without objective stimuli). The most common form of hallucination is visual and may present in simple forms such as flashes of light to fully formed scenes of people and animals. 'Lilliputian' hallucinations occur when patients see tiny animals or people jumping around on their beds.
- The hypoactive type of delirium is much less obvious as patients are withdrawn and do not react to their abnormal perceptual phenomena, which are easily detectable if an effort is made to recognize them. The hypoactive form of delirium is more common but can be easily missed and the patient classically presents as being drowsy, not interested in their environment, and eating and drinking poorly. If spoken to, speech is usually incoherent and they find it difficult to understand questions.

ICD-10 diagnostic criteria for delirium[1]

For a definite diagnosis, symptoms, mild or severe, should be present in each of the following areas:

- Impairment of consciousness and attention (ranging from clouding to coma, reduced ability to direct, focus, sustain and shift attention).
- Global disturbance of cognition (perceptual distortions, illusions and hallucinations—most often visual; impairment of abstract thinking and comprehension, with or without transient delusions, but typically with some degree of incoherence; impairment of immediate recall and of recent memory, but with relatively intact remote memory; disorientation for time as well as, in more severe cases, for people and persons).
- Psychomotor disturbance (hypo- or hyperactivity and unpredictable shifts from one to the other; increased reaction time; increased or decreased flow of speech; enhanced startle reaction).

- Disturbance of sleep/wake cycle (insomnia or, in more severe cases, total sleep loss or reversal of sleep/wake cycle; daytime drowsiness; nocturnal worsening of symptoms; disturbing dreams or nightmares, which may continue as hallucinations after waking).
- Emotional disturbances, for example, depression, anxiety or fear, irritability, euphoria, apathy, or wondering perplexity.

1 World Health Organization (1992). *The ICD-10 classification of mental and behavioural disorders. Diagnostic criteria for research.* WHO, Geneva.

Case example of delirium

An acutely disturbed 70-year-old in a care home

You receive a fax marked 'URGENT' from a local general practice. It states that a 70-year-old gentleman who has been a resident at a care home for the last few years has suddenly become 'aggressive' towards the staff. The routine physical examination is not suggestive of an acute physical illness and his blood results and MSU are normal. He has been prescribed some promazine 25mg up to three times a day but this is not helping to calm him down. He is known to have hypertension, ischaemic heart disease, and TIAs but has been stable on medication.

On your visit to the care home, the staff, who have known the patient for some years, inform you that the patient has not been sleeping at night, wandering in the corridors and getting into the bedrooms of other residents in the middle of the night. He has been physically aggressive towards members of staff on a couple of occasions when they tried to persuade him to go back to his room. During the daytime, he has been noted to be drowsy, not interested in eating and drinking and sitting quietly in front of the television in the lounge all day.

You try to interview the patient but he appears very drowsy and disinterested in the conversation. He finds it difficult to keep his eyes open, tries to respond to some of your questions but it is difficult to make sense of what he is saying. Despite repeated attempts, you are unable to do a formal mental state examination or test his cognitive function.

Looking at the list of his previous and current medication, you notice that there have been no major changes apart from a recent stoppage of his regular dose of laxative (lactulose) 2 weeks ago, following a brief episode of diarrhoea. On enquiring from the staff about the patient's bowel habits, you learn that he has been constipated since the lactulose was stopped recently.

You do a PR examination to find that the rectum is full of hard faeces. You ring the GP practice nurse to enquire if she would be able to give the patient an enema and restart him on his regular dose of lactulose.

You ring up the care home after the weekend to enquire about the patient's condition and are told that he had a huge bowel movement after the enema and his behaviour has gradually improved over the last 2 days. The staff have, however, been giving him promazine three times a day, which makes him drowsy during the daytime. You suggest omitting the morning and afternoon dose of promazine and keeping the night-time dose for a few more days until the sleep cycle comes back to normal.

Common causes of delirium[1]

Predisposing factors in delirium
- Old age (over 65 years).
- Male sex.
- Visual impairment.
- Presence of dementia.
- Severity of dementia.
- Depression.
- Functional dependence.
- Immobility.
- Hip fracture.
- Dehydration.
- Alcoholism.
- Physical frailty.
- Deafness.
- Malnutrition.

Precipitating factors in delirium
- Lower respiratory tract infections.
- Urinary tract infections.
- Catheterization.
- Constipation.
- Electrolyte imbalance.
- Orthopaedic surgery.
- Cardiac surgery.
- Pain and sleep deprivation.

Drugs that may cause delirium
- Drugs with high anticholinergic activity:
  - Cimetidine
  - Prednisolone
  - Theophylline
  - Tricyclic antidepressants (e.g. amitriptyline)
  - Digoxin
  - Nifedipine
  - Antipsychotics (e.g. chlorpromazine)
  - Furosemide
  - Ranitidine
  - Isosorbide dinitrate
  - Warfarin
  - Codeine
  - Captopril
- Other drugs associated with delirium:
  - Benzodiazepines
  - Narcotics
  - Antiparkinsonian agents (e.g. L-dopa)
  - NSAIDs

- Over-the-counter drugs associated with delirium:
  - Diphenhydramine (e.g. Benylin)
  - Chlorpheniramine (e.g. Piriton)
  - Promethazine (e.g. Phenergan, Night Nurse)
  - Antidiarrhoea drugs (containing belladona)
  - Irritable bowel syndrome drugs containing hyoscine (e.g. Buscopan)

1 Adapted from: Burns A, Gallagley A, Byrne J (2004). *J Neurol Neurosurg Psychiat*, **75**: 362–7; Young J, Inouye SK (2007). *BMJ*, **34**: 842–6.

Distinguishing delirium from other mental illnesses: 1, Dementia

Although delirium can occur in people suffering from any form of psychiatric illness, distinguishing delirium from dementia and psychosis are the two common clinical dilemmas.

Delirium and dementia overlap

In older people, distinguishing delirium from dementia can present as a clinical challenge as the two conditions have overlapping aetiology and clinical features (Table 3.1). Patients with dementia are known to be at an increased risk of developing delirium, and vice versa. Out of the three common types of dementia, distinguishing delirium from DLB can be most difficult as both illnesses present with prominent visual hallucinations and a fluctuating course.

The safest course of action in cases where there may be an overlap between the two illnesses is to consider delirium as the primary diagnosis and manage accordingly.

Table 3.1 Comparing delirium and dementia

Feature	Delirium	Dementia
Development	Sudden	Slow
Duration	Days to weeks	Months to years
Presence of other disorders or physical problems	Almost always present, may be a severe illness, drug use or withdrawal, or a problem with metabolism	Possibly none
Variation at night	Almost always worse	Often worse
Attention	Greatly impaired	Maintained until late stages
Level of consciousness	Fluctuates from lethargy to agitation	Normal until late stages
Orientation to surroundings	Varies	Impaired
Use of language	Slow, often incoherent and inappropriate	Sometimes difficulty finding the right word
Memory	Jumbled and confused	Deficient, especially for recent events
Mental function	Lost, variably and unpredictably	Lost, relatively consistently for all functions
Cause	Usually an acute illness or drugs. In older people, usually infection, dehydration, or drugs	Usually AD, VaD or DLB
Need for treatment	Emergency medical attention	Non-emergency attention

Distinguishing delirium from other mental illnesses: 2, Psychosis

Delirium and an acute psychotic illness can have a number of common presenting features and Table 3.2 should be helpful in distinguishing the two from each other. From a management point of view, however, as with dementia, all cases suspected of an overlap of delirium and psychosis should be managed with delirium being the primary diagnosis.

Table 3.2 Distinguishing dementia from psychosis

Clinical features of delirium	Common signs of delirium	Common signs of psychosis due to a psychiatric disorder
Orientation	Confusion about current time, date, place, or identity	Usually aware of time, date, place, and identity
Attention	Difficulty paying attention	Retention of ability to pay attention
Short-term memory	Loss of recent memory	Retention of recent memory
Abstract thinking	Inability to think logically	Inability to think logically
Concentration	Inability to perform simple calculations	Retention of ability to calculate
Delusions	Preoccupations commonly inconsistent	Preoccupations often fixed and consistent
Hallucinations	Hallucinations (if any) mostly visual or involving touch	Hallucinations (if any) mostly auditory
Physiology	Fever or other signs of infection	History of previous psychiatric disturbances
Drug use/abuse	Evidence of recent drug use	Drug use not necessarily involved

Managing the delirious patient in general hospital—principles

Delirium is a common condition seen in hospital patients. Its problems and incidence are particularly high in surgical in-patients, such as those undergoing cardiothoracic and orthopaedic procedures, in-patients undergoing cataract surgery, or those in intensive care units. High rates of delirium have also been reported in patients admitted to cancer units and those having dialysis due to renal failure.

Management

Delirium is a medical emergency with a high morbidity and mortality risk. Any patient suspected of having delirium requires prompt attention, while recent evidence suggests that the most successful approach to delirium should also concentrate on its prevention.

Strategies for delirium prevention

Identification of high-risk patients for developing delirium such as those with hip fractures, can lead to significant reductions in the incidence, severity, and duration of delirium. Evidence for delirium prevention strategies comes from non-randomized trials; it is estimated that 30–40% of cases may be preventable. The following strategies tailored according to the needs/risk factors of the individual patient can be used in delirium prevention:
- Orientating communication.
- Therapeutic activities.
- Early mobilization and walking.
- Maintaining nutrition and hydration.
- Adaptive equipment for vision and hearing impairment.
- Adequate pain management.
- Avoiding sedation.
- Use of non-pharmacological intervention for sleep disturbance.
- Early discharge.
- Home rehabilitation services.

Management of delirium

Identification of underlying cause and precipitating factors
- In practice, the commonest causes are infections, metabolic and fluid imbalance, cerebral hypoxia, pain, sensory deprivation, urinary retention, faecal impaction. and polypharmacy.
- A detailed history and examination along with review of the results of investigation provides a guide to understanding the cause. A raised white blood count or specific symptom (such as a fever) may indicate an infection process. Asymptomatic bacteruria is common in older people and a positive MSU does not necessarily mean that it is the only cause of the symptoms.
- Dehydration, cerebral hypoxia caused by congestive cardiac failure, and unrecognized severe pain should be ruled out in all in-patients with delirium.

Maintaining behaviours

Hospital in-patients, especially with hyperactive delirium, can be at risk of falls, non-compliance with medication/interventions leading to delayed/poor recovery, exposure to extremes of temperature, harm to self and others. Agitation, aggression, and wandering are the most common behavioural disturbances requiring pharmacological and non-pharmacological interventions.

Preventing complications and supporting functional needs

A number of strategies including adequate pain control, withdrawal of unnecessary drugs, supportive care including management of hypoxia, hydration, and nutrition along with mobilization, participation in ward activities such as physiotherapy and minimizing time spent lying in bed can all contribute to early resolution of delirium.

Management of delirium in a general hospital—key tips

- **Hospital admission:** identify high-risk cases, taking into account the possible predisposing and precipitating factors.
- **Use a standardized delirium assessment tool:** tools such as the Confusion Assessment Method (see box) can aid diagnosis
- **Perform a baseline mental and cognitive state examination:** observe for changes in mental and cognitive state.
- **Change observed in cognitive/mental state:** identify if the change is of acute onset or an aggravation of pre-existing illness such as dementia or psychosis.
- **For all acute changes in mental/cognitive state:** evaluate for the possibility of delirium using the diagnostic criteria. Try to rule out dementia, depression, and acute psychosis. Get specialist advice at this stage and don't wait for symptoms to become more complicated. Treat all acute changes/disturbance in mental and cognitive state as delirium.
- **Identify and eliminate predisposing and precipitating factors:** this process would include obtaining history for drug abuse and benzodiazepine use, monitoring vital signs, detailed physical and neurological examination, and laboratory tests which may include the following: MSU, FBC, B_{12} and folic levels, TFT, LFT, blood gas levels, ECG, lumbar puncture, and neuroimaging.
- **Review medications:** try to eliminate or alter all unnecessary medications that might contribute to delirium.
- **Prevent complications:** this would include procedures such as protecting the airways, preventing aspiration pneumonias, maintaining adequate hydration and nutritional support, skin care, mobilization, and prevention of deep-vein thrombosis.
- **Managing agitated patients actively:** only use pharmacological interventions for severely agitated patients, and as a general rule start with a low dose and titrate until the desired behavioural control is achieved. Try to use oral medication and use the parenteral route if oral medication is not possible.
- **Use non-pharmacological intervention** Environmental alterations and aids to reduce sensory deprivation such as eyeglasses and hearing aids are the most important.

The Confusion Assessment Method[1]

The diagnosis of delirium requires a present or abnormal rating for criteria 1 and 2 plus either 3 or 4.

1. Acute onset and fluctuating course

Is there evidence of an acute change in mental status from the patient's baseline? Did this behaviour fluctuate during the past day—that is, tend to come and go or increase and decrease in severity? (Usually requires information from a family member or carers.)

2. Inattention

Does the patient have difficulty focusing attention—for example, are they easily distracted or do they have difficulty keeping track of what is being said? (Inattention can be detected by the digit span test or asking for the days of the week to be recited backwards.)

3. Disorganized thinking

Is the patient's speech disorganized or incoherent, such as rambling or irrelevant conversation, unclear or illogical flow of ideas, or unpredictable switching between subjects? (Disorganized thinking and sleepiness can also be detected during conversation with the patient.)

4. Altered level of consciousness

Overall, would you rate this patient's level of consciousness as alert (normal), vigilant (hyperalert), lethargic (drowsy, easily aroused), stupor (difficult to arouse), or coma (cannot be roused)? All ratings except alert are scored as abnormal.

---

1 Adapted from: Inouye SK (2003). *The Confusion Assessment Method (CAM): training manual and coding guide*. Yale University School of Medicine, Boston; Young J, Inouye SK (2007). *BMJ*, **34**: 842–6.

Managing the delirious patient in a care home

Delirium in care homes is common and a number of factors including old age, medical comorbidity, polypharmacy, sensory impairments, and dementia can put care home residents at higher risk of developing delirium.

History and background information

- A careful history of the events leading up to the start of illness should be taken. The staff at the care home that have known the patient for some time are the best people to provide this information. Identification of the onset (acute or chronic), pattern of deterioration, sleep/wake cycle, food and fluid intake, changes in bowel habits, sensory deficits (deafness, cataracts, loss of spectacles and hearing aids) should be considered.
- A careful history of signs of acute infections, such as urinary tract infections, upper and lower respiratory tract infections, and skin infections should be taken.
- A detailed review of the patient's current list of medications, recent changes of dose/addition of new medications with possible deliriogenic effects should be made.
- Personal distress caused by pain and its causes, (varying from arthritis to metastatic cancer) should be taken into account. Chronic or acute on chronic constipation is a common cause of delirium and should always be considered in patients at care homes.

Past medical history

- Ischaemic heart disease and CVD along with metabolic disorders should be considered. An aggravation of an already existing chronic physical disease such as renal or hepatic failure could have precipitated delirium.
- Past history of psychiatric illnesses such as schizophrenia, bipolar affective disorder, depression, and anxiety is important in the assessment as they could complicate the clinical picture or the presentation might be due to a recurrence of a psychotic illness.

Mental state and cognitive examination

- There is no short cut to a detailed mental state and cognitive examination. As the diagnosis of delirium rests on the clinical skill of the physician, special emphasis should be laid on the patient's appearance, signs of agitation, perceptual abnormalities, and cognitive disturbances, including reduced attention and concentration and shifting attention.
- Use of diagnostic instruments can sometimes be helpful, and nursing staff can be trained to administer them. The Confusion Assessment Method (see Management of delirium in a general hospital—key tips) is a widely known instrument, which is easy to administer, and is available in long and short versions. The shorter version has only four questions and takes minutes to complete.

Investigations/management

- Routine investigations such as MSU, FBC, LFT, urine electrolyte levels, lipid profile and TFT should be carried out urgently. An ECG (although not always practically possible to carry out in care homes) could be helpful in ruling a recent cardiac event.
- Management should be a combination of environmental and pharmacological interventions.
- The staff should be made aware of the provisional diagnosis and environmental modifications required for the particular patient such as encouraging wakefulness during the day and replacement of spectacles or hearing aid, administration and timing of medication to control severely disturbed behaviours, and strategies to prevent escalation of agitation by using medication at the earliest signs of behavioural disturbance. The pharmacological interventions may also include a course of antibiotics for an ongoing infection, laxatives for relieving constipation, and painkillers for adequate pain control.
- Other management strategies might also include involving professionals from other disciplines in the patient's care, such as podiatrists to tackle painful/infected in-growing toenails, physiotherapists to provide exercise plans for arthritis, referrals to pain clinics for adequate pain relief with medications, skin patches, or acupuncture.

Follow-up

- It is essential that the treatment plan for delirious patients should include follow-up due to the high morbidity and mortality, especially in patients with underlying dementia.
- The follow-up should include a review of the results of investigations, effectiveness of the management plan (both pharmacological and non-pharmacological) and examining other interventions such as seeking specialist advice or hospital admission if the symptoms are not subsiding or are aggravating. This is especially important in a care home environment where patients can be more vulnerable than hospital inpatients and a contingency plan with the care home staff should be discussed, such as calling out emergency ambulance services if the condition deteriorates. Direct communication with the specialist/hospital staff by the referring doctor can be helpful in avoiding unnecessary delays by repeating investigations/assessment by the hospital staff.

Pharmacological management of delirium

Pharmacological management should be planned according to the symptomatology of an individual patient and would generally aim at control of symptoms (delusions and hallucinations), improving the sleep/wake cycle, and controlling agitation and aggression.

It is useful to formulate a management plan and clearly identify the symptoms/behaviours to be targeted with pharmacological intervention before prescribing medication.

The following steps are useful in making a pharmacological intervention plan:

- A careful analysis of the risks and benefits of drug treatment.
- A review of the current list of medication and consideration of stopping the possible 'deliriogenic' drugs may be useful.
- Making staff aware of early symptoms that could potentially escalate to cause behavioural disturbance can result in reduced use of medication.
- Oral administration of medication should be the preferred route of administration unless it is contraindicated or not possible due to lack of insight or behavioural disturbance.
- Administering medication parenterally (intramuscular or intravenous) can be challenging for the staff and a clear plan about the possible use of physical restraint can be useful. This is especially important if the staff are not trained to use restraint and may require the help of psychiatric nursing staff.
- Antipsychotics (typical and atypical) are the mainstay of treatment and are effective in all types of delirium.
- Amongst typical antipsychotics, haloperidol is usually the drug of choice. It has been found to be effective in a number of RCTs. It has a short duration of action and can cause extra-pyramidal side-effects and prolongation of the QT interval. It is usually safe in comorbid medical conditions but should be avoided in alcohol withdrawal syndrome and hepatic failure. The usual dose recommended for the elderly is 0.5–1mg twice a day orally with additional doses every 4 to 6h if required. In severely disturbed and aggressive patients it can be given intramuscularly (0.5–1mg) and repeated after 30–60 min until the behaviour is controlled. It can also be used intravenously in extremes of behavioural disturbance but should not be used IV as a routine because of its short duration of action.
- Among atypical antipsychotics, risperidone (0.5mg twice daily), olanzapine (2.5–5mg once daily) and quetiapine (25mg twice a day) can be used. The evidence for their effectiveness and safety comes from small uncontrolled studies. Risperidone and olanzapine have been associated with increased risk of cerebrovascular events and mortality in patients with dementia. These drugs have an advantage of having slightly less risk of causing extra-pyramidal side-effects compared with haloperidol. They do, however, prolong the QT interval.

- Benzodiazepines may be particularly helpful where the delirium is caused by withdrawal of alcohol or sedatives. Benzodiazepines with rapid onset and short duration of action, such as lorazepam, are preferred and can be given orally or in extreme emergencies, IV. Lorazepam (0.5–1mg) with additional doses every 4–6h can be used as a second-line agent in treating all forms of delirium and as a first-line agent in treating delirium due to sedative and alcohol withdrawal, Parkinson's disease, and neuroleptic malignant syndrome. It is known to sometimes cause over-sedation, respiratory depression, and sometimes, paradoxical excitation.
- Some other drugs such as trazodone, a tricyclic-related antidepressant, in doses of 25–150mg orally at bedtime may be useful (very limited evidence) in treating delirious patients with a disturbed sleep/wake cycle and night time disturbance. More recently some reports about the possible use of CHEIs in treating and preventing delirium have emerged but there have been no convincing controlled trials demonstrating their efficacy.

Non-pharmacological management of delirium

The non-pharmacological approach is equally, if not more, important than pharmacological interventions and should be an integral part of the management plan, tailored according to the needs of an individual patient.

Environmental modification

This aims at creating a calm and comfortable environment for the disturbed patient, taking into consideration the following:
- Noise control.
- Use of orientating influences, such as calendars, clocks, and familiar objects from home.
- Regular communication and reassurance by the staff and limiting room and staff changes.
- Involving family members in supportive care.
- Avoiding procedures such as venepuncture and catheterization at night-time to allow the patient to have uninterrupted periods of sleep.
- Encouraging normal sleep/wake cycles by dimming the lights and providing a calm environment at bed time and encouraging wakefulness and mobility during the day.
- Encouraging early mobilization, especially after orthopaedic surgical procedures, by involving physiotherapists and podiatrist to provide a structured routine of physical activity during the waking hours.

Sufferer's experience of delirium

Reports suggest that patients may recall their experience of delirium more vividly than expected from the profound disturbances in consciousness and awareness. These reports suggest that up to 80% of patients with delirium can recall their experiences (often in great detail) and a similarity between the experience of delirium and the recall of dreams has been noted. These observations emphasize the importance of non-pharmacological interventions such as patient listening, reassurance, and orientation techniques. Many such reports recall the experience of helplessness and terror common among patients with delirium; bear this in mind when organizing care.

Further reading

Burns A, Gallagley A, Byrne J (2004). *J Neurol Neurosurg Psychiat*, **75**: 362–7.

Fairburn AF (2002). Delirium – an overview. In: *Principles and practice of geriatric psychiatry*, 2nd edn (ed. JRM Copeland, MT Abou-Saleh and DG Blazer). John Wiley and Sons, Chichester, pp. 179–182.

Inouye SK (2006). Delirium in older persons. *N Engl J Med*, **354**: 1157–65.

Young J, Inouye SK (2007). *BMJ*, **34**: 842–6.

Mood disorders

Mood disorders—an overview 96
Diagnosing depression 97
Depression—epidemiology 98
Special presentations of depression in older people:
   1, Pseudodementia 99
Special presentations of depression in older people:
   2, Hypochondriasis 100
Special presentations of depression in older people:
   3, Severe retardation 101
Suicide in older people 102
Managing an older person after an overdose 104
Aetiology of depression in older people: 1, Biological
   factors 106
Aetiology of depression in older people: 2, Psychological and
   social factors 108
Management of depression among older people—drug treat-
   ment 109
Drug treatment of depression—alternatives to SSRIs 110
Drug treatment—second line 112
ECT 114
Psychological treatment of depression 115
Managing the recently bereaved 116
Managing depression in frail older people 117
Depression rating scales 118
GDS-15 119
Mania and bipolar illness 120
Managing mania and bipolar illness 121
Drugs for mania 122

Mood disorders—an overview

Depression

- Depression is the most common and important psychiatric disorder worldwide. It is also the most common disorder in older people, among whom community surveys show the prevalence of significant depression at 10–15%. It is important among older people because it is common, causes inherent suffering, is associated with suicide, and is clearly associated with poorer outcomes for physical illness. It also persists for longer in older people, among whom intervention now may be only 'just in time' in the context of a life course.
- Despite this, depressive illness is under-reported, under-detected and under-treated among older people. Reasons for this may lie with patients or services.
- Patients may be ashamed of reporting depression, may not recognize depression, may present with physical rather than emotional symptoms, or may manifest particular behaviours (for example throwing oneself on the floor, hypochondriasis, agitation) which are not typical of depression among younger people.
- Services may contribute through ignorance (a lack of training on depression among older people), apathy (a belief that depression is inevitable with the changes of old age or that change in a person's situation is futile), or misplaced altruism (a concern that the older person may be embarrassed by psychological inquiry or damaged by antidepressant treatment). Finally, secondary care services are often configured to deal with the more public face of mental health in old age—dementia; they may be less well placed to deal with depression.
- A focus in many countries on earlier recognition and management of depression, particularly in primary care, is welcome. The core skills to manage depression in older people are the same as for the young: clear history taking, examination of the mental state, prudent use of evidence-based treatments, good communication.

Mania

Classic mania, with elevated mood, self-important ideas and overactivity, may present for the first time in older age; graduation of patients with bipolar affective disorder from younger life is more common. When mania is associated with a clear organic illness the term secondary mania may be used. Medications used in treating mania, especially lithium, have increased side-effect and interaction potential in older people.

Diagnosing depression

Depressive symptoms are very common; the diagnosis of depressive illness is based on agreed thresholds for clusters of symptoms occurring together. These symptoms are recognized in DSM-IV and ICD-10 (despite some differences) and are the same in older age groups. A depressive illness is recognized when symptoms persist for several weeks and interfere with function. Major depression is a DSM-IV term often used to denote more severe disorders. The term minor depression is used to denote a less severe but troublesome level of depression which meets the general criterion for depressive disorders. Repeated studies have shown that significant depression, at a level considered worth treating by expert clinicians, is persistent, causes distress, and is associated with poor psychiatric, physical, and social outcomes. Diagnosis is based on careful history taking together with observation of core abnormalities of mental state. No reliable biological marker of depressive disorder is available.

Core symptoms
- Low mood.
- Reduced enjoyment.
- Reduced energy.

Psychological symptoms
- Poor self-esteem.
- Pessimistic, guilty, hopeless, or suicidal thinking.

Somatic (biological) symptoms
- Reduced appetite.
- Reduced weight.
- Diurnal variation of mood (lower in morning).
- Waking at least 2h early.
- Reduced concentration.
- Agitation or psychomotor retardation.

Severe/psychotic symptoms
- Delusions especially mood congruent delusions of a nihilistic type, failure, extreme guilt, deserving of punishment, hypochondriacal (e.g. has cancer).
- Hallucinations especially voices commenting on an individual's supposed failure, commands to self-harm, or olfactory hallucinations (e.g. of rotting flesh).
- Stupor; patient is mute, unresponsive and immobile but awake. This may be associated with risk of death from dehydration.

Presentations more likely in older than younger patients
- Agitation.
- Psychomotor retardation.
- Hypochondriasis/somatization (physical symptoms predominate for patient).
- Histrionic behaviour (e.g. throwing oneself on the floor).
- Dangerously poor food/fluid intake.
- Pseudodementia (depression presenting with significant cognitive impairment).

Depression—epidemiology

Prevalence: general
- Major depression (strict DSM-IV criteria) 1–3% in community elderly.
- Significant depression (considered worthy of treatment by a psychiatrist) 10–15%.

Prevalence in special groups
- Older medical inpatients 12–40%: particular groups with high prevalence of depression reported include post-MI, cancer patients, diabetic patients, patients with Parkinson's disease, and post-stroke patients.
- Residential/nursing home residents 20–40%: rates of detection and treatment of depression in this population are especially poor. Ignorance of depression among staff, pessimism about outcomes, and masking of the condition by dementia and physical illness may contribute.
- People with dementia 25%: a quarter of people with dementia will develop depressive illness at some point during the course of their illness. Depressive *symptoms* are common in dementia; these tend to fluctuate significantly over time.

Well-supported risk factors for depression
- Female gender.
- Poor health.
- Disability.
- Poor perceived social support.

Partially supported risk factors for depression
- Loneliness.
- Family history.
- Bereavement.

Outcomes
There is increasing evidence that the outcome of depression at all ages is less good than previously thought: chronicity, relapse, and recurrence are common. It is clear that depression has the following risks:
- Increased mortality, after controlling for medical illness burden.
- Increased suicide risk.
- 20% become chronic.
- 60% recover but have relapses/further episodes.
- 20% make full recovery.

Worse outcome if
- Depressive symptoms are severe.
- Abnormal personality.
- Severe burden of chronic physical illness.

Special presentations of depression in older people: 1, Pseudodementia

Case example

A 72-year-old woman is referred to psychiatric services with a 3-month history of poor self-care, 'confusion', poor eating, recent incontinence of urine, and poor performance on primary care screening tool for cognitive impairment. For some months she has also been low in mood, lacked confidence, and feels hopeless about the future. At clinic, she scores only 12/30 on MMSE, often answering 'I don't know'.

Pseudodementia is a term used for any non-organic cause of dementia which can resolve with resolution of the underlying problem. The term usually refers to depressive pseudodementia. The patient is likely to show poor self-care, lack of concentration, and may appear very forgetful. On testing, deficits are worst on attentional tasks, for example, concentration (e.g. serial sevens or 'WORLD' backward), retrieval of short-term memories, but less likely in 'cortical' tasks, e.g. apraxia/dysphasia. The latter deficits would strongly suggest organic dementia. In the 1980s pseudodementia was felt to be a common misdiagnosis. More recent work has shown that the majority of older people who present with serious cognitive deficits while depressed do not recover full cognitive function, while those who do are at increased risk of subsequent dementia.

Management points
- Clear history—which came first, depression or cognitive impairment?
- In mental state examination are there clear features of depression—sad appearance, hopelessness, retardation, or agitation?
- On cognitive testing, does the patient do worse on attentional tasks?
- Are there a lot of 'I don't know' answers?
- Is memory performance better with cueing (e.g. hinting at the answer)?
- If depressed, treat with therapeutic course of antidepressant, e.g. SSRI for 6–8 weeks before making a change.
- May be appropriate to do dementia screen in the interim (blood screen/neuroimaging) in anticipation of persistent cognitive deficits.

Special presentations of depression in older people: 2, Hypochondriasis

Case example

An 84-year-old man has a history of arthritis and congestive cardiac failure. He has been attending much more frequently than normal in primary care. He reports a headache and worries that he may have a brain tumour. He reports poor sleep, weight loss, and 'I just can't enjoy anything because of this'. His wife died 6 months previously.

Hypochondriasis means an unjustified morbid fear of illness. A closely related term is somatization, which refers to presentations to see a clinician with unexplained physical symptoms which cannot be explained by organic factors but don't respond to reassurance. Hypochondriacal presentations are just as common in older people and depression is the most important psychiatric association of these presentations. Depressive illness should be suspected in all such cases. Fear of cancer is particularly likely in older people with severe depression. Preoccupation may be total, leading to relentless pursuit of hospital tests and admission. The hypochondriacal ideas may reach delusional intensity. Such ideas will usually resolve when underlying depression is treated.

Management points

- Clarify the history clearly, especially evidence for depressive illness.
- It is often useful to examine the patient physically to reassure them, establish credibility of the clinician, and avoid surprises during treatment.
- Medically qualified clinicians may find uncertainty about symptoms easier to handle than other professionals, e.g. nurses.
- New investigation may still be needed; a parallel approach of investigating while treating underlying causes of hypochondriasis may in fact be appropriate.
- Treat underlying depression, e.g. with 8 weeks of SSRI or if this does not work use a mixed serotonin/noradrenaline active antidepressant, e.g. venlafaxine (can raise blood pressure) or mirtazepine (can sedate).
- If delusional, add low-dose antipsychotic, e.g. 2.5–5.0mg olanzapine daily.
- Set strict appointments and call a halt to further investigations.
- Use judgement if new symptoms arise; older people have much higher incidence of new physical illness.

Special presentations of depression in older people: 3, Severe retardation

Case example

A 79-year-old woman is referred with a history over several weeks of low mood, reduced appetite and weight, not going out, and poor communication. Primary care ask for an urgent psychiatric opinion as she has in last 3 days stopped most talking, is incontinent, eats barely any food, and is drinking only 500ml of fluids per day. On assessment, she is clinically dehydrated. She rocks back and forth on a chair and makes little eye contact. She constantly whispers 'it's no good, it's no good'. She refuses all offers of help from nurses, social services, and family.

Presentations of depression with severe retardation are more frequent in older people. Other features found are likely to include suicidal ideation, psychotic symptoms especially nihilistic, hypochondriacal, or guilty delusions, agitation (inner sense of restlessness associated with motor overactivity), and poor food and fluid intake. In older people, progression to malnutrition, and particularly to dehydration, is particularly likely and makes prompt assessment essential. These clinical features predict a favourable response to ECT, which may need to be given against the will of the patient.

Management points

- Urgent assessment is required.
- Assess nutrition and hydration status of patient—look for dry lips and tongue, low blood pressure, weak rapid pulse, change in skin turgor, diminished consciousness.
- Admission to hospital usually required, if necessary compulsorily, e.g. under Section 2 of Mental Health Act England and Wales.
- Baseline investigations in hospital should include those needed to assess anaesthetic fitness—physical examination, U&E, full blood count, ECG, chest X-ray.
- Arrange fluid balance chart and parenteral rehydration if needed.
- Assess suicidal ideas in deciding observation required on ward—suicide risk may increase as retardation lessens but depressive ideation remains.
- Choice of treatment likely to be between ECT or a combination of antidepressant with antipsychotic.

Suicide in older people

Epidemiology

Around 500 people aged over the age of 65 commit suicide each year in the UK. The usual mode of suicide is overdose, whereas in other countries, e.g. the USA, more lethal methods (hanging, shooting) are most common. In the elderly, completed suicide is more common among men, while attempts are found equally among men and women. Suicide rates overall have fallen in a number of Western countries (including the UK) from 1970s on. This fall has been more pronounced among older people, for reasons that are not understood. The most important risk factors remain male gender, depressive illness, and painful physical illness.

Definite higher risk

- Male gender (3–4 times more likely to commit suicide).
- Depressive illness (at least two-thirds of completed suicides).
- Physical illness, especially if painful.

Probable higher risk

- Socially isolated.
- Widowed (for male widowers; women appear protected from this risk).
- Abnormal personality.
- Alcohol abuse.

No clear association

- Dementia.

Lower risk

- Residential care.
- Currently married.
- Female gender.

Compared with younger people

- Suicide attempts among older people are generally more serious than among younger people. A higher proportion of attempts are genuine attempts to die. When followed up, older people who have attempted suicide (self-harmed) are more likely to kill themselves than younger people. Predictors of completed suicide are male gender, and a history of depression.

Prevention

- Primary prevention—remove lethal means, e.g. banning coproxamol, replacing tricyclic antidepressants with SSRIs, catalytic converters (catalytic converters on exhausts make it harder to commit suicide through carbon monoxide poisoning).
- Secondary prevention—screening for depression in primary care, or among older medical inpatients, combined with education of clinicians.

Managing an older person after an overdose

General principles
- Manage medical consequences of overdose as a priority.
- Assess further risk.
- Identify psychiatric disorder.
- Identify life problems which can be meaningfully addressed.

Background
- In history taking, also get a collateral history from another person (especially family members).
- Does he/she have symptoms of depression (low mood, hopelessness, sleep/appetite/weight disturbance/diurnal variation)?
- Is he/she widowed?
- What are his/her social contacts?
- Any previous history of suicide attempts?
- Is he/she in pain?
- Has he/she suffered recent losses?

The attempt
- Was it planned or spontaneous?
- How long had she/he been feeling like this?
- Did she/he think the method would be fatal?
- Were there any final acts (making a will, writing a note)?
- Did she/he conceal the attempt?
- Was she/he found by accident?

Current attitude
- Does he/she wish he/she had died?
- How does he/she feel about the future?
- How does he/she feel others would be affected?
- Does he/she want to live? Does he/she plan to do it again?
- Are there depressive features in the mental state (agitation, retardation, sad expression, hopelessness, suicidal ideas)?
- Has anything about situation changed?

Decide risk
- Need to decide if risk is high or low, in short term and longer term.
- Classic high-risk patient: male sex, widowed, bone cancer, depressive illness, on tricyclic antidepressants, planned attempt, survived by luck, wishes he had died, ambivalent about repetition.
- Classic low-risk patient: female sex, married, spontaneous attempt after stress, mild depressive illness, good support, guilty about worrying family, physically well.

Where to manage the patient?

For high-risk patients, transfer to a psychiatric unit may be needed, in some cases under compulsion. For lower-risk patients, discharge home with support, e.g. family, community mental health team, day hospital, general practitioner is appropriate.

Who will manage the patient?

In any case where risk appears substantial, assessment by a specialist (nurse or doctor from mental health service) is appropriate. The specialist can advise on precise risk status and arrange ongoing management. If the patient appears high risk and insists on leaving, compulsion to remain until specialist assessment is appropriate.

Intervene to achieve change

- Treat any depressive disorder.
- Increase analgesia and refer to pain clinic if in pain.
- Arrange social support, e.g. day centre, if isolated.
- Psychological treatment, e.g. bereavement counselling.

Aetiology of depression in older people: 1, Biological factors

Biological factors which may cause depressive illness have been very extensively researched in younger people—especially genetics, neuroendocrine studies and functional imaging. Key findings in depression include enhanced genetic risk, diminished monoamine neurotransmission, enhanced glucocorticoid neurotransmission, and abnormalities in certain cortical areas on functional imaging. It remains unclear whether these changes are primary or secondary to depression. Such research has often excluded older people. It is known that monoamine neurotransmission changes in older age; often but not always in a way similar to that seen in depression. Below are outlined findings particularly relevant to older people with depression.

Genetics

It is clear that genetic risk is lower in later life; people with late-onset depression have fewer than half as many relatives with a history of depression as among younger-onset depression.

Physical illness

A vital risk factor which operates independently of age. Most physical illnesses increase the risk of depression among older people. Conditions which may cause cortical and subcortical brain lesions including stroke, Parkinson's disease, and dementia increase the risk of depression substantially.

Disability and handicap

It is clear that, independent of physical illness, the handicap that older people with physical illness experience in functioning in society is a very important risk factor for depression. This has important implications for primary and secondary prevention of depression.

Depression and dementia

It is clear that depression is more common in people with dementia. Similarly, depression can be the first clinical presentation of dementia—sometimes as an understandable response to a diagnosis, sometimes in a patient unaware of cognitive problems. Depression may also be a risk factor for dementia; putative shared causes include elevated glucocorticoids and loss of monoamine neurotransmitters.

Vascular depression

Vascular depression is a term essentially describing the hypothesis that in old age, depression may be primarily caused by small vessel cerebrovascular disease. It has led to a search for confirmatory evidence and a focus on interventions for vascular disease as a secondary intervention for some people with depression. The key focus is on deep white matter lesions (DWMLs) in orbito-frontal circuits and in the basal ganglia. Not all studies confirm the hypothesis but the balance of evidence shows:

- Depression is commoner in post-stroke patients.
- MRI DWMLs are more common in depressed than non-depressed older people.
- DWMLs are more common in late-onset than early onset depression.
- DWMLs predict a poorer response to treatment of depression.
- Post-mortem studies tend to confirm imaging findings.

At present, looking for the presence of DWMLs on MRI is not supported as a routine investigation in late-onset depression unless another indication exists; vigorous treatment of depression and of vascular conditions like diabetes, atrial fibrillation. and hypertension remain common-sense interventions.

Aetiology of depression in older people: 2, Psychological and social factors

Old age is a time of considerable readjustment; to frailty, to loss of family/partners, to changes in accommodation. It is a myth to contend that depression or even demoralization are normal in old age—psychological studies show that older people are at least as happy and well adjusted as younger people and psychiatric studies show the prevalence of depressive illness is the same. Non-biological factors do have well-known effects on mood which are important both in considering individual cases and in establishing high-risk populations. These include:

- Bereavement.
- Isolation/loneliness.
- Disability.
- Life events including moving house, financial, relationship events.
- Social role changes, e.g. ceasing caring role as childminder.
- Caring role, especially for person with dementia.
- Residence—residential home versus own home.
- Personality type/psychological style.

Table 4.1 summarizes these factors.

Table 4.1 Factors to look for in formulating an individual case of depression in old age

	Biological	Psychological	Social
Predisposing	Genetic (family history)	Early parental loss/trauma	Lower social class
Precipitating	Stroke, MI	Bereavement	Change of accommodation
Perpetuating	Pain Deep white matter changes in cortex on MRI	Abnormal personality	Handicap from disability
Protective	Compliance with medication, pain relief	Family support	Social contact

Management of depression among older people—drug treatment

General principles

Most antidepressants are of about the same efficacy, and most patients who benefit from an antidepressant recover after 6–8 weeks. There is no convincing evidence that any one antidepressant works better, or more quickly, than others. Differences between drugs are largely around side-effects and to some extent cost. Particular considerations for older people are medical comorbidity, potential drug interactions, changes in pharma-cokinetic handling of the drug, and seriousness of side-effects. A particular consideration in recurrent depression is what has worked before—you need a good reason not to use it again if it has worked before.

SSRIs

These are a class of antidepressants which became widely prescribed during the 1990s and are now the most common antidepressants used at any age. They work by preventing reuptake of the key monoamine neu-rotransmitter serotonin (5-HT), thus promoting serotonergic neurotrans-mission. A number have been shown to work in trials specifically among older people. They have fewer serious side-effects than older drugs and are considerably safer in overdose. SSRIs have been recommended in NICE guidance on treatment of depression as first-line drug treatment for depression among adults of all ages in the UK.

SSRI name	Target daily dose
Fluoxetine	20mg
Citalopram	20mg
Escitalopram	10mg
Sertraline	100mg
Paroxetine	20mg
Fluvoxamine	100–200mg (divided doses over 100mg)

Most older people can tolerate initiation on the once-daily full thera-peutic dose of fluoxetine, citalopram, escitalopram, and paroxetine. Start sertraline at 50mg daily. Fluoxetine has a long half-life so can be stopped abruptly. Paroxetine has shortest half-life so must be stopped gradually to avoid withdrawal reactions which may be severe. Fluvoxamine is rarely used in the UK and probably causes most gastrointestinal side-effects. All may cause early anxiety and gastrointestinal discomfort and all may cause hyponatraemia (stop antidepressant, refer to general medicine if serum Na remains below 125mmol/L). There is some increased risk of gastroin-testinal haemorrhage among older people on SSRIs.

Drug treatment of depression— alternatives to SSRIs

Serotonin/noradrenaline active drugs

- Venlafaxine is a SNRI (serotonin/noradrenaline reuptake inhibitor) which is effective in treating depressive illness. The target dose is 112.5–150mg/day. There is a concern about raised blood pressure at the higher doses. A concern has been expressed about cardiac risk on venlafaxine but it can be freely prescribed in UK without specialist opinion.
- Mirtazepine (target dose 30–45mg/day) is a serotonin/noradrenaline active agent which is particularly useful in sleepless patients. Monitoring of FBC may be needed as it may cause blood dyscrasias.
- Duloxetine (target dose 60mg/day) also works by preventing reuptake of both serotonin and noradrenaline. It is generally well tolerated.

Tricyclic antidepressants

This class of drug led the era of antidepressant prescribing from the 1950s, when imipramine was introduced. These drugs are undoubtedly effective in depression and appear to exert their effect by preventing reuptake of serotonin and noradrenaline into pre-synaptic nerve endings. They have many other effects including α-receptor blockade (hypotension), anticholinergic effects (dry mouth, urinary retention, constipation), drowsiness, and in higher doses destabilization of the cardiac membrane, making them particularly dangerous in overdose. Equally effective agents with fewer side-effects have made new prescriptions less common. Commonly used tricyclic antidepressants include imipramine, amitryptiline, clomipramine, dothiepin, trimipramine, and a more modern tricyclic called lofepramine (target dose 70–210mg/day), which has fewer toxic effects. In older people, tricyclic antidepressants should be started at low doses (e.g. 25mg/day for amitryptiline, 10mg/day for clomipramine or imipramine) and built up slowly, warning the patient about likely side-effects.

Monoamine oxidase inhibitors (MAOIs)

This class of drug was introduced in the 1950s but has fallen out of favour due to potential interaction with certain drugs, e.g. other antidepressants, nasal decongestants, and opiate analgesics, and with tyramine-containing foods, which may precipitate a hypertensive crisis. A newer reversible and selective MAOI, moclobemide, has fewer restrictions on use and is a useful alternative to older MAOIs such as phenelzine and tranylcypromine.

Drug treatment—second line

In general, expect 60–70% of older people with depressive disorders to respond to a full course of an adequate dose of an antidepressant. For those who do not, a change in treatment strategy is needed. This may include a change to a non-drug treatment like ECT or psychological treatment (such as CBT)

Options include to
- Increase dose.
- Switch class.
- Augment.

Increase dose

Rarely likely to be helpful if a therapeutic dose has been achieved (e.g. already on 20mg/day of citalopram, fluoxetine, or paroxetine). Increasing to higher doses should only be tried with frequent monitoring for side-effects and when there has been at least partial response to initial course of antidepressant.

Switch class

A switch of class of agent is appropriate. A sensible initial strategy is to switch from a first-line SSRI to a noradrenaline/serotonin active agent or vice versa. Some patients will respond to a switch to a tricyclic antidepressant but the new drug should be started at a lower dose and weekly review to increase dose and review response and side-effects is recommended. Switching to a MAOI requires precise washout periods and particular expertise and should always be done after referral to a specialist.

Augment antidepressant

Augmentation involves the addition of a new agent to an existing antidepressant drug. The most common agent used in augmentation has been lithium. Small controlled trials support the usefulness of this strategy but lithium interacts with many commonly prescribed drugs among older people, including SSRIs and thiazide diuretics (both increasing the risk of lithium neurotoxicity) so this is another manoeuvre only to be used with specialist review.

Other augmentation strategies include the addition of atypical antipsychotics (especially useful in patients with delusions) or triiodothyronine (T3). Combinations of two antidepressants are sometimes used; this should only be done in specialist hands due to risks of hypertension and severe serotinergic side-effects.

How long to treat for?

- Depressive illness usually takes 6–8 weeks for a full recovery.
- Older people are at significant risk of relapse (within 6 months) and recurrence (after 6 months).
- The full dose of antidepressant used to make them well, if tolerated, should be used for at least 6 months, then gradually withdrawn.

- Observe for re-emergence of depression on withdrawal.
- For those with recurrent depressive disorder, permanent maintenance therapy at full dose is appropriate.
- Maintenance treatment is superior to placebo for up to 2 years in older people, even in first-onset cases.
- Consider maintenance treatment in any older person you feel is at risk.

ECT

ECT is a proven and generally safe treatment for depression including among older people. The main indication is likely to be severe depressive illness, especially where clinical features include delusions, refusal to eat or drink, and severe retardation, all presentations found more commonly among older people. The problems of ECT are no different in older people, but issues to consider include anaesthetic fitness and management of cognitive impairment associated with ECT.

Pre-treatment considerations

- Consent to treatment (incompetent patients, or those refusing but in need of ECT, may require detention under mental health legislation).
- Medications used - particular cautions with benzodiazepines (raise seizure threshold), lithium (confusion and lithium toxicity), clozapine (may lower seizure threshold).
- Anaesthetic fitness.
- Previous anaesthetic/treatment response.

Investigations

- ECG, chest X-ray, U&E, FBC, physical examination.
- Cognitive examination (e.g. of anterograde memory; the MMSE may be too crude for this task).

Day of treatment

- Nil by mouth.
- Reassure patient.
- Oxygenation.
- Record seizure duration.

Recovery

- Monitor during recovery.
- Post-treatment cognitive impairment (reassure) and headache (use simple analgesia, e.g. paracetamol).

Between treatments

- Assess clinical response to each treatment.
If cognitively impaired
- Reduce frequency of treatment.
- Unilateral electrode placement.
- Alternative treatment (antidepressants, psychological treatment).

Psychological treatment of depression

While social interventions such as attendance at day centres are often initiated for older people with depression, psychological treatment is underused. Reasons for this may include lack of provision of services, a perception that older people do less well in psychological therapy (Freud described older people as 'ineducable'), a perception that older people may not want psychological treatment, or a belief that cognitive impairment will interfere with progress in treatment. Though the vast majority of trials of psychological treatment for depression have been among younger adults, it is now clear that psychotherapy is an effective treatment among older people, with effects about the same as antidepressants and the same as psychological treatment in younger people.

Deciding on psychological treatment

- Does the patient have cognitive impairment which would make treatment difficult?
- What is the treatment preference of the patient?
- What psychological treatment is available?
- Group versus individual therapy—there is no evidence one better than another so depends on availability and preference. Group therapy is a dominant mode of treatment for depression in day hospitals for older people.
- Mode of therapy—the main types of psychological treatment appear equally effective among older people.

CBT

Based on Aaron Beck's principle that how we think and how we act can influence our mood, rather than other way round. Therapy typically lasts for 6–20 weekly sessions. Unhelpful beliefs and behaviours are identified and countered cognitively (cognitive therapy) or behaviourally.

Analytic psychotherapy

Originated from work of Freud a century ago. Assumes that psychological distress arises from unresolved unconscious conflicts. Uses techniques including free association and focus on transference (emotional relationship of patient to therapist) to work through major issues. Can last for years.

Counselling

Term describes a brief therapy where ventilation of distress is encouraged, direct information may be imparted, problem-solving by the patient is encouraged by the therapist. Counselling is probably appropriate for mild to moderate depression, especially when it has arisen in the context of life stress. It is often provided privately or in primary care.

Social management

In the UK, depression in older people is often managed by a community mental health team. Engagement of the patient in social activity to counter absence of positive experiences, regular monitoring of mental state and risks, monitoring of drug dose/side-effects, and direct contact with mental health professional are all likely to contribute to patient benefit.

Managing the recently bereaved

The main point is to know when intervention is necessary. Older people are much more likely to have bereavements than younger people—their siblings/peers are older and those who are currently older people came from larger families.

Normal grieving

Early reactions are disbelief, numbness, shock, and sometimes denial (carrying on as if nothing has happened). This gives way to a combination of anger, sadness, crying, insomnia, appetite loss, preoccupation with the person lost, or guilt (the bereaved person may seek reassurance that they have done everything possible). A significant minority may experience true hallucinations of the lost person. Gradually, these feelings subside as acceptance of the loss occurs, with readjustment of life plans. Grieving usually lasts for 3–12 months—this varies greatly and in some cultures much longer periods are normal.

Pathological grieving

Also known as morbid or abnormal grief, this term is used when grief is either completely absent or is excessively severe or prolonged. Marked hopelessness, strong suicidal ideas, psychomotor retardation, guilt of delusional intensity, or severe weight loss all indicate pathological grief and warrant intervention.

A debate has long existed as to the status of grief—is it a psychiatric disorder or an essential part of human experience? Some feel it is a dismally ignored mental illness, others a necessary part of spiritual renewal. Freud wrote of the similarity between grief and depression in *Mourning and melancholia*. A combination of common sense and experience should make decisions in this area easier.

What to do with a bereaved person

- Sympathize with the loss.
- Understand what is experienced in normal grief.
- Arrange timely review for high-risk people—those with previous depressive disorder, those suddenly bereaved or those socially isolated.
- Look for warning signs of pathological grief—significant weight loss, psychomotor retardation, suicidal and delusional thinking.
- For people with directly bereavement-related distress, counselling at primary care level or with specialist volunteers (e.g. CRUSE, 🖳http://www.crusebereavementcare.org.uk/) may be appropriate.
- For those with clear depressive symptoms, initiate antidepressant treatment and/or psychotherapy (first-line supportive type, consider more specialized therapy including CBT if little progress).
- Optimism is appropriate; vigorous treatment of late-life depression following bereavement has been clearly shown to be effective.

Managing depression in frail older people

Frail older people have a number of risk factors for new depressive disorders—physical illness, disability, higher risk of institutionalization. Managing depression in frail older people requires a vigorous treatment approach and mindfulness of particular problems with treatments. Outcomes of depression among older people with physical illness are no worse than among older people with fewer physical illnesses, despite assertions to the contrary.

Problems with drug treatment in depression

- Compliance issues—reading prescriptions, muddling multiple drugs.
- Swallowing tablets may require assistance or supervision of liquid doses.
- Reduced body mass and deficient renal excretion may lead to greater plasma concentrations and more side-effects early.
- Multiple medications may mean higher risks of interactions, e.g. warfarin effect may be increased by SSRIs, which also diminish hepatic metabolism so may enhance concentrations of other psychotropic drugs and antiepileptics, and can lead to CNS excitation when combined with selegiline.
- Inadequate dosing has been a major problem with tricyclic antidepressants—much less so with SSRIs.

Problems with psychological treatment in frail older people with depression

- Cognitive impairment—either temporary (pseudodementia) or permanent (underlying dementia) may make concentration on psychological treatment difficult.
- Availability of trained therapists is often limited.
- Length of treatment (10–20 weeks) may be too long in frail people with limited life expectancy.
- Apathy and incorrect belief that psychological treatment will not work in older people.
- In some older people, surprise at proposed approach.

Key points in managing frail older people with depression

- In mild cases 'watchful waiting' is appropriate—wait a week to see if it persists.
- Treat underlying pain and relieve physical disability.
- Maximize hydration and nutrition (particular care needed to ensure frail people can actually swallow food).
- Use adequate doses of antidepressant, e.g. start on 10mg/day of citalopram, increasing to 20mg after a week if tolerated and adequate renal function.
- Use liquid form of antidepressant or ask carer to deliver 50–100ml of fluid needed to swallow a tablet.
- Review progress regularly.
- Maintain treatment at full dose for at least 6 months after recovery and permanently in people with previous episodes or at high risk of recurrence.

Depression rating scales

Geriatric Depression Scale (GDS)[1]

Probably the best known and most widely used instrument for detection of depression among older people and is particularly appropriate for screening. It takes about 5 min (15-item version) and can be self- or rater-administered. The original version[1] has 30 items and tends to avoid physical/somatic items which will be endorsed by people with physical illness. It has been developed as a 15-, 10- and even 4-item version. All have been shown to be valid and reliable, though reliability is lowered in more severe dementia. The 15-item version is now widely used including in primary care.

Centre for Epidemiological Studies–Depression Scale (CES-D)[2]

This 20-item scale is self-administered and takes about 5 min to complete. Originally developed for general populations, it is more popular for use with older people. Validity against traditional instruments is established, though caution is advised with visually or cognitively impaired people.

Hamilton Depression Rating Scale (HDRS)[3]

One of the best known depression rating scales and the commonest scale used in trials of antidepressant medication[3]. It takes about 20 min for an interviewer to administer and establishes the severity of symptoms in 17 domains. The time required and the number of physical symptoms may limit its practical usefulness in older clinical populations.

Montgomery and Asberg Depression Rating Scale (MADRS)[4]

Well-validated scale needing an interviewer to spend 20 min with the patient. It rates severity of symptoms in 10 important areas. This scale was designed to be sensitive to change and is especially useful in establishing the effects of treatment. Psychological items dominate, making it suitable for use in older people.

Patient Health Questionnaire 9 (PHQ-9)[5]

Scale widely used in UK primary care. Nine-item self report developed mainly for use in primary care. Probably less well validated among older people than other measures. Easy to use and has demonstrated sensitivity to change.

1 Yesavage J, Brink T, Rose T, Lum O, Adey M, Leirer O (1983). Development and validation of a geriatric depression screening scale: a preliminary report. *J Psychiat Res* **17**: 37–49.

2 Radloff L, Teri L (1986). Use of the Centre for Epidemiological Studies Depression Scale with older adults. *Clin Gerontol* **5**: 119–37.

3 Hamilton M (1960). A rating scale for depression. *J Neurol Neurosurg Psychiatr* **23**: 56–62.

4 Montgomery S, Asberg M (1979). A new depression scale designed to be sensitive to change. *Br J Psychiatr* **134**: 382–9.

5 Kroenke K, Spitzer RC, Williams JBW (2001). The PHQ-9. *J Gen Intern Med* **16**: 606–13.

GDS-15[1]

Undertake the test orally (can be given as a self-rated sheet—omit bold print for this). Ask the patient to reply indicating how they have felt over the past week. Get a clear yes or no reply. Bold answers score one point.

> 1. Are you basically satisfied with your life? Yes/**No**
> 2. Have you dropped many of your activities and interests? **Yes**/No
> 3. Do you feel happy most of the time? Yes/**No**
> 4. Do you prefer to stay at home rather than going out and doing new things? **Yes**/No
> 5. Do you feel that life is empty? **Yes**/No
> 6. Do you often get bored? **Yes**/No
> 7. Are you in good spirits most of the time? Yes/**No**
> 8. Are you afraid that something bad is going to happen to you? **Yes**/No
> 9. Do you feel helpless? **Yes**/No
> 10. Do you feel that you have more problems with memory than most? **Yes**/No
> 11. Do you think it is wonderful to be alive? Yes/**No**
> 12. Do you fee pretty worthless the way you are now? **Yes**/No
> 13. Do you feel full of energy? Yes/**No**
> 14. Do you feel that your situation is hopeless? **Yes**/No
> 15. Do you think that most people are better off than you are? **Yes**/No
>
> *Scoring*
> 0–4   No depression
> 5–8   Mild depression
> 10+   Severe depression

1 Sheikh JL, Yesavage JA (1986). Geriatric Depression Scale (GDS): recent evidence and development of shorter versions. *Clin Gerontol* 819–820.

Mania and bipolar illness

- Bipolar disorder refers to an illness in which patients have episodes of mania (high mood) and depression (low mood). The great majority of those who have a manic episode will go on to have a depressive episode; hence one manic episode is enough for the diagnosis of bipolar disorder (unlike a single depressive episode). Diagnostic issues are the same in older people—the diagnosis is based on at least one week of elevated mood, overactivity, and self-important ideas. Patients are often sleepless, irritable, disregard social norms, spend excessively, and may be pressured in speech. In severe cases grandiose delusions, hallucinations, frenzied overactivity, and violence may be seen. Insight is almost always absent.
- The lifetime incidence of bipolar disorder is just over 0.5%. Most cases begin in the third or fourth decade. New cases in old age are relatively rare. Late-onset cases are less likely to have a family history and more likely to have a diagnosable brain disease. Clinical features are identical and a history of depression is usual. The incidence in older people is unknown—a second peak related to brain disease appears to occur in late life. When found in conjunction with a new brain insult this is known as secondary mania.

Causes of secondary mania

- Stroke (commonest cause and particularly right-sided lesions).
- Tumour.
- Head injury.
- Endocrine conditions.
- HIV infection.
- Medication including steroids and anti-parkinsonian drugs.

Outcome of mania

The outcome of manic episodes among older people is the same as younger people—with treatment, full recovery within 1–2 months is usual. Issues thereafter relate to the particular importance of compliance with mood-stabilizing medication and the general need to monitor patients at high risk of further illness. Cycling directly into severe depression carries particular risks for older people, while in all age groups, when treating for bipolar depression, watch for the risk of precipitating a manic episode.

Managing mania and bipolar illness

General approach

- Assess risk levels—aggression, self-neglect, overspending, legal problems, deterioration, stress to carers.
- Decide where to treat—under the Mental Health Act if necessary.
- Ensure adequate hydration.
- Baseline blood tests to include U&E, FBC, and TFT.
- If mild illness, use a mood stabilizer alone—lithium, carbamazepine, or valproic acid.
- If more severe initiate antipsychotic treatment, e.g. haloperidol 5–20mg/day in divided doses or olanzapine 10mg/day.
- Consider using parenteral treatment if non-compliant (e.g. intramuscular haloperidol or olanzapine).
- If long-term prophylaxis needed, initiate a mood stabilizer at same time.
- Maintain observation in in-patients until absconsion/non-compliance risks are acceptable.
- Observe closely for emergence of depressive symptoms during treatment and particularly for suicidal ideas.

Case example

An 85-year-old patient with a history of recurrent depressive disorder has recently changed: the GP refers her to specialist services. Her husband is exhausted, and reports she has slept poorly, been spending more money, giving money away to local youths, and has been irritable. She denies there is anything wrong. At interview, she is irritable, voluble and somewhat euphoric. Her speech is pressured. She has no grandiose ideas but is certain that there is nothing wrong. Cognitively, she scores only 21 on MMSE, losing points on concentration tasks in particular. She agrees to admission, believing it is for medical reasons. U&E is normal and she is initiated on lithium and olanzapine. Her sleep improves rapidly and mania subsides. After 2 months, back home, she remains psychiatrically well but is gaining weight. She comes off olanzapine but remains on lithium, with a diagnosis of bipolar affective disorder. She has 3-monthly blood tests. Her urea oscillates between 6.0 and 8.0, and creatinine between 90 and 130. Her lithium level varies between 0.4 and 0.6 mmol/L. She develops a slight tremor of the upper limbs. Eventually she moves to a care home after her husband dies, and a district nurse keeps regular lithium testing going.

Drugs for mania

Lithium

- Lithium has been known since the late 1940s to have antimanic action. It took nearly three decades to be widely used as clinicians were concerned by its toxicity which had been demonstrated in the 1940s when lithium was used as an alternative to sodium chloride in the diet of people with hypertension. Lithium is antimanic, has mood-stabilizing effects for people with bipolar disorders, can be used to augment the effects of antidepressants, and may have prophylactic effects in recurrent unipolar depression. It is waning in popularity due to a concern over side-effects, but remains the best-supported prophylactic treatment in bipolar affective disorder. At normal levels (usually clinicians aim for blood levels of 0.4–0.8mmol/L 12h post-dose), lithium causes tremor, a metallic taste, some diuresis, and can cause hypothyroidism. Used long term, lithium causes declining renal function in some patients, probably due to renal parenchymal damage.
- It has an unknown mode of action. Usually given as a carbonate once at night. At normal levels (blood concentration 0.4–0.8mmol/L) causes tremor, metallic taste, diuresis, hypothyroidism, may worsen renal function. At toxic levels (over 1.5mmol/L) causes diarrhoea and vomiting, coarse tremor, confusion, convulsions, coma, and death. Toxicity is more likely in patients on NSAIDs, thiazide diuretics, and in those dehydrated. It may be more likely in older people, who use these drugs more often. Avoidance of toxicity depends on regular blood tests (3-monthly lithium levels taken around 12h after usual dose) and counselling about symptoms.

Suggested lithium regime

- Baseline U&E, TFTs.
- 200–400mg nocte of lithium carbonate, depending on renal function.
- Lithium level to be taken 5–7 days later, 12h post dose (in morning).
- Adjust dose to establish level between 0.4 and 0.8 mmol/L.
- Repeat lithium level after 1–2 weeks more.
- 3-monthly blood tests—lithium level, TFTs, U&E.

Carbamazepine

An excitatory neurotransmitter blocker, though its exact mode of action in mania unclear. Therapeutic window less clear-cut than with lithium. Main problems are likely to be blood dyscrasias (regular FBC recommended though patients should be aware of symptoms), hyponatraemia (probably more common in older people, regular U&E needed), and dose-related dizziness and unsteadiness. Carbamazepine is a liver enzyme inducer; it may decrease the effect of warfarin, some analgesics, and antibiotics. Doses should be started low (100–200mg/day) and increased in steps of 100–200mg/day.

Valproic acid

Another anticonvulsant drug which enhances gabaergic inhibition of neuro-transmission. It is often given as Depakote (semisodium valproate). Valproic acid can cause gastric irritation, weight gain, drowsiness, and blood dyscra-sias. Its main problem is the potential for serious hepatic dysfunction—it should not be started without baseline LFTs. Fulminant liver failure is rare, transient increases in LFTs are more common. Doses should start low (250mg/day of Depakote) and be increased carefully.

Antipsychotics

Antipsychotics undoubtedly have antimanic effects and may work faster than mood stabilizers alone. Atypical antipsychotics also show some evidence of prophylactic effects in bipolar affective disorder. The antimanic effects are probably due to antidopaminergic action. Higher doses may be needed than for later paraphrenia, especially in acute manic episodes Older patients with mood disorders are at high risk of tardive dyskinesia and other risks to consider are known cardiovascular/mortality risks in presence of dementia, and weight gain with olanzapine used long term.

Useful reference

NICE (2004). Depression: management of depression in primary and secondary care. NICE, London (http://www.nice.org.uk/).

Anxiety and behaviour disorders

Anxiety presentations 126
The main anxiety disorders 128
Somatoform disorders and somatization 130
Drug treatments for anxiety disorders 132
Non-drug treatment for anxiety disorders 133
Alcohol in older people 134
Alcohol and cognitive impairment 135
Management of alcohol misuse among older people 136
Benzodiazepines 138
Managing insomnia in older people 139
Sexuality in older age 140
Squalor/neglect 142

Anxiety presentations

Anxiety as a word refers to a marked subjective emotional state of apprehension and fear. This can be a normal, even helpful, response to stress/threat. More severe anxiety is a common symptom of a number of psychiatric disorders. When anxiety is the dominant symptom, the disorders are usually classified as anxiety or (sometimes) neurotic disorders. Different patterns of anxiety in terms of clinical picture and precipitants lead to characteristic diagnoses; the pattern within individuals tends to run true over a long period.

Symptoms of anxiety

Emotional
A sense of fearful foreboding, which may focus on a particular object or situation (in phobias) or may be independent of particular precipitants.

Physiological
• Autonomic symptoms include dry mouth, tachycardia, palpitations, sweating, dizziness.
• Muscle tension causes tremor, inability to sit still, headache ('tension' type), muscle aches.
• Hyperventilation.
• Paraesthesia in extremities and feelings of dizziness.

Cognitive
Characteristic thoughts are of negative evaluation ('I will make a fool of myself'), catastrophe, or hypochondriacal type ('I am going to collapse', 'I am having a heart attack').

Behavioural
Characteristic behaviours include *escape* from the situation one feels anxious in or *avoidance* of feared situations.

Epidemiology

New diagnoses of anxiety disorders are comparatively rare among older people. Reasons for this may include a true decrease in incidence, resolution of early life cases, selective mortality, or diagnostic difficulties in patients with physical disease or depressive disorder. Phobia is probably the most common of the anxiety disorders in older populations, affecting 3–6% of older people. Outcomes of anxiety disorders in older people have been little studied; probably fewer than half of cases resolve after 3–20 years.

Relationship with other illnesses

Depression
Anxiety and depressed mood frequently coexist. Anxiety symptoms are very common in depressive disorder. Careful history taking to establish which symptoms dominate and which came first will usually decide the diagnosis. New-onset anxiety symptoms in older age should strongly suggest a depressive disorder. Depressive symptoms, or even incident depressive disorder of case level, are common in many anxiety disorders, especially OCD and PTSD.

Dementia

Anxiety symptoms are found very commonly in people with dementia. These may be found in the early stages of the condition as an understandable reaction to developing deficits or as a direct behavioural symptom of moderate to severe dementia, probably as a result of depletion in monoamine neurotransmission. Up to 80% of people with dementia experience significant anxiety symptoms during the course of the dementia. As anxiety may be a presenting complaint in early dementia, cognitive screening should be carried out in such cases. Anxiety may of course artificially depress cognitive performance.

One possible explanation for the decreased incidence of anxiety disorders in older people is that such cases develop dementia which then 'hides' the anxiety disorder; this theory is as yet unsupported by evidence.

The main anxiety disorders

Phobias

Phobias are disorders in which anxiety arises mainly, or only, in situations which are not dangerous. The situation provokes a variety of anxiety symptoms and is both dreaded and avoided. Simple phobias are of particular objects or experiences, e.g. dogs, spiders, dentists. These usually arise in childhood and may persist for a lifetime. Social phobia is anxiety provoked by social encounters and is disabling. It usually arises in adolescence. Agoraphobia has a lay meaning of fear of open spaces but refers to a fear of uncontrollable outside situations, often with crowds of people and difficult to get away from. It may arise independently in adult life or after a panic attack; if associated with true panic attacks it is known as agoraphobia with panic disorder. In either case, onset is in adult life, later than other phobias. This pattern is most common in older people, often following a distressing event while out alone, and may cause the patient to be housebound.

Generalized anxiety disorder (GAD)

In this disorder, anxiety is chronic and persistent (often described as 'free-floating'). It does not occur in discrete bursts, unlike panic disorder.

Panic disorder

Anxiety occurs in discrete bursts, recurs, and is not linked to particular situations (unless in agoraphobic patients). Attacks are unpredictable, sudden and very severe. Predominant subsequent fears are of further attacks.

Obsessive–compulsive disorder (OCD)

This disorder is often classified with the other anxiety disorders, a convention open to criticism. While anxiety may be part of the clinical picture, the dominant symptoms are powerful intrusive thoughts/images which come to the patient's mind despite resistance and a recognition that they are the patient's own, and compulsive rituals, where a sequence of actions, e.g. handwashing, must be carried out repeatedly, again despite recognition that the compulsion is irrational. OCD usually starts in early adult life, and if severe may run a chronic fluctuating course, lasting a lifetime. New cases in old age appear very rare, and depressive disorder should be suspected in such presentations. A distinction from the purposeless, repetitive behaviours often seen in dementia should be made; such behaviours are found in moderate to severe dementia.

Post-traumatic stress disorder (PTSD)

- Studies of the psychological impact of the great wars of the 20th century have revealed the characteristic symptoms of this disorder. In PTSD, a significant traumatic event, such as an assault, direct threat, or witnessing catastrophe, is followed by persistent symptoms of
  - **Intrusion**: the event comes repeatedly to the patient's mind in the form of images, flashbacks (re-experiencing the original trauma), or dreams.

- **Arousal**: poor concentration, anxiety, irritability.
- **Avoidance**: emotional detachment, numbness, failure to consciously recall the trauma, avoidance of places/situations reminiscent of the event.

- The epidemiology of the condition has been examined. Most people experience a potentially traumatic event during a lifetime but fewer than 1 in 20 have PTSD at any stage. Severe cases often persist for many years and in certain cultures may be suffered without complaint. More severe trauma is associated with higher risk, while direct personal injury/threat increases risk further.

- Among older people new onset is relatively rare. Studies of World War II veterans show high rates of PTSD. Among servicemen interned in POW camps in WWII, 60–80% still report some symptoms of PTSD. Clinical experience suggests that such symptoms may be triggered by lesser but still stressful life events suffered in later life.

Somatoform disorders and somatization

- Somatization refers to the expression of psychological distress through physical symptoms. Patients report unexplained or poorly defined but troublesome physical symptoms which are negatively investigated. Symptoms persist despite reassurance. A distinction is sometimes made between hypochondriasis, where a particular illness is feared (e.g. a person believing that their weight loss and abdominal cramps must indicate cancer), and somatization, in which the focus is on symptoms rather than a feared illness. An underlying psychiatric disorder is often present, usually depressive disorder or an anxiety disorder. When the unexplained symptoms are present in the absence of other psychiatric disorder, a somatoform disorder may be diagnosed.
- Somatization is common at all ages and the prevalence among older community and primary care samples has been found to be 1–8%. Among older people, a very strong association with depressive disorder has been confirmed. Depressed older people may present with any physical symptoms but some are characteristic. These include:
  - Faintness
  - Muscle pain
  - Weakness
  - Heavy limbs
  - Lump in throat

Case example

Mrs Smith is a 76-year-old woman who was widowed 5 months previously. She has been presenting to her GP every week for the last 2 months with fatigue, poor sleep, poor appetite, tension headaches, burning feelings on her skin, and dry eyes. She is convinced that she is going to die of a brain tumour and wants a brain scan.

An approach to management of somatized symptoms in older people

This approach draws on what is known to be effective among younger people with somatization. Older people have a high prevalence of physical illness, so a commonsense approach to management of new or uncharacteristic physical symptoms must be taken. It may be easier for medically qualified staff to tolerate uncertainty with such patients.

Is there a physical illness? Is it being adequately dealt with?

In the majority of cases the patient will be adequately investigated and treated before somatization is considered.

Is there a psychiatric illness?

In depressive disorder, the low mood and biological symptoms such as poor sleep, weight loss, poor appetite, poor concentration, and retardation/agitation usually precede the physical complaints. Patients usually admit to gloomy introspection and are likely to admit to depression rather than reject such suggestions.

Is it being adequately treated?

Antidepressant medication will usually resolve depression, with resolution of somatized symptoms.

Do somatized symptoms need independent treatment?

- Stop investigations and hospital referrals.
- Schedule regular appointments with the patient so they do not need to report symptoms in order to be seen.
- Explain that investigations have shown no condition that they cannot recover from.

Use cognitive behavioural techniques

- Identify dysfunctional beliefs ('headaches usually mean brain tumour' 'muscle aches mean exercise has damaged the muscle fibres') and dysfunctional behaviours ('I will stay in bed all weekend to give my muscles a chance to recover').
- Identify positive thinking and behaviour strategies, for example: demonstrate that holding a book in outstretched hand causes pain – to show effect of muscle tension 'Exercise increases blood flow and fitness of muscle fibres'.
- Schedule increasing levels of activity and record symptoms in a symptom diary.

Drug treatments for anxiety disorders

Tricyclic antidepressants

Imipramine was the first treatment shown to be effective for panic disorder. Tricyclics cause significant side-effects, especially anticholinergic side-effects (dry mouth, urinary retention, constipation), drowsiness, hypotension. In patients with anxiety disorders, very low doses, e.g. 10mg/day, need to be started with 10mg increments every few days to tolerable maximum in the range 75–150mg/day. Anxiolytic effects may take several weeks to be felt.

SSRIs

Fluoxetine (GAD, PTSD), citalopram (panic disorder), paroxetine (GAD, PTSD) have been licensed in the UK for treatment of anxiety disorders. Unlike tricyclic agents, the full therapeutic dose (similar to that used for depression) can usually be tolerated early by older patients. Patients need to be warned of a temporary increase in anxiety in first 1–2 weeks. In older patients, particular problems occur with hyponatraemia (severe caution if sodium falls below 125).

Serotonin/noradrenaline drugs

Venlafaxine, a SNRI has been licensed for GAD. Among older people a relative caution exists in people with established cardiac disease and blood pressure may be elevated at higher doses (usual effective dose 112.5–225mg/day).

Benzodiazepines

These drugs are widely prescribed for anxiety disorders despite limited evidence of effectiveness among older people. They can be particularly dangerous in older people, in whom they cause sedation, cognitive impairment, ataxia, falls, and delirium. For this reason long-acting benzodiazepines such as diazepam are best avoided due to their tendency to accumulate. Shorter-acting benzodiazepines such as lorazepam are less likely to accumulate and cause these toxic effects; their shorter duration of action means they are more likely to lead to dependence.

Buspirone

This 5-HT1A partial agonist is unrelated to other anxiolytics. It has some efficacy for anxiety disorders including GAD and is probably well tolerated by older people. Its onset of action is delayed (at least 2 weeks). It requires 2–3 times daily dosing and its long-term effects in older people (among whom anxiety tends to persist) are unknown.

Propranolol

A β-blocker sometimes used for relief of peripheral autonomic symptoms such as palpitations in low doses, e.g. 10mg twice a day. The many cautions on its use, e.g. asthma, cardiac failure, may limit use in older people.

Non-drug treatment for anxiety disorders

- Psychological treatment has a very prominent role in the treatment of the anxiety disorders, more so even than in other psychiatric conditions. The most common treatment techniques are based on cognitive and behavioural theories. They involve the identification of unhelpful automatic thoughts ('my racing heart means I am having a heart attack', 'If I go out something terrible may happen like last year') and behaviours (avoidance of going out, repeated visits to the doctor for reassurance); their replacement with more constructive thoughts and behaviours, and encouraging homework and review. These techniques are usually combined with anxiety management techniques of muscular relaxation and breathing exercises to allow mastery of somatic anxiety symptoms. Variants on these techniques include graded exposure to feared situations in phobia and response prevention in OCD.
- Among older people, these techniques have been subject to few controlled trials. A widespread and misplaced myth that older people are less likely to benefit from such interventions exists. Particular barriers to such techniques in older people may include physical disability, sensory impairment, and cognitive deficits. Cost-effective techniques include group treatment, which suits some older people accustomed to meeting in seniors groups/day centres.

Panic disorder

Anxiety management techniques and psychoeducation are appropriate. Patients may at least require some antidepressant drug treatment to hasten improvement.

GAD

Anxiety management is probably effective but adjunctive drug treatment is often required and there is a mixed prognosis.

Simple phobia

Drug treatment has no role in most cases. Graded exposure to a hierarchy of feared situations with anxiety management and cognitive techniques is the treatment of choice.

OCD

Exposure to the feared situation and response prevention (for patients with compulsive rituals) is the usual treatment. Serotinergic antidepressants are probably of equal value.

Agoraphobia

Psychological treatment will involve graded re-exposure to the outside world with anxiety management. Direct involvement of the community team or psychology staff is likely to be needed at home for housebound older people.

Alcohol in older people

There is a spectrum of use of alcohol at any age, from total abstinence, through moderate use and harmful use to dependence syndrome.

Usual quoted safe limits
- Under 14 units a week for women.
- Under 21 units a week for men.

Harm is likely
- Above 35 units a week for women.
- Above 50 units a week for men.
- 1 unit = 1 small glass of wine (100ml of 11% wine), 1 small measure of spirits (25ml 40% whiskey), or a half pint (284ml) of normal strength beer (4%).

Dependence syndrome has no intake limits but the following features
- Strong compulsion to drink alcohol.
- Difficulty controlling alcohol intake.
- Withdrawal symptoms on stopping drinking.
- Tolerance (larger and larger amounts needed to get same effect).
- Neglect of social obligations.
- Persistence of drinking despite clear evidence of harm.
- Reinstatement (immediate relapse into full dependence soon after a long period of abstinence).

Physiological effects of alcohol in older people (versus younger)
- Similar amounts of alcohol lead to higher blood alcohol concentrations.
- Similar alcohol levels have greater intoxicating effects.
- Body mass often smaller so less alcohol can be tolerated.
- Increased prevalence of conditions which may be worsened by alcohol.
- Increased incidence of polypharmacy so interactions more likely.

Alcohol use and misuse among older people
- Abstinence is more common among older people.
- Harmful use is less common among older people.
- Older people tend to reduce their alcohol intake as they age.
- Cohort effects apply—prevalence of harmful use is increasing with ageing of 'baby boomer' generation.
- Men are twice as likely as women to abuse alcohol.

The prevalence of harmful alcohol use among older people is estimated at 1–3% (Western community samples) and 4–20% (hospital in-patient/out-patient samples). Reasons for the reduced prevalence of alcohol disorders among older people include early death of people abusing alcohol in younger life, cohort effects, misdiagnosis due to masking by other medical problems, and strong social stigma against alcohol misuse by older people.

Alcohol and cognitive impairment

- The relationship between alcohol and cognitive impairment is complex. Alcohol abuse predisposes to important causes of cognitive impairment such as subdural haematoma. Alcoholic dementia is a condition found in heavy persistent drinkers which may be very difficult to distinguish in life from comorbid AD. Significant deficits in orientation, short-term memory, and ability to self-care are all found. CT brain scans will usually show generalized atrophy. Improvement in CT findings, as well as improvement in cognitive performance, have been reported on abstinence. The diagnosis is rarely made and the true prevalence is unclear.
- Wernicke–Korsakoff syndrome is found among heavy alcohol abusers. It is associated with deficient availability of thiamine (vitamin B_1), a vitamin important for the integrity of memory and other cognitive pathways. Characteristic neuropathology in strategic brain areas has been shown, including the mamillary bodies, thalamus, hypothalamus, and periaqueductal grey matter. In the acute Wernicke's presentation, patients present with
  - Disorientation and general cognitive impairment
  - Ataxia
  - Opthalmoplegia
  - Nystagmus
- Untreated, progression to chronic amnestic syndrome (also known as Korsakoff's syndrome) is usual and is characterized by
  - Severe deficit in short-term memory
  - Disorientation in time
  - Confabulation
  - Relative preservation of other cognitive functions

Can alcohol be good for people as they age?

Much media interest has been spurred by increasing evidence that moderate alcohol intake may have beneficial effects for health. Research continues but the following patterns emerge from epidemiological research:

- Alcohol abuse is associated with significant health risks including physical health (liver disease, hypertension, cardiomyopathy) and psychiatric disorders (dementia, suicide).
- Moderate alcohol intake (usually defined as up to 14 units per week)
  - Probably reduces the risk of cardiovascular disorder
  - Reduces platelet aggregation
  - Reduces arterial stiffness
  - Improves HDL/LDL cholesterol ratios
  - Probably reduces the risk of AD
  - Type of alcohol probably unimportant though most studies have focused on wine drinking

Management of alcohol misuse among older people

Immediate

Physical assessment

Myriad complications of alcohol may be found. In particular
- GI: liver disease, peptic ulceration.
- CNS: head injury, cerebellar degeneration, eye signs.
- CVS: cardiomyopathy, unstable pulse/blood pressure.

Cognitive assessment

Acute encephalopathy should be excluded. Immediate cognitive assessment should establish the presence of acute deficits and degree of anterograde memory impairment and disorientation in time.

Decide on location of detoxification

Community detoxification is increasingly available. Older people with significant comorbid physical illness and/or inadequate community social support are likely to need in-patient detoxification.

Short term

Initiate detoxification

Replacement of alcohol with a long-acting benzodiazepine or equivalent will reduce unpleasant withdrawal symptoms and reduce the risk of seizures. Diazepam (also available parenterally) or chlordiazepoxide are the usual drugs of choice. Other psychotropic drugs are not appropriate—antidepressants and antipsychotics should only be initiated for psychiatric symptoms persisting beyond the period of withdrawal. Anticonvulsants do not usually reach adequate blood levels until withdrawal has peaked so are inferior to benzodiazepines.

Typical chlordiazepoxide detoxification regime

Day one   20–30mg 3–4 times a day.
Day two   20mg 3–4 times a day.
Day three   40–50mg/day in 3–4 divided doses.
Day four   30–40mg/day in 3–4 divided doses.
Day five   20mg/day in divided doses.

Parenteral thiamine

Vitamin B$_1$ (thiamine) is poorly absorbed orally. Parenteral (IV or IM) thiamine should be offered to all patients undergoing alcohol detoxification and all patients who have abused alcohol who show signs of
- Opthalmoplegia.
- Acute confusion.
- Memory loss.
- Disorientation.
- Ataxia.
- Hypothermia and hypotension.

Anaphylactic reactions are rare; rates for IV infusion are about 1/250 000, for IM injection about 1/4 million. In psychiatric wards, the IM route is recommended.

Long-term maintenance

Alcoholics Anonymous (AA)

AA arose in the USA in the 1930s. AA provides a unique support programme based on admission of weakness, wish for abstinence, open
self-disclosure, and regular peer support. A 12-step programme model is
followed worldwide and groups are very widely available. The model does
not suit all personalities but all detoxified people should be encouraged
to consider attending.

Specialised services

Community/hospital-based services often accept older people. Practical
support and motivational interviewing can be effective in reducing
relapse.

Drug treatment

- Acamprosate centrally reduces craving for alcohol and may reduce
  relapse rates. It has been little evaluated in older people but is probably
  well tolerated. It needs to be initiated soon after abstinence achieved.
- Disulfiram causes acetaldehyde to accumulate in the presence of
  alcohol and has been used as an aversive treatment for some
  alcohol-dependent people. The reaction is exceptionally unpleasant
  and occasionally dangerous. Disulfiram is contraindicated in people
  with a history of hypertension, cardiac failure, stroke, or ischaemic
  heart disease so should be rarely used in older people.

Benzodiazepines

Benzodiazepine use is very common among older people and almost exclusively involves prescribed medication. Cross-sectional community surveys internationally show 10–30% of older people are prescribed benzodiazepines (the UK at the lower end of this range). Among older people, insomnia is the commonest indication. Prescription becomes more likely in extreme old age and half of new prescriptions lead to long-term use.

In older people

- Pharmacokinetic changes mean similar doses lead to higher plasma concentrations.
- Pharmacodynamic changes mean similar plasma levels cause greater sedation, cognitive impairment and ataxia.
- Adverse effects of benzodiazepines are more common among older people. In particular, ataxia, falls, cognitive impairment, sedation, and depression are caused.
- Dependence on benzodiazepines can develop after daily use over more than 6–8 weeks. Shorter-acting drugs such as lorazepam are more likely to lead to dependence. Other risk factors for dependence include use for insomnia (to which tolerance develops), other addictions, and abnormal personality.

Long-acting benzodiazepines
- Diazepam.
- Chlordiazepoxide.
- Clonazepam.
- Nitrazepam.

Short-acting benzodiazepines
- Lorazepam.
- Oxazepam.
- Temazepam.

Proper indications for benzodiazepines in older people

- Insomnia (short term use only: 2–4 weeks, when sleep hygiene and alternative treatments have not worked).
- Anxiety disorders.

Improper indications

- Behaviour problems in dementia (frequently used: there is no evidence that they are effective and they increase risk of falls and worsen cognitive impairment).

Managing insomnia in older people

Full history and examination

It is too easy to simply prescribe hypnotics for older people who complain of lack of sleep. Readily identifiable causes of insomnia, including psychiatric illness, ignorance of changing need for sleep, and physical illness may all be directly responsible.

Education

Older people require less sleep. This fact is not always known—mean hours sleep needed per night declines from 8 (20s), to 6 (60s) and 5 (80s and 90s).

Exclude other causes

- Pain.
- Depressive illness.
- Urinary problems.

Sleep hygiene

- Give written and verbal information.
- Avoid stimulants—caffeine, alcohol, nicotine.
- Regular sleeping hours.
- Environment suitable for sleep (temperature/noise/light).

Non-drug treatment of insomnia

CBT and sleep education groups have evidence for effectiveness, including among older people. Such interventions are not widely available, however.

Drug treatment of insomnia

Drugs should be considered after the above steps. Dependence is likely after 6 weeks of treatment, so prescriptions should not be for longer than 4 weeks. There is no evidence that the Z drugs (zolpidem, zaleplon and zopiclone) are different in efficacy, side-effects, or addiction potential from short-acting benzodiazepines (lorazepam, temazepam)[1].

- Offer temazepam 10–20mg or zolpidem 5mg nocte, for 3–4 weeks.
- Do not switch to another hypnotic unless side-effects preclude use of the first-line agent.

---

1 NICE (2004). *Insomnia—newer hypnotic drugs.* NICE, London (🔖http://www.nice.org.uk/TA077).

Sexuality in older age

Normal sexuality in older age

This area has been poorly researched. This partly reflects a lack of research interest, a reluctance to raise sexual issues with older people, and possibly cohort effects with older generations preferring to avoid such discussions. Societal changes and new medical treatments have combined to increase focus on this area.

Normal patterns of sexual behaviour

- At least 20% of people aged 65–75 years are sexually active (intercourse at least once a month).
- At least 20% of people aged over 80 years are sometimes sexually active.
- Sexual interest/pleasure is reported by a clear majority of older people.
- Cessation of sexual behaviour is usually due to bereavement or illness, not reduced interest.
- Reduced blood flow and loss of oestrogens reduces vasocongestion and lubrication in vaginal tissues.
- Direct atrophy of vaginal tissues may lead to increased incidence of pain/dryness during intercourse.
- Males have slower time to arousal, less firm and less sustained erections, and longer refractory periods after intercourse (e.g. >24h).
- Impotence affects 10–20% of men aged 70 years or over.

Medical causes of sexual dysfunction

General
- Arthritis.
- Parkinson's disease.
- Incontinence.
- Stroke.

Drugs causing erectile dysfunction
- Antihypertensives, especially thiazide diuretics, spironolactone, and β-blockers.
- Benzodiazepines.
- Alcohol.
- Antidepressants (trazodone may rarely cause priapism).
- Antiandrogens.
- Prostate surgery/medication.

Treatments for erectile dysfunction

- Phosphodiesterase inhibitors such as sildenafil relax smooth muscle, increasing blood flow. They are contraindicated for patients on nitrates and a caution exists for patients with history of ischaemic heart disease or CVD.
- Alternatives, including for people with vascular risk factors, include prostaglandin E1 treatments and intracavernosal injections.

Abnormal sexual behaviour in dementia

This problem is widely known, particularly in residential/nursing homes. It has not been systematically investigated. It may be a specific manifestation of frontal lobe pathology, or part of a more general behaviour disturbance, e.g. in AD. It may range from disinhibited touching of care staff, to exposure, public masturbation, or direct and dangerous sexual assault. A distinction between this and normal sexual behaviour between people unable to fully consent to intimacy should be drawn. The latter may cause embarrassment to relatives and carers but may not be inherently harmful. A balance between using opportunities for privacy to enhance the best interests of patients, against inability to consent and embarrassment, should be made for individual cases.

Treatments for hypersexuality in dementia (case series only)

- Antidepressants and antipsychotics may induce as a side-effect reduced sexual desire/performance.
- There is no systematic evidence for efficacy of benperidol, despite folklore to the contrary.
- Carbamazepine.
- Hormonal treatments, e.g. medroxyprogesterone acetate, cyproterone acetate.

Squalor/neglect

Any clinician dealing with older patients will come across cases of extreme self-neglect associated with domestic squalor. Various terms have been used to describe such situations. In the 1960s the accurate term 'senile breakdown in standards of personal and environmental cleanliness' was used to describe older people in extreme squalor, many of whom had mental illness. The more memorable term 'Diogenes syndrome' was introduced in the 1970s; the term refers to the cynic philosopher Diogenes who lived in a barrel 2000 years ago, rejecting possessions. Attention was being drawn in these descriptions to older people with unusual, aloof personalities who lived in appalling conditions but did not have mental illness and were strikingly unaware of their dire circumstances. Subsequent formal investigations of the presentation suggest that half of people in squalor are over 65 years, most have either mental or physical illness, and a majority are in fact aware of their plight.

Presentations

- Self neglect (skin/hair/clothing/nails).
- Hoarding (housing cluttered with accumulated individual items especially newsprint, food containers, personal dislike for allowing objects to be disposed of).
- Dirty accommodation (infestation, excrement, lack of cleaning).

Among people who self neglect

- Older age more common.
- Live alone.
- Socially isolated.
- High prevalence (70%) of mental illness.
- One-quarter have direct physical health problem contributing.
- May have unusual personalities.
- May show unawareness of neglect.

Case example

Mr D is a 72-year-old unmarried retired serviceman. He has lived alone in a council flat for 30 years and has lost contact with his family. He drinks three cans of normal strength beer a day. He rejects offers of social care assistance, stating 'I am perfectly all right'. Neighbours have complained of the smell from his flat and a social worker has observed rotting food, large piles of old newspaper, and evidence that he has soiled himself, has long dirty hair, has lost weight, and wears clothes unchanged for months. Under threat of eviction, he agrees to admission to a psychiatric unit. No mental illness is found, though he has mild deficits in short-term memory and is started on thiamine and advised not to drink. He reluctantly agrees to move into a sheltered housing complex. At all stages, he expresses surprise at the state he had got to.

Paranoid illness and schizophrenia

Clinical presentations—background 144
Clinical presentations—late-onset paranoid illness 146
Aetiology 147
Management principles 148
Antipsychotic prescribing 150
Graduates 152

Clinical presentations—background

Psychotic symptoms include any symptoms in which contact with reality is lost and include delusions and hallucinations. These may be found in a variety of illnesses—including schizophrenia, depression, mania, delirium, and dementia. When particular psychotic symptoms dominate the clinical picture, the terms paranoid illness or (loosely and confusingly) psychotic disorder, are often used. The most prominent diagnosis of this type is schizophrenia, while brief psychotic disorder and delusional disorder are also sometimes diagnosed. Among older people, nomenclature is even more confusing. *Graduate* is a term used for people with schizophrenia who have grown old. Late paraphrenia is a term for a late-onset (over 50) illness resembling schizophrenia in which delusions and hallucinations dominate the picture, but thought disorder and negative symptoms are less commonly found. Debate continues as to whether these late-onset cases are just schizophrenia with a better outcome, or represent a separate illness.

Causes of psychotic symptoms among older people

Organic brain disease
- AD (50% of cases have psychotic symptoms at some point in illness).
- DLB (90% of cases have psychotic symptoms).
- Delirium.
- Strategic lesions, e.g. infarction in optic radiations.

Functional mental illness
- Psychotic depression.
- Manic episode.
- Bereavement.

Primary psychotic illnesses
- Early onset schizophrenia.
- Late-onset psychotic illness (paraphrenia).

Medication
- Steroids.
- Dopaminergic agents.

Epidemiology

Lifetime incidence of schizophrenia is about 0.9%. Mortality among people with schizophrenia is increased but may be falling. Including late-onset schizophrenia-like illness, a bimodal incidence may be seen, with peak onsets in early life and among older people (Fig. 6.1). Among women, incidence is clearly highest with increasing age.

Outcomes

About half of cases do not respond to treatment, with 'encapsulation' of delusions (in a quarter) or complete resolution (a quarter) less likely. Positive prognostic markers include medication compliance, some social contact, absence of negative features, and a normal pre-morbid personality. The majority of people with late-onset psychotic illness do not go on to develop dementia.

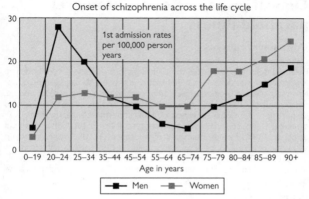

Fig. 6.1 Age and incident presentation of paranoid illness (reproduced with permission of R. Howard).

Clinical presentations—late-onset paranoid illness

Common symptoms

Delusions

Paranoid delusions dominate the clinical picture. The most common type is persecutory delusions—a belief that one is being damaged/spied upon/ adversely affected by another person or organization. Among older people, these delusions frequently involve neighbours and are often accompanied by 'partition' delusions—in which a usually impermeable barrier like a wall or ceiling is passed through by a person, radiation, or gas. Other paranoid delusions found include delusions of reference (in which one is spoken about or referred to by supposedly uninterested parties, e.g. strangers in public or TV newsreaders), control (the delusion that one's actions, moods or even thoughts are controlled from without), and grandiose delusions (delusions of excessive wealth, rank, or power).

Hallucinations

Auditory hallucinations are most common. These are usually frank hallucinations and may be of second person (a voice talking to the patient) or third person (voices discussing the patient) type, but are sometimes relatively uncomplicated, e.g. whirring or banging noises or the noise of machines or movement. Olfactory hallucinations usually accompany related delusions, e.g. of gas being pumped in to one's house. Visual hallucinations are rare and should suggest organic pathology, e.g. DLB or delirium.

Related (occasional) symptoms

Cognitive impairment

In some cases, paranoid symptoms may be the harbinger of early dementia. For most older people with late-onset schizophrenia, progression to dementia does not follow, and the majority of cases will perform normally on common cognitive tests, e.g. MMSE.

Mood symptoms

The relatively benign outcome, and presence of mood symptoms in up to half of cases, have led some to suggest that these cases are in fact psychotic mood disorders. Mild depression, apparently reactive to demoralization about persecution and failure to be believed, is common in late onset psychotic illness. Careful history will indicate for the majority that mood symptoms did not precede psychotic symptoms.

Uncommon symptoms (never or rarely found)
- Thought disorder.
- Negative symptoms.

Complications

Requests for rehousing, complaints to local authorities and police, and demands that relatives and friends endorse symptoms, are frequent. Serious complications, such as suicide or violent attack on supposed persecutors, are probably very rare. Neglect, social withdrawal, and chronic insightless suffering are very common.

Aetiology

Personality

Patients with late-onset paranoid illness have long been shown in retrospective case series to typically live alone, be of at least normal IQ, but to have aloof, paranoid, and schizoid personality traits. Later data from well-controlled studies building pictures of the pre-morbid personality of such cases have confirmed reticence, lack of sociability, shyness, and hostility to be common. Social isolation may follow for such people which makes symptoms harder to eradicate.

Gender

Among late-onset cases, new presentations are much more common among women.

Family history

A positive family history is much less common among relatives of people with late-onset paranoid illness than among younger people. No useful genetic marker has been established.

Sensory deficits

Deafness is associated at all ages with increased risk of paranoid illness and auditory hallucinations in particular. In late-onset paranoid illnesses, deafness has been consistently and specifically shown to be associated. It is presumed that auditory hallucinations become more likely, while relative social isolation will make delusions become more firmly held, as opportunities to refute the supposed origin of symptoms are fewer, and social encounters are withdrawn from.

Brain changes

Structural neuroimaging

CT and MRI scanning studies have demonstrated that among late-onset paranoid illness
- Increased ventricular size can be demonstrated.
- This increased ventricular size is not of a degree useful in diagnosing individual patients.
- Infarction and DWML are no more common than among controls.

Functional neuroimaging

- SPET studies show some hypoperfusion in frontal and temporal areas, suggestive of vascular deficits.
- PET studies have failed to demonstrate primary dopaminergic overactivity.

Neuropsychological findings

- Paranoid symptoms may be found among patients with profound cognitive deficits of dementia.
- No consistent cognitive deficit has been shown in patients with late-onset paranoid illness.
- Prospective work shows that most cases do not progress to dementia.

Management principles

Assessment
- Establish diagnosis—exclude depression and dementia.
- Identify sensory deficits and social isolation.
- Clarify degree of insight/likelihood of compliance.
- Quantify risk—of neglect/deterioration/violence/suicide/pestering police and social services.

Set goals of treatment
- Resolution of delusions *or*
- Encapsulation of delusions.
- Containment of complaints/requests for rehousing.
- Building therapeutic alliance.
- Allow ventilation of distress.
- Reduce social isolation.

Compulsion
Use of compulsory powers, e.g. the Mental Health Act 1983 in England and Wales, may be appropriate in the following circumstances:
- Total lack of insight and refusal of treatment.
- Risk of suicide or violent attack on supposed persecutor.
- Risk of serious deterioration if not detained in hospital (and reasonable prospect of improvement on treatment).
- Social threat to patient, e.g. threat of eviction for persistent complaining.
- Failure of all attempts to manage case in community.

Antipsychotic drug treatment
- Antipsychotic drugs are undoubtedly effective in the management of schizophrenia in younger people. A limited number of controlled studies with older people support the use of haloperidol, quetiapine, risperidone, and olanzapine. Around half of patients will respond to sustained antipsychotic treatment; this modest success rate should be born in mind when considering compulsory treatment.
- Older patients are especially prone to extrapyramidal side-effects of antipsychotics; doses should be started low and the atypical class is likely to have fewer such side-effects. Target doses for risperidone should be 2mg/day, for olanzapine 5 mg/day, for quetiapine 100mg/day. Higher doses should be used with caution and with specialist advice.
- Among patients with dementia there is now evidence that antipsychotics may worsen the underlying condition, while among those with DLB extreme susceptibility to extrapyramidal side-effects makes complete avoidance of antipsychotics wise.

Non drug treatment
- Rehousing is a common response to requests by the patient. Evidence of efficacy is lacking; clinical experience and common sense suggest recurrence of symptoms in the new environment is inevitable; such requests should be refused if possible.

- Correcting sensory deficits is a sensible intervention; in particular hearing aids should be sought for deaf patients. Again, evidence of efficacy is lacking but the attempt is at least rational.
- Community team support is likely to be valuable. Allowing visits from a community nurse or social worker may allow opportunities for ventilation of distress, minimize unhelpful complaints to police or housing authorities, and allow monitoring of drug compliance and for deterioration. Social interventions such as day centre attendance are frequently resisted but may allow positive social interactions.
- Specific cognitive intervention is rarely offered—there is limited evidence that insight and social function may be improved in chronic schizophrenia among older people. There is no reason to suppose that CBT used for residual symptoms among younger patients would not work with non-demented older patients.

Antipsychotic prescribing

Indications

Antipsychotics may be used in older people for the following reasons:
- Treatment of paranoid illness.
- Adjunctive treatment (with antidepressants) of psychotic depression.
- Treatment of mania and maintenance of bipolar affective disorder.
- Management of behaviour problems in people with dementia.
- Empirical treatment for anxiolytic and sedative qualities.

General issues among older people

- First-pass liver metabolism is lower among older people, e.g. chlorpromazine should be used in lower doses.
- Glomerular and renal tubule excretion are lower.
- Polypharmacy is much more likely.
- Adverse reactions are more common.
- Anticholinergic effects are likely.
- Physical illness is commoner, affecting drug handling and increasing the risk of adverse reactions.
- Older people are more prone to develop tardive dyskinesia with prolonged use of antipsychotics.
- Class effect concern—among people with dementia antipsychotics may worsen prognosis, including by increasing risk of stroke.

Selected drugs

Haloperidol

A butyrophenone drug in use for many decades. A profound dopamine receptor blocker, it is a highly effective antipsychotic but dopamine blockade in the nigrostriatal pathway makes parkinsonian side-effects very likely. It has few anticholinergic effects and can be given orally, intramuscularly and intravenously. It is still used among older people, particularly with delirium, for this reason. Low doses, e.g. 0.5mg 2–3 times a day, should be initiated with cautious increases to usual maximum of 5–10mg/day. Avoid routine parallel use of anticholinergics to prevent extrapyramidal reactions.

Chlorpromazine

Phenothiazine and the first effective antipsychotic. Strong dopamine blockade; effective but marked antiadrenergic effects (causing postural hypotension) and anticholinergic effects (dry mouth, urinary retention, constipation) make its use among older people troublesome.

Thioxanthines

These drugs, e.g. fluphenazine decanoate, zuclopenthixol decanoate, are often given as depot preparations, e.g. IM injections each 1–4 weeks for maintenance treatment in schizophrenia. This has benefits in ensuring compliance among some older people with chronic schizophrenia. Lower doses than among younger people may be used but tardive dyskinesia is a common side-effect.

Olanzapine

An atypical antipsychotic with good efficacy and mixture of dopaminergic, serotinergic, and antihistamine effects. Can be initiated in low doses, e.g. 2.5mg/day and increased to maximum among older people of 10mg/day. Causes a degree of somnolence and likely to cause weight gain. Lower risk of extrapyramidal side-effects than older drugs. Avoid in patients with dementia due to increased risk of CVA.

Risperidone

A bensizoxazole drug with significant serotinergic and dopaminergic effects. An effective antipsychotic, it has been shown to have some effect for behavioural problems in dementia and has been a drug of choice for this indication. Recent concern over increased CVA risk mean that it should be avoided for this indication unless a clear benefit/risk analysis has been made. Moderate risk of extrapyramidal side-effects mean low doses, i.e. 1–3mg/day, are preferred in older people.

Quetiapine

Atypical antipsychotic drug with low propensity to cause extrapyramidal side-effects. Twice daily dosing is needed due to short half-life. Doses up to 100–200mg/day are generally tolerated. It is unclear whether there is an increased risk of CVA in people with dementia.

Graduates

'Dementia praecox' was a term used by Kraeplin to describe the illness we now call schizophrenia. The term emphasizes the widespread belief that cognitive decline and general deterioration were inevitable in schizophrenia. Remarkably, not until the 1950s was it recognized that older psychiatric hospital populations included both people with dementia and those with disabling but non-progressive illnesses—mood disorders and schizophrenia. *Graduates* is a term used for people who have had a diagnosis of major mental illness in earlier life and have grown older. Technically the term could apply to any significant mental illness, though usually is only used to describe ageing schizophrenics. Originally it was used to describe people resident in long-stay psychiatric wards, at a time (the early 1980s) when there was widespread concern about their prospects with the impending moves to the community seen in the UK and other countries. The outcome was less negative than feared, but this group still all too frequently falls between psychiatric and social service arrangements which do not cater to its needs.

Clinical features

• Patients meet diagnostic criteria for schizophrenia.
• More than one diagnosis may have been recorded in old notes.
• Prominent negative symptoms including social withdrawal, lack of volition, poverty of speech, and blunted affect.
• Inability to self-care successfully in many.
• Positive symptoms such as delusions, hallucinations, and hostility may be found but only intermittently dominate the clinical picture.
• Performance on cognitive tests tends to be poor but progression to dementia is not usual.
• Poor physical health, heavy smoking, and movement disorders, including tardive dyskinesia, very common.

Management

• Treatment goals likely to be limited—complete symptom resolution most unlikely.
• Positive symptoms are more likely than negative symptoms to respond to antipsychotic treatment.
• Compliance issues are likely to be aided by use of depot antipsychotic medication, e.g. flupenthixol decanoate 20–40mg each 2–4 weeks IM.
• Regular contact with community nurse to monitor compliance is beneficial. Regular assessment of physical health, movement problems (especially tardive dyskinesia), and treatment response can be coordinated by community nursing staff.
• Specialist long-stay/rehabilitation residential units are sometimes required for those with severe enduring positive and negative symptoms which mean community living is impractical.

Case example

John is a 72-year-old man who lives in a nursing home. He was first admitted to a psychiatric hospital at 19 and was given diagnoses of 'psychotic depression' and 'schizoaffective disorder' before a final diagnosis of schizophrenia. His last admission was 8 years ago, since which a community psychiatric nurse (CPN) has visited him to administer his depot zuclopenthixol decanoate 200mg every 2 weeks. He had to move into the nursing home 4 years ago due to self-neglect. He has needed prompting to wash/shave for about 5 years, but goes into town alone on the bus most days. He smokes heavily but takes treatment for emphysema and angina. When pressed, he admits to hearing voices from the heating system and to believing 'the tax people' are monitoring him, but rarely expresses distress. He is happiest alone, and can only tolerate short interviews. He has an increasing degree of orofacial involuntary movement noticed by his CPN over the last 2 years.

Further reading

Broadway J and Mintzer J (2007). The many faces of psychosis in the elderly. *Curr Opin Psychiatr* **20:** 551–8.

Services

Services—overview 156
Specialist services—young-onset dementia (YOD) 158
Specialist services—old age liaison psychiatry 160
Specialist services—day hospitals 161
Specialist services—memory clinics 162
Care homes 164

Services—overview

Only since the 1950s has it been clearly recognized that abnormal mental states in older people were due to a variety of conditions, with very different outcomes and some eminently amenable to treatment. Since this time, services catering for older people with mental illness have rapidly evolved from asylum-based long-stay ward facilities to a primarily community model of care, parallel to similar developments in services for younger people. A key difference has been the effective withdrawal (in the UK) of the state from provision of long-stay beds for the mentally ill elderly, chiefly those with dementia. Most of this provision now comes from the private sector in the form of care home places. Particularly close working relationships between health and social services are necessary as the need for social care among people with dementia is huge and increasing. The UK is unusual in having comprehensive provision of specialist old age psychiatry services. In other western countries, management of older people with psychiatric disorders, especially dementia, may fall more to general psychiatrists, neurologists, geriatricians, and primary care physicians, as well as social services.

Specialist psychiatric services in the UK are usually provided by mental health/community care health trusts; most will accept referrals from primary care (e.g. from a GP), from secondary care colleagues (e.g. from other medical specialities), social services, the voluntary sector (e.g. care workers with charity service providers like MIND and the Alzheimer's Society), and even self-referral. UK services have traditionally had some barriers to referral, e.g. the need for community referrals to be made by GPs, but such barriers are reducing. Local arrangements still vary considerably.

Community mental health teams

There are several hundred community mental health teams for older people in the UK, covering almost all of the population. In almost all cases, they cater for older people with the full range of psychiatric disorder, both organic illness, mainly dementia, and functional illness including depressive illness, anxiety disorder, and schizophrenia. Exact configurations differ according to local arrangements but some combination of the following core staff is likely.

Community psychiatric nurses (CPNs)

Nurses with specialist experience in psychiatric care of older people; roles include screening and assessment in crises, monitoring medication compliance, commissioning packages of social care, counselling carers, administration of depot medication.

Occupational therapists

Provide expert assessment of the functional abilities of patients and recommendations on how environment (the built environment, care packages, social engagement, assistive technology, activities) may maximize function.

Social workers

May be employed by health or social services. Particularly concentrate on carer support, commissioning and reviewing packages of care, protection of vulnerable people (e.g. financial or physical abuse), and statutory tasks such as Mental Health Act work.

Old age psychiatrists

Medical professionals specializing in the assessment, investigation, and treatment of psychiatric disorders among older people. In UK, it is likely that around half of new referrals seen have dementia and half have functional disorders such as depressive illness and schizophrenia. The psychiatrist's role is likely to include leadership of in-patient care and more generally of diagnosis and treatment decisions.

Clinical psychologists

Professionals trained in expert assessment of psychological functioning and the use of psychological therapies. Particular roles include neuropsychological assessment in the diagnostic work-up of people with dementia and provision of psychotherapies such as CBT.

Specialist services—young-onset dementia (YOD)

Dementia is rare among people under the age of 65 years. Among people aged 50–60, incidence (new cases per year) of dementia is below 0.1% compared with 3.0% among those aged 80–84 and 7.0% among those aged over 90. The range of diagnoses found differs significantly. Among YOD cases AD remains the most common diagnosis, but higher rates of cases of alcohol-related dementia, fronto-temporal dementia, Huntington's disease, dementia complicating Down's syndrome, HIV, and acquired brain injury are found. There may be particular diagnostic difficulty with border-line cases, e.g. MCI, among whom prospective evaluation may be the only option. Particular issues for services providing for younger people include the following:

• **Genetics**: younger-onset cases are more likely to have a strong family pedigree of dementia, whether due to AD, a fronto-temporal dementia, or Huntington's disease. Liaison with, or provision of, genetic counselling is much more likely to be needed.
• **Deficient specialist services**: people with YOD may be inappropriately admitted to day care or residential care with much older people, with whom they have little physically or socially in common.
• **Family dynamics**: unlike older-onset cases, patients with YOD are likely to be working, to have dependent families, and to have spouse carers with severe stress.
• **Physical**: younger-onset cases are less likely to have any physical illness and more likely to be physically powerful. This may present particular risks to the patient and especially to carers.

Specialist services have sprung up to reflect these needs. Many provide specialist day care providing for the needs of younger onset cases and some provide specialist in-patient assessment and respite. Residential and nursing home care for younger-onset cases is almost always more expensive than that for older people, and specialist involvement in commissioning and monitoring care packages is usual.

Case example

John is a 56-year-old accountant with a wife and two adult children. He presents to a neurologist with a 1-year history of forgetfulness, coarse behaviour causing social embarrassment, for example urinating in the garden in daylight, driving while over the limit for alcohol, and making sexually suggestive remarks to colleagues. He has been missing work deadlines and his boss has expressed concerns about accounts he has signed off on as auditor. He is currently suspended from work. He does not admit to any problems and is very reluctant to be seen. He has no medical or psychiatric history. He recalls his father 'retiring early—he may have had dementia'. Physical examination is normal. He allows a cognitive examination by the clinical psychologist linked to the neurology team. His CAMCOG score is 80/104 (usual cut-off for dementia 79) and MMSE 25/30. His deficits are primarily in new learning, visuo-spatial skills, and time orientation. MRI of his brain shows diffuse cerebral atrophy and some particular hippocampal atrophy. Blood investigations are normal.

The neurologist gives him a diagnosis of AD. He is angry when asked to stop driving. Local arrangements do not allow for anti-dementia drugs to be continued without psychiatric services input and his wife is desperate for some social help. The neurologist refers him to the local YOD team. They gain permission from pharmacy to initiate donepezil (despite his being in the mild range for the condition) and monitor this with a CPN visit every 3 months. The consultant in the YOD team writes a medical report which leads to his receiving medical retirement. The community nurse organizes a specialist activity group for YOD sufferers, which John eventually joins. His wife joins a local Alzheimer's Society carers educational and support group and starts campaigning for better services locally. The family are offered genetic counselling but refuse this. On donepezil, he maintains his cognitive performance for 2 years, while behavioural outbursts become less frequent, though he remains irritable with his wife on occasions, eventually necessitating respite stays at his daughter's home.

Specialist services—old age liaison psychiatry

- Two-thirds of general hospital beds in the UK are occupied by people aged over 65 years. Half of these older people have a psychiatric disorder, most commonly dementia, delirium, and depression. A typical 1000-bed general hospital would expect to have 6000 admissions of older people with a significant psychiatric illness per year, but rates of detection and management of these disorders have been low. Psychiatric disorders among older general hospital patients predict poorer outcomes including
  - Increased mortality
  - Longer hospital stays
  - Increased costs
- Liaison psychiatry services for older people have arisen to meet this need. The liaison model involves a dedicated team, often including nurses, doctors, and social workers, who work closely with general hospital staff to assertively find new cases of psychiatric disorder, jointly manage disorders such as depression and delirium, and plan for future care needs. Education of general hospital staff is a core role.
- Compared with a traditional consultation model, in which individual cases are referred to a general community service, liaison services
  - Achieve quicker assessment
  - Are proactive rather than passive
  - Have a directly educational role
  - Achieve shorter bed stays

Case example

An 82-year-old woman is described as 'confused' when admitted through A&E to a general medical ward. Her presumed UTI is treated with antibiotics. Ward staff ask for a liaison psychiatry assessment to prepare for move to a care home. The liaison team nurse establishes from the family that she was recently completely independent and deteriorated quickly. Suspecting delirium, she asks the ward nurses to complete twice daily AMT scoring which shows significant fluctuation. A diagnosis of delirium is made. She is moved to a side room and staff agree to use familiar faces and a consistent style of communication of orientation and treatment information to her. Once her UTI is treated and dehydration corrected, she returns to her normal state and is able to be discharged home with family support only. The liaison team nurse writes a brief report to the patient's GP, advising referral to community old age psychiatry services should mental health problems reappear.

Specialist services—day hospitals

Day hospitals are provided in the majority of old age psychiatry services in the UK, with over 400 such hospitals. These allow the admission, assessment, and treatment of older people with both organic and functional psychiatric disorders. A particular focus is on group interventions; groups providing supportive psychotherapy, exercise, CBT for depression, anxiety management, cognitive training, and reminiscence are common. The role of occupational therapy and physiotherapy, both in assessment and provision of activities, is likely to be very prominent.

- The majority of day hospitals provide 10–20 places per day.[1]
- Most provide for both organic and functional psychiatric disorders.
- Most patients receive NHS transport.
- Over half of admissions are for over 6 months.
- A third of admissions last over 1 year.

The effectiveness of day hospitals has been questioned. Trials of rehabilitative care in older frail people show no advantage for rehabilitation in day hospitals versus day care or community over day care or home care. No good-quality evidence is available to indicate the effectiveness of psychiatric day hospitals for older people, though patients have been shown to be improved by the end of admissions.

Problems in day hospitals include

- Prolonged admission.
- Heterogeneity of patient group and reasons for admission.
- Dependency.
- Short therapy hours.
- Insufficient day care places to discharge to.
- Need to provide transport.

Case example

An 83-year-old woman is referred by a community nurse to a psychiatric day hospital for older people. The referral letter states she is 'widowed, lonely and low…she could do with company and structure…and an assessment'. She settles in quickly, enjoying company, meals, and group activities. Assessment shows no clear sign of depression and cognitive assessment is normal. At review after 12 weeks she expresses reluctance to try a day centre and her daughter asks that she stay at the day hospital. Repeated attempts to move to a day centre are met with anxiety and weepiness. Eventually a discharge date 3 months in the future is set and day hospital staff accompany her on three occasions to the day centre.

---

1 Royal College of Psychiatrists (2001). *Old age psychiatry day hospital survey*. Royal College of Psychiatrists, London.

Specialist services—memory clinics

Memory assessment services (also known as memory clinics) have multiplied in the UK since the 1980s. Spurs to their development included the realization that the vast majority of people with dementia were never known to specialist services, and the need for structured clinics to service the then dawning age of controlled trials of antidementia treatments. Key goals of memory clinics include the early detection of dementia and instigation and monitoring of treatment. Memory clinics vary in emphasis but assessment is likely to include

- Structured history taking, including from a relative or carer.
- Detailed neuropsychological testing, including instruments such as MMSE and CAMCOG.
- Neuroimaging with MRI or CT scanning.
- Blood test screening for treatable causes of dementia.
- Feedback of diagnostic information to patients and carers.

It will be clear that these features do not radically differ from more generic services. The emphasis on investigation, early referral, detailed investigation, and exclusion of functional illness leads to different referral patterns. Compared with generic services, patients are younger, have milder cognitive impairment, and are less likely to refuse assessments. Memory clinics appear to lead to greater detection rates for dementia.

Case example

A 74-year-old man, a retired engineer, is referred by his GP to local old age psychiatry services for memory loss. A CPN does a screening home visit but he reacts poorly to this, refusing to perform the MMSE and stating 'there is no point to this… you are making me feel like a child'. The CPN refers him to a memory clinic at a local general hospital, jointly run by the geriatricians and old age psychiatrists. He is willing to come to clinic. He is interviewed by a junior doctor, has CAMCOG done by a psychologist and a full dementia blood screen. A CT brain scan is booked for 2 weeks later and he returns to memory clinic to receive results after a month. The results are fed back to his wife and him; these indicate early AD. He reluctantly accepts this information but agrees to participate in a local research project which follows people with AD prospectively. He agrees to try a CHEI and to return to memory clinic in 4 months.

Care homes

One of the responses to a steadily ageing population in Western countries in the latter part of the 20th century was the expansion in the number of care home places for older people. This was partly driven by the closure of long-stay state care homes and hospital beds and partly by commercial entrepreneurism. In the UK, around 450 000 places are available in care homes for older people. This represents about 5% of all older people. The care home population may have peaked in the last decade, possibly due to policies to deliver care in recipients' own homes where possible.

Mental disorders in care homes

- The majority of people living in care homes have some form of psychiatric disorder. Repeated surveys show that over half of all care home residents have dementia, including in care homes specializing in the care of physical frailty. This figure approaches 100% in care homes specializing in dementia care.
- The prevalence of clinically significant depression, among non-demented residents, has been shown to be 20–40%. Incidence of depression (new cases) is about 5–10% per year. Treatment of depression among care home residents is inadequate and outcomes are often very poor, fewer than half of new cases resolving within a year. Specialist services often do not liaise with care homes unless specific referrals are made, but the ability to detect and understand psychiatric disorder is low among care home staff.
- Older people entering care homes come from acute hospital beds in a half of cases. Decisions are often made quickly and with minimal choice for the older person and their carers. Decisions are often irreversible; under half of those admitted to care homes are likely ever to leave institutional care.
- People with dementia live longer in care homes than non-demented new entrants, reflecting their better physical health. Particular concern has been raised about overmedication in care homes. Surveys in Europe and USA in 1980s and 1990s showed multiple psychotropic prescriptions, use of high-dose major tranquilizers, and oversedation to be common. Legislation, national warnings over specific drug side-effects, and pharmacy involvement have all been shown to reduce inappropriate use of psychotropic medication in care homes.
- In some countries, especially the Netherlands, specialist medical services for care home residents have been established.

Case example

A 78-year-old woman loses her husband. Her daughters have had to take over a lot of care, including paying bills, cooking, and laundry. Her husband had probably covered up her cognitive impairment for some time. She falls and fractures her neck of femur. After successful surgery, she rehabilitates fairly well on a surgical ward. Her family express concern they can't cope at home and social services indicate that they cannot provide sufficient care to keep her safe. Under pressure from the bed manager, the hospital social worker finds two care home places, one out of her home town and away from family. The family visit on a Thursday evening and feel compelled to accept the other place. She is admitted there the following day. She settles reasonably but continually asks 'when am I going home? She survives 18 months, declining in the final 6 months with poor appetite, weight loss, going off her legs, and 'giving up' in the words of the carers. No referral to psychiatric services is made.

Services to care homes

Some local services in the UK provide specialist liaison to care homes. This may include reviewing all cases in a care home, training of care home staff, screening for dementia and depression, intensive involvement in management of behaviour disturbance in individual residents or even taking over the clinical leadership of failing care homes. More commonly, a care home will engage a GP to provide general medical services. Involvement of mental health services will then depend on referral of such cases by GPs.

Netherlands model of care

In the Netherlands, around 57 000 nursing home places are offered. These units are typically large, averaging 200 places each. Since 1989, a new medical speciality of nursing home physicians has been introduced. Around 1000 such physicians have since had a specialist 2-year training in physical medicine, psychogeriatric assessment, and limitation of handicap. The role is probably unique. Direct costs of the service are probably offset by reduced costs from hospitalization.

Further reading

Royal College of Psychiatrists (2005). *Who cares wins*. Royal College of Psychiatrists, London.

Ethical and legal issues

Elder abuse 168
Types of abuse 169
Approach to possible cases of abuse 170
Crime and older people 171
Capacity/competence—general principles 172
Tips for those assessing capacity 174
Capacity to make a will 176
Capacity to make health care decisions 178
Capacity to make social care decisions 180
Financial capacity 182
The Mental Capacity Act (2005) 184
Mental health legislation 186
Mental Health Act—in-patient issues 187
Mental Health Act—community issues 188
End-of-life issues 190

Elder abuse

Elder abuse is the term most often used to describe maltreatment of older people. Many acts of commission or omission can lead to harm for an older person. Technically, abuse refers to an act of commission causing harm, e.g. stealing, punching, shouting at, or sexually assaulting a victim. Neglect refers to an act of omission which leads to harm; examples may be withholding food or ignoring cries for help. We will use the term abuse to cover all such acts. Abuse may also be thought of as emotional, verbal, humiliation, financial, violent, or sexual, or oversedation, restraint, or omission of care. There is greatly increased interest in the area; partly due to older people's advocacy groups, partly because of public awareness of the scale of the problem; it has been estimated that at least 2 million older people in the USA (population 300 million) and 500 000 older people in the UK (population 60 million), experience significant abuse per year. Estimates of the true scale of the problem often depend on proxy measures such as helpline reports or selective surveys, and depend greatly on the definition of abuse. The reliability of reports of people with memory problems may be called into question.

Always abuse
- Violence including hitting, pushing, kicking.
- Sexual assault.
- Financial abuse including stealing, forging cheques.
- Deliberate omission of provision of food, warmth, medical care.

Often abuse
- Bed sores.
- Oversedation with psychoactive drugs.
- Restraint.
- Restriction of food/access to money/privacy.
- Altering of will in favour of new person.

Where does abuse occur?
- Action on Elder Abuse estimate (2004 figures) that 67% of abuse takes place in the older persons home, 5% in hospitals, and 22% in residential or nursing homes.
- In care homes, yearly prevalence of abuse reported as 6–10% physical abuse, 11–40% psychological abuse.
- Among community carers of people with dementia, 5–47% yearly prevalence figures are reported for violence against a person with dementia.
- Rates of violence against carers by people with dementia are estimated at close to 100% in residential homes, i.e. professional carers in these settings endure regular physical aggression.

Types of abuse

Financial abuse

This may take many forms. Direct stealing of money by a carer or local youth, failing to return change when shopping is done as a service, excessive pressure on older people to sign to a poorly understood financial commitment, signing cheques on the account of an older person for personal use, running up of large premium rate phone bills on an older person's phone may all be seen. More subtly, a new carer may influence an older person to alter the terms of a will in his/her favour. In some cases, this may be disputed by family, and judgements of the capacity of the person with dementia to make a will (testamentary capacity) may be required. Prosecution is often difficult due to lack of reliable evidence. The new Mental Capacity Act (MCA, 2005), enacted in England and Wales in 2007, provides for protection in this area: as before, people may donate power of attorney over financial matters (now known as lasting power of attorney), the court of protection may appoint deputies to manage financial affairs for an incapacitated person, and a specific criminal offence of ill-treatment or neglect of a person who lacks capacity has been introduced.

Sexual abuse

The prevalence of sexual abuse of older people is unknown, but represents under 10% of cases of elder abuse. Serious sexual assaults are less common than on younger people; serious offenders against older people are likely to have significant psychological disturbance and may be incarcerated for long periods for treatment and public safety. Signs of sexual abuse may include unexplained sexual disease or anal/vaginal bleeding and bruising.

Physical abuse

Including all forms of physical abuse, violence between older people, especially those with dementia, and their carers, is common. In specialist care home settings, assault of staff by patients is commonplace, often daily. Physical abuse of residents by staff is reported in up to 10% of residents per year in care homes and up to 50% in community settings. The distinction between self-protection and violence, and the status of use of gentle force in ensuring personal care, is often a matter of judgement.

Approach to possible cases of abuse

- Get a clear history.
- Decide if local vulnerable adults procedures should be invoked.
- Establish capacity of victim to participate in decision-making.
- Establish carer characteristics and account of events.
- Get specific expertise if needed, e.g. financial advocate, solicitor, police.
- Arrange multidisciplinary case conference.
- Consider help required by carer—treatment, psychological assessment, relief from care burden.
- Decide if legal proceedings are needed.
- Protect both parties by establishing third-party support, e.g. independent deputy appointed by court of protection.
- Relocate vulnerable person, e.g. to new care home, if appropriate.

Case example

Mrs R is an 84-year-old woman with a 3-year history of AD. She lives alone and is cared for by a 50-year-old unmarried son who has a history of alcohol abuse. Neighbours express a concern that she is losing weight, her clothes are not being changed, and her medications are being given chaotically. The son permits carers only to give a meal daily and give medication. She later has bruises that both he and she explain are due to 'a fall'. He refuses help for his alcohol use and won't allow her to have a respite admission to a care home. She says she is 'not bothered' and wants to stay at home. A multidisciplinary vulnerable adults case conference is held, led by social services. The son, her case worker from social services, a police officer, a neighbour, a manager of the care agency, and an old age psychiatrist who has seen her on four occasions are present. The GP has sent a report expressing her concern about well-being. The outcome is that a letter is sent to him stating that he must allow two carers access to his mother three times a day and a respite admission to a care home each 8 weeks. Legal proceedings to take his mother into care will be started if he does not comply. The social worker obtains all eligible financial benefits to offset the costs of the extra care and he is offered help from the community alcohol team. No criminal charges are brought.

Crime and older people

Older people and offending
- Older people in the UK represent under 1% of all those convicted of an offence.
- The number of older people convicted of an offence is rising.
- The prison population of those over 60 years is rising.
- A tenth of convictions among older people are for sexual offences.

Psychiatric disorder and crime in older people
- Among convicted people, rates of psychiatric disorder are very low.
- Most assaults by people with dementia are unreported.
- There is no evidence that paranoid illness, mood disorder, or dementia increase the risk of offending among older people.
- Alcohol may precipitate offending in older people.
- Drug-related crime is very rare.
- Abnormal personality traits are found less frequently among older offenders than among younger offenders.

The older psychiatric patient in court
Most countries will seek to divert older people from the criminal justice system. In particular, people with dementia who lack criminal responsibility or fitness to plead are unlikely to recover it with treatment and are unlikely to come to trial. Alternative disposals to prison may include care homes, probation, or psychiatric hospitalization.

Checklist in establishing fitness to plead in the UK (equivalent to 'competence to stand trial' in the USA)

Can the person
- Understand the charge s/he is answering?
- Understand what entering a plea means?
- Understand the consequences of a guilty and a not guilty plea?
- Follow evidence?
- Challenge proceedings?
- Challenge a juror?
- Instruct a lawyer?

Older people as victims of crime
Older people are much less likely to be a victim of crime than younger people. In particular, they are much less likely to be a victim of violent crime. It is widely held that fear of crime is higher among older people but the best evidence does not support this, showing older people to have a realistic appraisal of risk. Some older people lose confidence and may become housebound or even institutionalized after becoming a victim of crime. This is more likely among women and the socially isolated.

Capacity/competence—general principles

- Capacity is a legal concept technically meaning the ability to enter into a contract. It has the same meaning as the clinical concept of competence. Health care professionals, especially doctors, are frequently called upon to make judgements about capacity. Particular expertise is expected from those who specialize in dementia care, e.g. psychogeriatricians. In many countries, including the UK, an assumption is made that adults have capacity. It is also widely recognized that certain groups in society are likely to lack capacity to make important decisions; these may include children, those with learning disability, and, among older people, those with dementia. Among adults, older people are much more likely to lack capacity, mainly due to the much higher prevalence of dementia in old age. Particular legislation is available in some countries to assist in making decisions about capacity (e.g. the MCA 2005 in England and Wales), while professional bodies offer advice and guidance to members and the public (e.g. the General Medical Council in the UK).
- A number of important decisions likely to be made in late life lead to queries about capacity. These include capacity to make a will, capacity to consent to a medical procedure, capacity to manage financial affairs, capacity to appoint someone as an agent, e.g. donating lasting power of attorney, capacity to decide to remain at home rather than move to a care home. For people lacking capacity, various clinical and legislative options are available. A general principle is that staff will always act in the best interests of the patient.

MCA (2005) test of capacity

- Does the person have an impairment of, or a disturbance in the functioning of, their mind or brain?
- Does the impairment or disturbance mean that the person is unable to make a specific decision when they need to?

General fundamentals of capacity to make a decision

A person with capacity should

- Understand the decision to be made.
- Believe information given.[1]
- Understand the alternative choices and their consequences.
- Retain information long enough to decide.
- Weigh up the options.
- Communicate a decision.
- Not be subject to undue influence.[1]

---

1 Part of traditional assessment of capacity; not strictly necessary for current (England and Wales) definition of capacity within the MCA 2005.

Tips for those assessing capacity

Capacity should be assumed

It is not acceptable to assume a lack of capacity in an individual. UK law is quite clear: adults are assumed to have capacity until proven otherwise. Any professional making a judgement about capacity has to give the reasons why they believe capacity is not present. It is unfortunately common for an assumption to be made that people with dementia lack capacity to make important decisions. In reality, in early dementia, capacity is retained or may be regained with reasonable effort by the assessor.

Capacity for one decision does not imply capacity for another

It is sometimes mistakenly believed that a person either has or does not have capacity to make important decisions, i.e. they are either competent or incompetent. In fact, an individual may have capacity to make one decision, e.g. to accept a particular drug or operation, but simultaneously lack capacity for another decision, e.g. to make a will. Capacity must be judged for each decision to be made. There are of course people, e.g. those with advanced dementia, who lack all capacities; the assessor should still state the reasons why capacities are absent.

Capacity can change in an individual

Capacity can vary considerable in a short space of time. Rehydrating an elderly person admitted from home with self-neglect, treating a chest infection which has caused delirium, going back to see a newly admitted patient after a period of rest, or simply waiting a few days or weeks before seeing a borderline case again may lead to a different assessment of capacity.

Do everything possible to increase capacity

The assessor should make sure that medical problems interfering with capacity are resolved, e.g. dehydration/infection/pain. Excessive sedation should be reduced. Severe depression should be treated before decisions are made about capacity. Full information about the decision should be given in a manner understandable to the patient. If at all possible, discussions should take place in a quiet room with minimal distraction.

Maximize information

The professional assessing capacity needs to ensure they know the relevant facts. What are the financial circumstances of the patient? What is the family structure? What are the actual risks inherent in going home from hospital rather than to a care home? What were the wishes of the person expressed throughout their life? What are the wishes of the nearest relatives?

Establish the expressed wishes of the patient

Find out what the patient would have wanted. Have they written an advanced directive? Have they repeatedly expressed a particular wish when well? These matters will assist in deciding on best interests rather than on capacity *per se*.

Does anything influence capacity?

If the person has a mental illness, might it affect capacity? For people with dementia, is the memory deficit and deterioration in judgement and concentration sufficient to mean they cannot understand, retain, or weigh up the information given? For people with paranoid delusions, do the delusions influence their choice of where to live or to whom to leave assets in a will? Mentally ill people may well retain capacity for the decision at hand.

Is there undue external influence?

Might a person or persons be influencing a vulnerable person unduly? Could they have forced them to sign a will? Could they clearly benefit from a particular decision? In many cases an interested party, e.g. a child, would of course benefit from a decision but there will be no evidence of undue influence.

Capacity to make a will

This capacity is known as testamentary capacity. Doctors may be asked to witness a will. It is probably wise to avoid this unless the doctor is confident that the person signing the will has capacity and the doctor is willing to say so in a court of law. The most common scenario where this capacity may be questioned arises when an older person has made a will which excludes someone who may reasonably have expected to benefit. This person may challenge the will on the grounds that the person with dementia lacks testamentary capacity. It is much easier to argue on these matters if the capacity is clearly established prospectively, that is, by an examination of the patient at or around the time of making the will. Deciding on capacity retrospectively on the basis of contemporaneous notes is likely to be very difficult and contentious. Psychogeriatricians are quite frequently asked to comment on this capacity for people with dementia in the UK. The criteria for testamentary capacity have been clearly established in English law since 1870. They are:

The patient should understand the nature of the act

The patient needs to know they are signing a will and that this will decide what happens to their assets after their death. They also need to understand that the new will replaces any old one so should understand how the new will differs.

The patient should understand the extent of their estate

They need to know what they have to leave. This doesn't mean knowing the exact values of a bank account, investment, or house, but the patient needs to be aware of what their main assets are, including a house and any major investments.

The patient needs to know who has claims upon their estate

Specifically, who is being included and excluded. For example, the patient should be able to identify any first-degree relative such as a spouse or children. They should be able to state why individuals are being disinherited. It does not matter if the decision appears foolish or capricious; only that they are aware who might benefit and give a non-delusional reason for exclusion.

Case example

A 82-year-old man has a mild case of dementia, diagnosed 18 months previously. He is widowed and has four children. One was long estranged but has come back to live with his father after 30 years. The father rewrites his will to exclude the other three children, who object. It is clear to the family solicitor that there is a major rift between the children. The solicitor writes to the old age psychiatrist who monitors the patient's care. The instructions given include a request to judge capacity to make a will and a statement of the criteria for these. The solicitor also informs her that the man owns a house worth about £400 000, about £25 000 in shares and about £14 000 in savings. The old age psychiatrist last saw the patient 4 months previously. MMSE at that time was 19. There was no evidence of delusions but the patient was being cared for by the original three children. She can't make a full judgement just from the notes so arranges to visit him again. At interview, he states clearly that he knows what a will is and says his assets are 'my house... I reckon it's worth £300 000', 'some shares and about £10 000 in the bank'. He states he knows the other three are fed up but his son who returned 'is like a prodigal... the others are well set in life; they don't need the money'. 'They will come round eventually, I hope'. She writes to the solicitor to conclude that he does have testamentary capacity.

This case illustrates the value of careful contemporaneous notes in deciding on capacity.

Capacity to make health care decisions

Two-thirds of people in general hospital beds in the UK are over 65 years old, a pattern found in most developed countries. Older people are much more likely to need invasive and/or serious procedures, so capacity to decide whether to have a procedure is commonly assessed. Doubt about this capacity is particularly likely when very frail or demented older people require serious procedures, e.g. PEG tube insertion, ECT, or major surgery. For common procedures such as accepting medication, having a blood test, or being physically examined, simple verbal consent, whether explicit or tacit (consent assumed as no objection is made) is acceptable. For the more significant procedures, explicit criteria should be met, as outlined below. A common error is to assume that a signed consent form means informed consent was obtained; it in fact records no more than a discussion having occurred.

To give informed consent the patient should

Understand why a procedure is proposed
They need to understand what condition the procedure is for. It is not necessary that they be exact about this, e.g. a patient saying 'bad infection' when they have *Clostridium difficile* sepsis, may be sufficient in many cases.

Understand the nature of the procedure
They need to know what procedure will be done. For example, ECT needs to be understood as electrical treatment under anaesthetic which works by causing a short seizure.

Understand the choice available
They need to know what the alternatives to the treatment are, including no treatment. Understanding that they have a choice of surgery, or chemotherapy for cancer, with no treatment being their ultimate choice, usually suffices.

Understand the benefits and risks of each course of action
They need to be aware in broad terms of the consequences of each choice. It isn't necessary for them to know 5-year survival rates in breast cancer surgical options, but knowing that a radical mastectomy may carry a longer survival than local surgery is needed.

Believe the information given
Patients with severe depression may believe that they are doomed whatever the choice made, or patients with schizophrenia may believe themselves conspired against. Every effort should be made to establish whether mental illness may directly affect the cognitive processes necessary to give informed consent. This may not affect the legal test of capacity of the 2005 MCA, but is an important principle in medical consent.

Retain the information for long enough to make a decision
Patients with dementia may be unable to explain the main points back after say 5 min; retention of details for hours or days is not needed but the minutes for weighing up and deciding are important. It is wise to retest (if necessary giving the information again) in doubtful cases.

Weigh it up and communicate a decision
The patient should be able to judge pros and cons and be able to indicate clearly what choice they have made, by whatever means.

Case example

A man aged 84 years with established dementia is admitted to a geriatric ward with falls and poor eating. He refuses all food and fluids and won't take medication. An old age psychiatrist is asked to 'authorize' a PEG tube. The patient has persistently stated that he wants to die to join his wife. He has refused most food and care from home carers for a year. When asked what will happen if he carries on he says 'I will die'. He is not clinically depressed. He knows that the procedure is 'a tube in my stomach to give me stuff'. His MMSE is 18 on the ward. The old age psychiatrist sees him again the next day but his views are unchanged. The psychiatrist writes in the medical notes that 'This man has undoubted dementia but understands the procedure, the reasons for it and what will happen if he carries on without it. He is adamant he does not want it and is not in my view clinically depressed. I believe he has capacity to decide on this issue and that therefore a PEG tube cannot be inserted'.

Capacity to make social care decisions

Many older people may be fiercely independent, even in the face of mounting evidence that they will need more social care. In hospital, the most common dilemma involves an older person, usually with dementia, who faces obvious risks if they go home but insists they do not want to enter a care home. In the community, the same situation applies, in which older people refuse either care being introduced to them at home or to enter a care home. These situations involve risk, and doctors may be asked to comment on the person's capacity to decide this. One common misconception is that any risk is unacceptable. There is in fact no risk-free circumstance, just greater and lesser risk. Deciding that someone lacks capacity does not automatically mean that compulsion is justified; a careful weighing of the risks of not introducing care versus the distress of forcible care, e.g. in a care home, should be made for each individual.

Patients should

Understand what care is proposed

For example, that a move to a care home is needed, or that a carer will come in twice a day to ensure medication is taken and that they have a hot meal.

Understand why care is needed

This equates to some appreciation of risk—the older person may flatly deny an obvious risk, while another may acknowledge that they may fall but they still don't want to leave home.

Understand the consequences of decision

Appreciate what will happen if they accept the care and if they refuse it. For example, in a care home they may fall just as often but at least someone will be around to pick them up. Accepting a home carer may mean they will take their tablets regularly, and they may need them to control pain.

Professionals should ponder

Has every alternative been explored?

The least restrictive option should be explored. Negotiation will often lead to voluntary admission to a care home or acceptance of partial care, e.g. a carer visiting once a day may allow them to trust more frequent visitors.

What will cause the most distress?

A weighing of relative risk and distress to patient/family/professional carers (if they stay at home) versus distress to the patient (if they are compelled into care) should be made.

Case example

A 90-year-old lady is frail and may have cognitive impairment; she has never been diagnosed with dementia. She lives alone and wants 'to die at home'. The carers organized by her social worker find blood on her sheets every day (she has a probable rectal carcinoma but is not considered a candidate for active treatment) and she is losing weight, eating very little. The social worker calls her GP out to see her, asking that she be forcibly admitted to a care home. The GP has known her a long time. She is a committed Christian and says 'I look forward to dying'. She scores 23/30 on MMSE. She says 'I know I can't look after myself but I want to end my days at home'. The social worker is unwilling to take further risks and the GP reluctantly calls for a MHA assessment. The lady is removed to a care home under guardianship arrangements and dies, unhappy, 11 days later.

Financial capacity

Much concern is often expressed about the ability of older people to manage their financial affairs. These abilities are focused on in old age for a number of reasons; these include sensory deficits, frailty due to physical illness, increased prevalence of dementia, and the reality of major financial decisions such as paying for care or making a will. There is no standard established method for testing financial capacity. Indeed, one cannot speak of a general capacity for financial decision-making; rather an individual may or may not have capacity for an individual decision. The capacity to manage the transaction of buying a newspaper is clearly not the same as that required to negotiate the sale of a house.

The questions below cover a range of abilities relevant to financial decision-making in old age; it will be clear that financial capacity is not 'all or nothing' and capacity in these areas will vary among both cognitively impaired and cognitively intact older people.

- Does the person have basic skills to manage money—identifying currency, adding notes/coins by value?
- Can the person correctly state what change they would expect for one or more items of differing value?
- Can they understand what a bank account, a cheque book, a cash card, and a credit card are?
- Can they identify the parts of a cheque and its stub and complete a dummy transaction?
- Can they explain the parts of their bank statement?
- Can they identify solicitation by advert (post/email) for legitimate and bogus (spam) financial transactions?

In dealing with lack of financial capacity, use of legal manoeuvres may be unnecessary. Family members often take over financial affairs such as paying bills, which are now commonly paid by direct debit, reducing the number of transactions needed. Family will often also supervise shopping. In disputed cases, many jurisdictions allow for an agent to be appointed to manage financial affairs. Common sense holds that this should be done in advance of incapacity supervening. In England and Wales, a power known as lasting power of attorney (LPA) could be signed over, usually to a close relative, which is signed by a person in full capacity and registered after capacity is lost, e.g. after stroke or dementia develops. In practice, even those who have signed powers of attorney in England and Wales are often not registered even after the individual becomes incapacitated.

Conditions for donating LPA

The donor (the patient) must understand that:

- The attorney will be able to assume complete control over the donor's affairs.
- The attorney will be able to do almost anything with the donor's money which the donor would have done in the past.

- The attorney's power will continue after donor becomes incapable, by reason of mental disorder, of managing their money and property.
- The donor can in such circumstances never reverse the power.

It will be clear that some people with dementia do not have this capacity; the test of capacity is a stringent one, as the stakes are high. But it remains the case that many people with dementia do have this capacity, even if they lack capacity to make financial decisions.

The Mental Capacity Act (2005)

In the UK, a combination of case law and specific courts have governed dealings with incapacitated persons. The situation left very wide scope for doctors to act in the 'best interests' of patients. Courts dealt primarily with financial competence issues and emergency cases. In Scotland, the Adults with Incapacity (Scotland) Act 2000 is in force, and in 2007 the MCA (2005)[1] came into legal force for England and Wales. The latter act expands existing court powers to include health care as well as financial decision-making, clarifies exactly who can make what decisions and when, and introduces mandatory procedures for assessing capacity. Five principles underlie the act:

- A presumption of capacity.
- The right for individuals to be supported in making decisions.
- Individuals retain the right to make unusual decisions, however unwise.
- Best interests will always determine what is done for incapacitated persons.
- The least restrictive option is always sought for those without capacity.

Assessing capacity

A single test is done for capacity to make one decision at one time; there will be no presumption of incapacity based on age, appearance, or diagnosis.

Best interests

The act provides a checklist for deciding what is in an individual's best interests. Those assessing it must consider any advance directive/written statement made by the person and must consult with carers or family members

Acts in connection with care/treatment

The act clarifies that no clinician/carer would be legally liable for actions like injection or restraint (technically, a deprivation of liberty) if they had carefully considered capacity and best interests and were acting in a caring capacity.

Research

The act clarifies that people lacking capacity may be involved in research projects if they agree to the research, if a carer agrees they would have wanted to be part of the research, if the research will directly benefit them, or if it will not, that it could not be carried out with people who had capacity.

New terms likely to be encountered by professionals

Independent mental capacity advocates (IMCAs)

These are individuals appointed by the court to speak for someone who lacks capacity but has no-one to speak for them. They may challenge a clinician or carer, and represent the person's wishes and feelings; though their decisions are not legally binding, only to be considered.

Lasting power of attorney (LPA)

LPA replaces enduring power of attorney (EPA) but conveys similar powers. The LPA persists after capacity is lost and cannot then be revoked. A key difference is that it now applies to health care decisions as well as financial decisions.

Deputies

The Court of Protection may appoint deputies (these replace the old system of receiverships) who can make decisions about financial, health, and social care. They cannot refuse life-saving treatment. Deputies will only be appointed if recurrent decisions are likely, so the court cannot rule as a one-off.

1 Mental Capacity Act 2005 ▣http://www.justice.gov.uk/guidance/mental-capacity.htm

Mental health legislation

- Most countries have some form of mental health legislation. The purpose of such legislation is to provide protections from harm for people with mental disorders, to protect others from the effects of mental disorder, to protect people with mental disorder, a vulnerable group, from mistreatment and excessive detention, and in some cases, to assist in the care of people unable by reason of mental disorder to make informed decisions about health care.
- In the UK, formal legislation has been available since the early 19th century. For any legislation, common themes are likely to be some definition of mental disorder, specification of grounds for detention and compulsory treatment, clear legal redress including grounds for appeal, and provision for scrutiny of the application of the law. There is often confusion around when mental health law should be applied and when considerations of capacity issues apply; practice varies between countries.

Mental Health Act 1983

In England and Wales, the Mental Health Act 1983 applies; a new act (2007) provides some amendments. The main sections encountered in clinical practice include

- **Section 5(4)**: nurse holding powers—power of nurses to hold a patient for up to 6h until a doctor arrives.
- **Section 5(2)**: power of a doctor to detain a patient in a hospital for up to 72h because of mental disorder; decision on further detention must be made in this time.
- **Section 2**: power of three professionals to detain a person with mental disorder in a hospital for up to 28 days for assessment.
- **Section 3**: power of three professionals to detain a person with mental disorder in a hospital for up to 6 months for treatment of the mental disorder.

In Scotland and Northern Ireland, there is independent legislation which largely follows the same principles as England and Wales. Scottish law already provides for limited community treatment orders. Northern Irish law allows initial detention periods of up to 7 days, followed by treatment up to 6 months. In the Republic of Ireland, the Mental Health Act 2001 allows certain people including doctors and police officers to detain a person in a psychiatric hospital for a short period before a consultant psychiatrist applies to extend the period of detention.

Mental Health Act 2007

A new mental health bill has been proposed for some years for England and Wales. Extensive consultation has led to substantial amendments. The bill became law in 2007; the principal changes include:

- Introduction of limited community treatment orders.
- Simplifying the definition of mental disorder.
- Changing the definition of treatability.
- Broadening the range of professionals allowed to make decisions about detention.
- Making appeals compulsory after long periods of detention.

Mental Health Act—in-patient issues

Likely issues in a general hospital

Among older general hospital in-patients, the MHA may occasionally be used to assist with patients who are delirious and require administration of calming medication and prevention from leaving the ward. Physicians may sometimes erroneously request that in-patients with a mental disorder (usually dementia) be detained to allow treatment of a physical illness which they cannot consent to. Among older psychiatric in-patients, people with dementia may initially consent to admission but need regular restraint to prevent them leaving. People with depression may deteriorate to the point that ECT is required but is either refused or capacity is absent.

Scenario 1

A 73-year-old woman is an in-patient with peripheral vascular disease. She has established moderate dementia and lives in a care home. She requires a below-knee amputation of the right lower limb or gangrene is likely, in the opinion of the vascular surgeon treating her. She refuses surgery but cannot give informed consent. A psychiatrist is asked to 'section' her. The psychiatrist writes: 'This woman has established Alzheimer's disease of moderate severity. She lacks capacity to give informed consent and there is no prospect of this being recovered. She refuses the surgery on the grounds of "not wanting an operation". The Mental Health Act cannot be used to treat a physical condition, unless that condition is clearly the cause of her mental disorder (dementia). It is up to the treating team to decide whether this operation is in the best interests of this patient, after consulting with family in usual way.'

Scenario 2

A 65-year-old man was admitted to a medical ward with an overdose of 35 paracetamol tablets. He agreed to transfer to a psychiatric unit for assessment on a Friday night, once medically fit. On Sunday morning he states 'I am going home'. He has severe osteoarthritis and an alcohol problem, and has been depressed for 3 months since his wife died. He won't answer questions about whether he will do this again. A duty doctor writes in his notes 'This man appears clinically depressed and took a substantial recent overdose. His suicide risk is high and I am detaining him on section 5(2) of the Mental Health Act to allow further assessment, pending consultant review tomorrow morning.'

Mental Health Act—community issues

Among older psychiatric patients in the community, common issues involve patients with dementia who neglect themselves, refuse social care, or refuse to enter a care home. As with younger people, older people with serious mental illness including depressive illness, mania, and schizophrenia may refuse services/treatment and represent a high risk, needing compulsory admission. Some older people have physical frailty which may increase the urgency of assessment, for example patients with congestive cardiac failure may refuse diuretics when depressed, putting themselves at risk.

Scenario 1

A 81-year-old man has a history of recurrent depressive disorder and now mild dementia. He is followed up by a community mental health team. In recent months he has become low in mood, apathetic, eats poorly, and fails to take antidepressant and antihypertensive medication regularly. His wife is now very worried as he is eating poorly, losing weight, and not drinking enough fluid. When seen by the community team he states 'there is no point to treatment; I don't deserve it. They are better off without me'. His community nurse contacts medical and social work colleagues to request a Mental Health Act assessment 'This man is deteriorating quickly and neither myself nor his wife can get him to eat or drink. I believe he is at risk of renal failure and we cannot get medication in reliably. I have no choice but to request urgent Mental Health Act assessment'.

Scenario 2

A 77-year-old woman is referred to a psychiatrist by her GP. She has had no previous physical or mental health problems but her daughter reports she has been very suspicious about the neighbours recently and thinks her food may be poisoned. She tells the psychiatrist that new neighbours are pumping gas in and contaminating her water supplies. She hears them 'interfering with the plumbing at night'. She adamantly refuses treatment 'there is nothing wrong with me'. She is terrified of admission to 'the loony bin'. The psychiatrist writes 'The diagnosis is of late-onset schizophrenia and the symptoms are typical. There is no evidence of dementia. She is adamantly opposed to treatment. In theory she could be detained and treated with antipsychotic medication in hospital but I do not think we should do this as: 1. The response rate to such treatment is modest, 2. She is able to lead a reasonable quality of life despite her symptoms, 3. She would be extremely upset by forcible admission to hospital, 4. There is very low risk of her acting forcibly against the neighbour, other than complaints. We will follow her up through our community team in case of deterioration'.

End-of-life issues

Palliative care

This term palliative care[1] refers to care which is holistic, i.e. offers care for the body, mind, and spirit and which is not primarily directed towards cure. It is given to patients in whom death is expected in the near future and key goals including preparing the patient and family for the death and making the most of the time left. Specific services have been set up in many countries to provide such care. In the UK they are known as palliative care teams and are best known for dealing with terminal stages of cancer in both young and old, and management of progressive neurological conditions like motor neuron disease. There is increased interest in how the palliative care model may help people with dementia. Dementia of whatever cause is usually progressive and fatal. Mean time from diagnosis to death in dementia is 5–8 years. Some organizations deliver palliative care to people/families with dementia, e.g. Admiral Nurses in the UK, who are specialist dementia nurses with a role supporting the family and carers of people with dementia .

Where people die

Clear trends can be seen in location of death for older people. As the populations of Western countries age, increasing proportions live in residential and nursing homes. In the last two decades, there has been a significant fall in the proportion of older people in the UK dying at home (now about a quarter) with increases in those dying in hospital (over half) and in care homes (a sixth). US research also shows that the place of death of those with dementia is much more likely to be a care home (67%) than for those with cancer. Individual choice should be accommodated if possible; many older people will be surprisingly keen on dying in an institutional setting, it seems the presence of loved ones, and not being a burden, may outweigh any wishes to die in their own homes.

Psychological care of the dying

The majority of older people probably die a good death, that is, without evidence of distressing pain or other physical discomfort and without severe psychological distress. Older people who are dying may undergo anticipatory changes in preparation for death which resemble a grief reaction, including disbelief, shock and bewilderment, bargaining, depression, and resolution. In dementia, realization of impending death may be absent. For relatives, anticipatory grief is common. The family may have been robbed of the person they knew by the dementia so rehearsing and undergoing grieving during life is understandable and may allow easier coping with death itself. It is unusual to have to use specific psychiatric skills with families, other than sympathy, listening, and answering questions.

To feed or not to feed?

In the last 20 years, nutritional support in the form of enteral feeding has become widely available. The most common intervention is nasogastric tube feeding, but PEG tubes are also available. PEG tubes are usually considered for medium- to longer-term feeding in those unlikely to recover the ability to eat due to dysphagia. Complications of PEG tubes include

gastrointestinal tract perforation, bleeding, inhalation, infection, and consequences of sedation. The procedure is sometimes proposed for people
with dementia who are losing weight due to dementia. Several hundred
such procedures are carried out per year in the UK. This raises important
clinical and ethical issues:

- It is widely held that PEG tubing removes the risk of inhalation
  pneumonias—this is untrue and the rate of such infections is
  unchanged after PEG.
- PEG tubing in dementia has been shown not to improve quality of life,
  infection rate, bedsores, or survival.
- While withholding nutrition is legally counted the same as removing
  treatment, there is no obligation to introduce treatments which are
  futile, i.e. cannot lead to a meaningful improvement in quality of life.

1 Hughes JC, Jolley D, Jordan A, Sampson EL (2007). Palliative care in dementia: issues and evidence. Adv Psychiat Treatment **13**: 251–60.

See also: General Medical Council http://www.gmc-uk.org/

Prescribing issues in older people

Pharmacokinetics *194*
Pharmacodynamics *195*
Polypharmacy *196*
Aggression in the elderly *198*
Assessing aggressive patients *199*
Specific management of aggression *200*
Sleep disorders/insomnia *202*
Prescribing for insomnia *204*
Psychosis in Parkinson's disease *206*
Post-stroke depression *207*
Post-stroke mania *208*
Other post-stroke disorders *209*

Pharmacokinetics

Pharmacokinetics is the study of the metabolism and action of drugs, with particular emphasis on time required for absorption, duration of action, distribution in the body, and method of excretion. The ageing process can bring about changes in the following pharmacokinetic parameters:

Absorption

The absorption of drugs may be slowed down or delayed in older people due to a number of factors including reduction in gastric pH, decrease of the size of the intestinal absorption area, reduced blood flow to the digestive system due to an overall decrease in cardiac output. All these factors can contribute to an overall decreased bioavailability of drugs in older people.

Distribution

The distribution of drugs is influenced by the composition of the body. In older people, a number of changes in body composition could influence drug distribution. An increased proportion of fat tissue in older people can increase the volume of distribution of drugs, and as most psychotropic medications are stored in fat tissue, their elimination half-life is consequently increased. A decrease in the lean body mass and water content can result in higher concentrations of drugs such as alcohol that are distributed throughout the body fluids. A decrease in the overall albumen concentration can result in high concentration of free (not bound with plasma proteins) levels of drug, thus resulting in high levels of drugs crossing the blood–brain barrier and producing more side-effects. In some cases, a decrease in cerebral blood flow may result in decreased levels of drugs in the brain.

Metabolism

Most psychotropic drugs are metabolized in the liver, with the notable exception of lithium which is renally excreted. Hepatic blood flow is known to decrease with age thus increasing the elimination half-life of drugs metabolized in the liver. As a consequence a prolongation of action after a single dose and delayed accumulation on multiple doses can be seen in older people.

Excretion

A reduction in renal function is common in advanced age. Average renal excretion declines by a third from youth to old age. Individual older people may have perfectly normal excretion, but some, especially those with concomitant physical illness, may have difficulties with water-soluble drugs such as lithium. Guidelines for lithium prescription recommend using a single bedtime dosing regimen, regular monitoring of blood lithium levels and renal function, and dose adjustments according to declining renal function.

Pharmacodynamics

- Pharmacodynamics deals with the mechanisms by which drugs exert their actions on the body. In other words, it is the study of how drugs act at target sites of action in the body. A number of pharmacodynamic changes in old age tend to alter sensitivity to drugs, even when plasma concentrations are similar to those in younger people.
- The elderly are particularly sensitive to sedatives, antiparkinsonian drugs, and drugs with anticholinergic properties (Table 9.1). Ageing brain cells are more vulnerable to the excitotoxicity caused by glutamate overactivity. Age-associated changes in the brain result in general changes in cellular metabolism. These result in deficits in dopamine, acetylcholine, serotonin, and noradrenalin neurotransmitter systems resulting in diminished efficiency of homeostatic mechanisms in the ageing brain. Any direct influence of ageing itself on drug binding at individual receptors, and subsequent post-synaptic effects, is poorly understood.
- The above-mentioned factors contribute to a reduction in normal regulatory processes within the brain and make it more vulnerable to develop severe reactions with drugs. It is probable that the majority of adverse reactions to drugs which are common among older people are related to the presence of physical illness, and increased prescribing, rather than to pharmacodynamic changes *per se*.

Table 9.1 Pharmacodynamic factors in the ageing brain

Neurotransmitter	Age changes	Consequences
GABA system	Receptor changes Declining mitochondrial function	Increased susceptibility to sedatives, e.g. benzodiazepines
Dopamine system	Decreased dopamine production Decreased number of neurons in nigro-striatal system	Increased susceptibility to drug-induced parkinsonism
Acetylcholine system	Cortical degeneration Decreased nicotine affinity Decreased acetylcholine production	Increased risk of delirium Increased susceptibility to anticholinergic drugs
Nor-adrenalin system	Degeneration of locus ceruleus Depletion of nor-adrenaline Compensatory activation of other noradrenergic neurons	Slowed cognition Sensitivity to yohimbine
Serotonin system	Reduction in 5HT2 receptors Reduction in serotonin uptake sites	Decreased effectiveness of serotonergic drugs, e.g. SSRIs
Glutamate system	Decreased NMDA receptors Impairment of cellular energy metabolism	Cognitive decline Neurotoxicity

Polypharmacy

- The incidence of both psychiatric disorders and medical illnesses is higher among older people. These conditions frequently occur simultaneously and are often chronic, lasting for the lifetime of the individual; consequently, it is not uncommon in clinical practice to find elderly patients requiring more medications than younger people. Older people also tend to be higher consumers of over-the-counter drugs.
- A combination of use of multiple drugs for medical and psychiatric illness along with over-the-counter preparations and the pharmacokinetic and dynamic changes in the body makes older people vulnerable to a wide range of side-effects. The dilemma faced by the physician is how to treat an illness without causing more harm than good. This is not helped by the fact that most research studies on the use and safety of drugs are conducted on younger people and physicians caring for older people have to generalize those findings to their older patients.
- These problems can result in a reluctance to prescribe or treat a problem. This can be positive, as it tends to encourage us to look for non-pharmacological methods of management in disorders such as BPSD or psychological interventions for depression and anxiety. It can, however, also lead to a delay in the alleviation of distress, leading to poor quality of life and sometimes to increased risk.
- It is, therefore, important for physicians to realize that the response to treatment is generally good in older people with specific psychiatric disorders such as a major depressive episode, and that the risk of not treating or under-treating (low doses) can be greater than the potential risks of treatment. Although the choice of safest combination of medications would ultimately depend on the characteristics of the individual patient, the following strategies might be useful in avoiding harmful effects of polypharmacy:

Antidepressants

Tricyclic antidepressants:

- Tricyclics are not recommended as a first-line treatment of depression or mixed depression and anxiety states.
- Some patients may still be treated with tricyclics if they have been stable on them for many years or for other reasons, such as chronic pain and neuralgia.
- Their tendency to cause sedation and postural hypotension may increase the risk of falls and excessive sedation if combined with benzodiazepines and antipsychotics.
- Their combination with analgesics containing opioid derivatives such as cocodamol may cause/aggravate constipation.

SSRIs:
- Most SSRIs compete for the same metabolic pathway used by β-blockers, benzodiazepines, and some antiarrhythmics.
- SSRIs in combination with aspirin might increase a tendency to gastrointestinal bleeds/ulceration especially in very old (85+) patients.

MAOIs:
- A class of antidepressants rarely used nowadays due to dangerous interactions with opiate analgesics (especially pethidine), nasal decongestants (like pseudoephedrine), and other antidepressants (risk of hypertensive crisis) and tyramine-containing foods.
- Moclobemide is a safer modern alternative MAOI.

Antipsychotics

Conventional antipsychotics:
- Carry a high risk of causing movement disorders.
- Have a tendency to cause sedation and postural hypotension that in combination with other sedating drugs, such as benzodiazepines; tricyclic antidepressant, and mirtazapine may increase the risk of falls.

Atypical antipsychotics:
- Recommended first-line treatment for psychotic symptoms.
- Olanzapine has a tendency to disturb glucose and lipid metabolism and can aggravate/disturb treatment of diabetic patients on oral hypoglycaemics and insulin.
- Quetiapine has a tendency to cause sedation and postural hypotension, which might increase the risk of falls in combination with other drugs with sedating side-effects.

Aggression in the elderly

Being asked to see an aggressive elderly patient is common, both in liaison and community settings. Aggression is usually seen in one of the following four clinical scenarios.

Aggression in dementia

In most cases the reasons for aggression cannot be explained by the patient nor do they have any memory of their aggressive behaviour. The episodes of aggression are unpredictable and occur impulsively. The usual scenario is of a patient becoming physically or verbally aggressive while receiving care from staff or relatives, for example in personal hygiene. The patient can often simply be distracted from the target of aggression. This type of aggressive behaviour can be persistent and cause a strain on carers. It is one of the commonest reasons for placement in nursing homes for patients with dementia.

Aggression in delirium

The aggressive behaviour, either physical or verbal, appears to be random and unpredictable. The course is fluctuating and patients appear to be more disturbed and aggressive at night-time. The aggressive behaviour may be in response to delusions or hallucinations combined with the disorientation caused by an alien environment if the patient is in hospital.

Aggression in delirium can put the patient at risk of harm to themselves due to lack of cooperation with the staff in taking medication and accepting care, failure to eat and drink adequately, and exposure to extremes of weather.

Aggression in depression

This type of aggression usually occurs in the setting of irritability. Patients are usually aware of their irritability and may be angry with themselves and want to be left alone. Irritability/agitation/aggression in depression has to be taken seriously, requiring a detailed risk assessment of harm to self or others.

Aggression in psychosis/paranoid patients

Here the aggression usually occurs in response to the patient's delusional beliefs and perceptual abnormalities, such as auditory hallucinations. The patient usually expresses reasons for being aggressive, is likely to have a good recollection of the aggressive episodes, and may express remorse/guilt afterwards. It is important to recognize that the patient may be aggressive as a defence against profound fear and insecurity. Aggression with psychosis warrants a detailed risk assessment of harm to self or others and not just prescription of antipsychotic medication.

Assessing aggressive patients

- Management of all aggressive patients should involve a thorough assessment and not just prescription of psychotropic medications.
- Aggressive patients are vulnerable to self-harm, harm to others, neglect, abuse, and inappropriate placements for future care.

Assessment

A comprehensive assessment of an aggressive patient should include the following:

- A detailed history of the aggressive behaviour is extremely important, as aggression is a loose term and can have different meanings for people from different professional backgrounds.
- One of the useful ways of assessing episodes of aggression could be by dividing each episode into antecedents, behaviour, and consequences (the so-called ABC approach). With this simple approach, each episode of aggression can be analysed with useful information about the possible causes/provocations of aggressive behaviour, the actual nature of the behaviour (verbal/physical aggression and its severity), and the consequences of that behaviour, i.e. is it putting the patient or carers at risk of harm, is it resulting in isolation/neglect of the patient, is the behaviour reinforced by attention or by failure to challenge the patient? The 'ABC technique' is especially helpful in specialist dementia care homes.
- A detailed history of present and past illness, looking at the pattern of aggression (acute or chronic), symptoms of associated psychiatric disorders (depression, dementia, psychosis), and past history of mental disorders.
- A detailed mental state examination, including cognitive assessment is key to the management plan, as it will pick up signs and symptoms of associated psychiatric disorders.
- A list of baseline laboratory investigations (MSU, blood counts and metabolic profile) can be useful to rule out delirium or associated medical problems. A typical example of an underlying medical problem causing episodes of aggression/agitation would be a diabetic patient becoming aggressive during episodes of hypoglycaemia.

Case example

An 89-year-old woman with established dementia lives in a care home. She requires near total care. In recent weeks, she has become aggressive to the care staff when they attempt to bathe or dress her. The GP prescribes risperidone 0.5mg twice daily. Carers report her to be calmer but less verbally able and no longer walking. A CPN is called and visits. Her report states 'the patient has painful arthritic hands which need improved analgesia'. On tramadol, she is in far less pain and is not constipated. Risperidone is successfully removed and she is more alert. A senior care assistant assists junior staff with personal care.

Specific management of aggression

Pharmacological management

Use of psychotropic medication should only be considered as one component of the management plan for the individual patient, keeping in mind that fact that these drugs tend to be frequently overused and can cause a number of serious side-effects.

Antipsychotic medication

Antipsychotics are the drug of choice for aggression associated with psychosis, although they can also be effective in treating aggression/agitation in delirium and dementia. They are least effective in treating behavioural disturbances such as wandering, excessive vocalization, and sexual disinhibition. The atypical antipsychotics such as risperidone and olanzapine and, amongst typicals, haloperidol are most commonly used due to their high potency and low dose requirement.

Antidepressants

These can be used in aggressive patients with an underlying depression. SSRIs such as citalopram are drugs of first choice due to their better side-effect profile. The usefulness of antidepressants such as trazodone has also been reported in aggressive patients with dementia where there is a possibility of underlying depression (limited data).

Benzodiazepines

Short-acting benzodiazepines such as lorazepam can be useful in controlling acute episodes of aggression in conjunction with antipsychotics or on their own when there is a medical reason for not prescribing antipsychotics. Their long-term use, however, is not recommended. There are no controlled trial data to support this strategy.

Non-pharmacological Interventions

- These are planned and tailored according to the needs of the individual patient keeping in mind the underlying diagnosis, the nature of the aggression, and the associated risk of harm to self and others.
- Environmental influences and the nature of relationships with carers are important considerations in managing aggression. The first step in this process is to decide whether the current environment is safe for the patient and, if not, what would be the most suitable environment for them to be managed. For instance, some psychotic or depressed patients might require management in an acute in-patient facility.
- For aggressive patients with underlying dementia, it is useful to assess whether the current environment and skills of the carers are adequate to manage their difficult behaviour or whether they require in-patient management in hospital and discharge to a care facility with a more suitable environment and staff to deal with their behavioural difficulties.
- For dementia patients with a tendency to aggression, simple techniques like regular orientation in their environment, and a step by step approach with explanation when providing personal care such as changing clothes and bathing, is appropriate as a first-level intervention. Familiar nursing staff that can form a relationship with the patient and have knowledge of their background help in dealing with most patients with mild to moderate levels of aggression.

Aggression Reported

Background information gathering:

- Nature of Aggression: verbal/physical/frequency
- History of mental illness: mood disorder/psychosis/dementia/drug abuse
- History of physical illness: pain/constipation/head injury
- Setting: home/care home/general hospital
- Onset: acute/chronic

Mental and Cognitive State Examination

No mental illness	Mood disorders	Psychosis	Dementia	Delirium
• Consider possibility of abuse	• Assess suicide risk	• Assess risk of harm	• Assess risk of abuse	• Baseline investigations
Yes **No**	• Consider hospital admission	• Consider hospital admission	• Consider environmental causes & poss. changes	• Consider admission in general hospital
Report to: Report to: • Police • Referring authority	• Consider use of MHA*/admission against will	• Consider use of MHA*/admission against will	• ABC** technique to plan management	• Antibiotics
• Local authority	• Antipsychotics	• Consider environmental causes & poss. changes	• Antipsychotics	• Antipsychotics
	• Antidepressants	• Antipsychotics	• Antidepressants	• Benzodiazepines

* Mental Health Act

** Antecedents, Behaviours and Consequences

Fig 9.1 Management of aggression

Sleep disorders/insomnia

Sleep complaints are common in the elderly with up to 40% being affected by insomnia. Sleep disturbance in the elderly can be caused by a number of factors acting in isolation or in combination such as physiological changes associated with ageing, poor sleep, hygiene, medical illnesses, and psychiatric conditions causing secondary or primary sleep disorders. Secondary sleep disorders may result from psychiatric conditions such as depression, anxiety, and dementia. Primary sleep disorders include sleep apnoea, REM sleep behaviour disorder, and primary insomnia.

Treatment of insomnia

- A disproportionately large number of elderly people are prescribed sedative hypnotics. A number of studies have shown that in the UK and North America between 5% and 33% of elderly people are prescribed hypnotics for sleep problems. Benzodiazepines or benzodiazepine receptor agonists are the most commonly used drugs. These drugs are associated with increased risk of ataxia, falls, and memory impairment, which become more important in the very old age group. It is important to look at all possible causes of sleep disturbance before prescribing hypnotics.
- Excessive time in bed with regular sleeping hours, noisy environments, lack of exercise, and excessive intake of stimulants such as caffeine are all common causes for poor sleep hygiene and can be easily altered without prescription of hypnotics.
- It is also important to assess the total amount of sleep in 24h as sleep requirement decreases with advancing age and some retired older people tend to take afternoon naps that reduce the sleep requirement at night-time.
- Sleep disturbance caused by pain—especially due to musculoskeletal disorders is one of the common causes of insomnia and can easily be treated with a bedtime dose of NSAID medication.
- Bladder problems resulting in nocturia commonly contribute to sleep disturbance, falls, and hip fractures. When present, nocturia should prompt investigations for diabetes, prostate disease in men, and bladder prolapse in women.
- Patients with obstructive lung disease can present with sleep disturbance and may respond better to the use of long-acting β-agonists that minimize disruptive nocturnal dyspnoea.
- GI reflux can cause sleep disturbance and, if present, requires dietary counselling and the use of a proton pump inhibitor.
- Chronic congestive cardiac failure can also present with sleep disturbance and its aggressive treatment to prevent nocturnal dyspnoea and orthopnoea can enhance sleep quality.
- Depressed patients with marked sleep disturbance can be treated with sedating antidepressants such as mirtazapine and trazodone.
- Patients with dementia having sleep disturbance usually require a combination of behavioural and environmental measures such as reassurance, late day limitation of external stimulation, familiar and restful environments, along with hypnotic medication.

Basic principles of good sleep hygiene

Active measures to improve sleep:
- Use the bedroom only for sleep and sex.
- Go to bed at a regular time every day.
- Make the bedroom calm, quiet, and protected from noise.
- Make the bed as comfortable as possible.
- Regular daytime exercise.
- Warm baths, soft music, and meditation help with relaxation before going to bed.
- Food including warm milk and carbohydrates can help with sleep.

Things to avoid for improving sleep:
- Napping during the daytime/afternoon.
- Going to bed early in the evening.
- Avoid stimulating drinks (tea, coffee, cola) before going to bed.
- Avoid smoking and alcohol consumption before going to bed.
- Heavy eating.
- Active exercise before bed time.
- Stimulating thoughts/problem solving while in bed.

Further reading

Wolkove, N, Elkholy, O, Baltzan, M, Palayew, M (2007). Sleep and aging: 2. Management of sleep disorders in older people. *CMAJ* **176(10)**: 1449–1454.

Prescribing for insomnia

- In primary insomnia, benzodiazepines have been the most commonly used hypnotics in older people (Table 9.2). They can be roughly divided into three groups; long-acting, intermediate-acting, and short-acting according to their half-lives. They decrease sleep latency and nocturnal awakening but should be used with caution as older people with advancing age become more sensitive to the effects of benzodiazepines. In some cases, they can cause amnesia, night-time wandering, and paradoxical agitation. Improved sleep may not justify the increased risk in older people, especially if they have additional risk factors for cognitive deterioration and falls.

- As a general principle, for sleep onset problems, a short-acting agent such as lorazepam or oxazepam may be effective. There have, however, been case reports of confusion, amnesia, and behaviour problems with these agents. In patients with early morning wakefulness an intermediate agent such as temazepam may be more useful. Long-acting benzodiazepines such as diazepam, flurazepam, and chlordiazepoxide are not recommended for insomnia in older patients.

- The new non-benzodiazepine agents have become more popular recently and have been shown to be effective in short-term treatment of insomnia. They have a relatively short half-life and are less likely to cause daytime sedation. They have an added advantage of lesser impairment of psychomotor and cognitive performance as compared with benzodiazepines. They have also been shown to be less disruptive of the normal sleep pattern. Commonly used non-benzodiazepine agents include zolpidem, zaleplon, and zopiclone.

Table 9.2 Hypnotics

Drug	Recommended daily dose for older people
Benzodiazepines	
Short acting	
Lorazepam	0.5–1mg
Oxazepam	15–30mg
Intermediate acting	
Nitrazepam	2.5–5mg
Temazepam	10mg
Long acting	
Chlordiazepoxide	5mg
Clonazepam	0.25–0.5mg
Diazepam	2–5mg
Flurazepam	15mg
Non-benzodiazepines	
Zopiclone	3.75–7.5mg
Zaleplon	5mg
Zolpidem	5mg

Psychosis in Parkinson's disease

- About 10–15% of patients with Parkinson's disease develop psychotic symptoms, of which visual hallucinations and persecutory delusions are the most common. Treatment of psychosis associated with Parkinson's disease is challenging because a clinician is faced with what is described as the 'motion–emotion' conundrum. The dopaminergic drugs that improve movement are known to aggravate psychotic symptoms and, conversely, the use of antipsychotics aggravates the movement disorder.
- Clozapine and the new atypical antipsychotics are most commonly used to treat these symptoms. Most early studies on treatment of psychosis in Parkinson's disease were done on clozapine and found it to be effective in ameliorating these symptoms. The recommended dose range is between 6.25 and 50mg/day with most patients benefiting from a daily dose of 25mg without having a negative impact on cognition. Clozapine carries a risk of causing agranulocytosis that increases with age and some patients might not be able to comply with the strict requirements of blood tests associated with the treatment.
- More recently, other atypical antipsychotics with a lesser propensity to cause extrapyramidal side-effects, including olanzapine, quetiapine, and risperidone, have been reported to be effective in lower doses but there have been no substantial randomized controlled trials. Olanzapine in small doses (5mg) has been reported to be effective in treating psychotic symptoms, but some patients may benefit from even lower doses of 2.5mg. Risperidone and quetiapine may also be beneficial in lower doses and it is generally recommended that any of the three should be started at the lowest possible dose.
- Aripiprazole, a novel antipsychotic with a partial agonist action on dopamine D2 receptors, has been reported to be useful in psychotic symptoms associated with Parkinson's disease (small series). It has a lower likelihood of aggravating motor symptoms. It has the added advantage of being available in liquid form and can be started at a dose as low as 2.5mg/day and then titrated up to 5 or 10mg.

In psychosis in Parkinson's disease

- Clozapine has some controlled trial evidence of effectiveness for psychosis in Parkinson's disease.
- Clozapine does not worsen movement disorder in Parkinson's disease.
- The risk of agranulocytosis limits the use of clozapine.
- Other atypical antipsychotics have less evidence of effectiveness and safety.
- Major neuroleptics should be avoided.

Post-stroke depression

Psychiatric illness complicating the post-stroke period is common. The first 6 months after the stroke is considered a high-risk period for developing a psychiatric illness. Past and family history of psychiatric illness and suicidal behaviour are important pointers.

Post-stroke depression

- A distinction from post-stroke emotionalism, a syndrome of dysregulation of emotional responses due to damage after stroke, should be made. Similar phenomena may be seen in other neurological disorders, e.g. motor neuron disease. On discussion of emotional issues, patients become emotional, crying easily, but can usually recover poise quickly. It is easily mistaken for depressive illness. SSRIs have been shown to reduce emotionalism after stroke, should this be distressing the patient/carers.
- A number of reviews have reported the risk of post-stroke depression to be between 20 and 80%. Post-stroke patients are nearly twice as likely to develop major depression for up to 18 months after stroke as compared with the general population. It is important to recognize and aggressively treat post-stroke depression because it is associated with delayed functional recovery, decreased social function, and greater post-stroke mortality.
- In the literature, the usefulness of tricyclic antidepressants and SSRIs in post-stroke depression has been reported. There are fewer controlled trials conducted on other antidepressants such as venlafaxine and mirtazapine, but these are commonly used in clinical practice. SSRIs are recommended to be the first-line treatment in post-stroke depression because of better side-effect profile and less tendency to cause delirium and excessive sedation as compared with tricyclics.
- In the past some case reports had suggested that treatment with SSRIs might increase the risk of bleeding in some patients because of their effect on platelet function, but a major review conducted more recently did not report any causal relationship between the use of SSRIs and risk of bleeding after stroke.
- Among SSRIs there is little evidence to suggest the superiority of one over the other. As a general rule, treatment should be started at the lowest possible dose and increased gradually to higher doses with 1–2 week intervals. The recovery is expected to be slow and a trial of at least 6 weeks with a therapeutic dose is recommended before deciding whether the patient has responded to the treatment or not.
- If the patient responds, then the treatment should be continued for up to 12 months before deciding to gradually reduce the dose. If no clinical response is observed with treatment over 6 weeks or the medication is poorly tolerated, then the patient should be switched to a different class of antidepressant. The most commonly used second-line antidepressants are mirtazepine and venlafaxine.
- In resistant cases where two trials of antidepressant medications fail, the mood deteriorates further, or the patient becomes suicidal, a psychiatric consultation should be immediately considered with the possibility of using ECT along with antidepressants (would be contraindicated in cases of recent intracerebral bleeding).

Post-stroke mania

- Post-stroke manic illness is rare but well recognized. Some patients can present with mixed symptoms of mania and depression with episodes of expansive or irritable mood, recklessness, over-talkativeness, and poor judgement. Past and family history of bipolar disorder is important and all patients should be assessed for risk of suicide and aggression.
- These patients present with diagnostic and management challenges and should be referred for a psychiatric consultation. The treatment includes use of mood stabilizers with or without antipsychotic medication.
- In post-stroke patients, the use of lithium is not recommended, as they are more likely to have medical complications and possible renal disease.
- Valproic acid is known to be an effective antimanic agent in older people although there have been no trials on post-stroke mania. It has been reported to be well tolerated by older people and can be safely used in combination with antipsychotics. The recommended starting dose is 125mg twice a day, gradually increased to reach an optimum dose by monitoring blood levels.
- Carbamazepine is another well-known antimanic agent more widely studied in younger populations. Special attention should be paid to a past history of blood dyscrasias or liver disease as carbamazepine is known to cause bone marrow depression and hepatic toxicity. Starting dose recommended for older people is 200mg/day and gradually increasing to 400–600mg/day with monitoring of blood levels.
- Other anticonvulsants like gabapentin and lamotrigine have also been reported to be useful in managing acute mania in the adult population. Their use in post-stroke mania should only be considered as second- or third-line treatments where other treatments have either not worked or cannot be used due to poor tolerability.
- Amongst the atypical antipsychotics, olanzapine has been shown to be effective in management of acute mania. There have been few studies on other atypical antipsychotics but they can be potentially useful adjuncts in treatment of mania. Among older people with dementia, atypical antipsychotics are likely to increase the risk of CVA.
- Amongst benzodiazepines, lorazepam, a short-acting benzodiazepine has been shown to be effective in acute mania. It is commonly used as an adjunctive medication for control of behavioural symptoms of mania along with the mood stabilizers that take a longer time to exert their action. The other advantage of lorazepam is its availability in both oral and injectable form, which can be useful in episodes of acute disturbance. The recommended daily dose is 0.5–1mg oral or IM, which can be repeated up to three to four times in 24h.

Other post-stroke disorders[1]

Post-stroke anxiety disorder

Post-stroke anxiety disorders are common and present with increased anxiety, excessive sweating, worrying, and disturbed sleep. It is important to assess for the possibility for comorbid depression. SSRIs are the first-line medical treatment. Benzodiazepines should usually be avoided and buspirone can be used as a second-line or adjuvant therapy with antidepressants.

Post-stroke psychosis

- A psychotic illness after stroke should be clearly distinguished from delirium. Sometimes post-stroke depression can present with psychotic features.
- Because of the complexity of diagnostic possibilities and the risk of dangerous and disorganized behaviour, all patients with post-stroke psychosis should be referred for a psychiatric consultation.
- Atypical antipsychotics are suggested to be the first line of treatment due to their favourable side-effect profile.
- Concerns about the two most commonly used atypical antipsychotics (risperidone and olanzapine) with their possible role in increasing the risk of cerebrovascular disease and stroke has narrowed the choice of medication. More recent reviews have, however, suggested that the other atypical antipsychotics, including quetiapine and aripiprazole, may share the same risk factors and use of typical antipsychotics may prove more harmful due to their side-effects. In theory, non-demented patients have not been shown to share these risks.
- Patients with a past-history of psychotic illness may be treated with the same antipsychotic medication that helped in the past. Consideration of blood pressure, compliance, sedative and anticholinergic effects, and the marked increase in risk of extrapyramidal side-effects in the presence of brain disease should be weighed in the decision. Atypicals will usually be favoured.
- All new cases should be treated with atypical antipsychotics as first line with the choice of drug depending on the individual patient's situation. Olanzapine with its tendency to disturb glucose metabolism should be avoided in diabetic patients. Quetiapine requires a twice a day dose with slow-titration and is known to cause excessive sedation and postural hypertension. Risperidone has a higher tendency to cause extrapyramidal side-effects and may increase the risk of further strokes. Aripiprazole is one of the newly introduced atypicals, and hence the least studied. Its possible superior side-effect profile and convenient once daily dose might be useful in post-stroke patients who are likely to be on a number of medications and struggling to recover from their physical disabilities.

---

[1] For further information see Bourgeois JA et al. (2005). Post-stroke psychiatric syndromes: diagnosis and pharmacologic intervention. *Appl Neurol.* Published online 9 February 2005.

Index

A

Abbreviated Mental Test 5
ABC technique 199
AB peptide 44
abuse 168–9, 170
acamprosate 137
acetylcholine system 47, 56, 195
ageing
demographics 8
memory decline 22
normal 12
theories 12
aggression 17, 198–201
agnosia 17
agoraphobia 128, 133
alcoholic dementia 135
Alcoholics Anonymous (AA) 137
alcohol use and misuse 10, 134–6
alertness 76
Alzheimer's disease (AD) 35 see also dementia
'AD with CVD' 41
amyloid precursor protein (APP) 44, 46
apolipoprotein E (APOE) 46
behavioural and psychological symptoms (BPSD) 35
cerebral atrophy 44
cholinesterase inhibitors (CHEIs) 54, 56–60
diagnosis 35–6
donepezil (Aricept®) 54, 58, 65
Down's syndrome 46
'five As' 35
galantamine (Reminyl®) 54, 58, 65
genetics 46
gingko biloba 62
lecithin 56
memantine (Ebixa®) 54, 61, 65
memory impairment 35
molecular genetics 46
neurofibrillary tangles 44, 45
neuropathology 44–5
neurotransmitters 47
NICE guidance 65
NINCDS–ADRDA criteria 35

NSAIDs 62
personality 35
presenilin 46
rivastigmine (Exelon®) 54, 58, 65
senile (neuritic) plaques 44–5
sex hormones 63
signs and symptoms 35
stopping drug treatment 60
tacrine 56
vaccination 63
vitamin E 62
Alzheimer's Disease Assessment Scale (ADAS) 50
amnesia 17
amyloid 44
amyloid precursor protein (APP) 44, 46
analytic psychotherapy 115
antidementia drugs 54–5
antidepressant prescribing 196
see also specific drugs
antipsychotic prescribing 150, 197
see also specific drugs
anxiety
dementia and 127
depression and 126
drug treatment 132
epidemiology 10, 126
post-stroke 209
presentation 126
psychological treatment 133
aphasia 17
apolipoprotein E (APOE) 46
appearance 4, 28
apraxia 17
aripiprazole 206, 209
aromatherapy 66
assessment tips 4–6
auditory hallucinations 146–7

B

behaviour 4, 28
behavioural and psychological symptoms of dementia (BPSD) 17, 35, 66–8, 70

benzodiazepines 24, 92, 132, 138, 200, 204, 205,
bereavement 116
Binswanger's disease 48
bipolar illness 120–1
bright light therapy 66
Bristol Activities of Daily Living Scale (B-ADL scale) 50
buspirone 132

C

Cambridge Cognitive Examination (CAMCOG) 5
capacity 172, 174–182, 184
carbamazepine 68, 122, 208
care homes 3, 90, 164–5, 168
carers 72–3
carphologia 78
Centre for Epidemiological Studies–Depression Scale (CES–D) 118
cerebrovascular disease (CVD) 40
chlordiazepoxide 136, 205
chlorpromazine 150
cholinergic system 47, 56
cholinesterase inhibitors (CHEIs) 54, 56, 57, 58, 59, 56, 59, 60, 64, 66, 92
chronic amnestic syndrome 135
citalopram 109, 132, 200
Clinical Dementia Rating 50
clinical psychologists 157
clock-face drawing test 50–1
clonazepam 205
clouding of consciousness 24, 28
clozapine 64, 206
cognitive assessment 5, 29
cognitive behaviour therapy (CBT) 115
cognitive impairment 135, 146
community mental health teams 156
community psychiatric nurses (CPNs) 156
competence 172
compulsory powers 148
computed tomography (CT) 32
confidentiality 4

confusional state
  see delirium
Confusion Assessment
  Method 89
consent 178–9
Cornell scale for depression
  in dementia 50
cortical dementias 25
cortical Lewy body
  disease 48
counselling 115
crime 171

D

day hospitals 161
deafness 147, 148
death and dying 190
deep white matter
  lesions 107
delirium 76
  aggression 198
  alertness 76
  benzodiazepines 92
  care homes 90
  causes 82
  cholinesterase inhibitors
    (CHEIs) 92
  definition and
    description 76
  dementia overlap 24, 84
  depression 17, 66, 106
  diagnosis and differential
    diagnosis 18–24
  drug-induced 24
  EEG 33
  epidemiology 10, 34
  fronto-temporal (FTD) 49
  functional imaging 33
  hallucinations 17
  history 27
  HRT 63
  imaging 32
  investigations 30–1
  Lewy body (DLB) 42–3,
    48, 64
  management
    overview 54–5
  manifestation 17
  mental state
    examination 28
  mild cognitive impairment
    (MCI) 22–3
  mood 28
  MRI 32
  natural history 26
  neuroleptics 66, 68
  neuropsychiatric
    deficits 16–17
  neuropsychological
    deficits 16–17
  NICE guidance 65, 72
  olanzapine 70
  paranoid ideation 17
  Parkinson's disease 64
  perceptions 28
  PET 33
  physical examination 30
  prevalence in different
    settings 3
  quetiapine 70
  rare causes 25
  reversible causes 30
  risk factors 52
  risperidone 70
  sex hormones 63
  sexual behaviour 141
  signs and symptoms 26
  SPECT/SPET 33
  speech 28
  subcortical 25
  syndrome 16–17
  thought content 28
  valproic acid 68
  vascular (VaD) 25,
    38–41, 48, 64
  wandering 17
  young-onset (YOD) 158–9
dementia praecox 152
Depakote 123
depression
  aggression 198
  analytic
    psychotherapy 115
  anxiety 126
  augmentation
    strategies 112
  biological factors 106, 108
  cognitive behaviour
    therapy (CBT) 115
  counselling 115
  in dementia 17, 66, 106
  diagnosis 97
  disability 106
  drug treatment
    109–12, 117
  ECT 114
  epidemiology 10, 98
  frail older people 117
  genetics 106
  handicap 106
  hypochondriasis 100
  lithium augmentation 112
  major 97
  minor 97
  monoamine oxidase
    inhibitors
    (MAOIs) 110
  outcomes 98
  overview 96
  physical illness 106
  post-stroke 207
  prevalence 3, 98
  pseudodementia 20–1, 99
  psychological
    factors 108
  psychological
    treatment 115, 117
  rating scales 118–19
  risk factors 98

activities of daily
  living 16–17
aggression 17, 198
agnosia 17
alcoholic 135
amnesia 17
antidementia drugs 54–5
antipsychotics 70
anxiety 127
aphasia 17
appearance 28
apraxia 17
aromatherapy 66
assessment scales 50–1
behavioural and
  psychological
  symptoms (BPSD)
  17, 66–8, 70
bright light therapy 66
carbamazepine 68
carers 72–3
cognition 29
cortical 25
costs 9, 34
CT 32
definition 16
delirium overlap 24, 84
dementia 16 see also
  Alzheimer's disease
delusions 5, 27, 97, 146

serotonin/noradrenaline
    active drugs 110
severe retardation 101
social factors 108
social management 115
SSRIs 109
symptoms 20, 97
tricyclic
    antidepressants 110
underdiagnosis and
    treatment 9
vascular 107
deputies 185
detoxification 136
developing world 3, 8–9
diazepam 205
Diogenes syndrome 142
disability 106
disorientation 76
disulfiram 137
donepezil (Aricept®)
    54, 58, 64–5
dopamine system 195
Down's syndrome 24, 46
drug abuse 10
drug prescribing 194
duloxetine 110
dying 190
dyspraxia 27

E

elder abuse 168–70
electroconvulsive therapy
    (ECT) 114
electroencephalogram
    (EEG) 33
end-of-life care 190
enteral feeding 190
environmental
    modification 94
epidemiology 10
    see also under specific
    conditions
erectile dysfunction 140
escitalopram 109
ethical issues c08

F

financial abuse 169
financial capacity 182
fluoxetine 109, 132
flurazepam 205
fluvoxamine 109
fronto-temporal
    dementia (FTD) 49

G

gabapentin 208
GABA system 47, 195

galantamine (Reminyl®)
    54, 58, 64–5
generalized anxiety disorder
    (GAD) 128, 132–3
genetics 46, 106
Geriatric Depression Scale
    (GDS) 118–19
gingko biloba 62
Global Deterioration
    Scale 50
glutamate system 47, 195
graduates 144, 152–3
grief 116, 190

H

Hachinski score 38, 39
hallucinations 17, 27, 78, 97,
    146, 147
haloperidol 92, 150, 200
Hamilton Depression Rating
    Scale (HDRS) 118
handicap 106
hearing loss 147, 148
history, collateral 4
hormone replacement
    therapy (HRT) 63
hyperactive delirium 78
hypoactive delirium 78
hypochondriasis 100

I

illusions 78
imipramine 132
independent mental
    capacity advocates
    (IMCAs) 184
informed consent 178–9
insomnia 76, 139, 202, 203,
    204, 205

K

Korsakoff's syndrome 135

L

lamotrigine 208
language see speech
lasting power of
    attorney 169,
    182, 185
late paraphrenia 144
learning disability 24
lecithin 56
legal issues 165
leukoaraiosis 48
Lewy bodies 48
Lewy body dementia
    (DLB) 42–3, 48, 64
liaison service 160

lithium 122
    augmentation 112
lofepramine 110
lorazepam 92, 200, 204,
    205, 208

M

magnetic resonance
    imaging (MRI) 32
mania 96, 120–2, 208
memantine (Ebixa®)
    54, 61, 65
memory clinics 162
memory problems 17, 22,
    35, 76
Mental Capacity Act (MCA,
    2005) 169, 184
mental health 9
Mental Health Act
    (1983/2007) 186–8
mental health
    legislation 186
mental state examination
    4, 28
mild cognitive impairment
    (MCI) 22–3
Mini-Mental State
    Examination (MMSE)
    5, 50
mirtazepine 110
moclobemide 110
molecular genetics 46
monoamine oxidase
    inhibitors (MAOIs)
    110, 197
Montgomery and Asberg
    Depression Rating Scale
    (MADRS) 118
mood disorders 96
    see also specific disorders
mood symptoms 28, 146

N

nasogastric tubes 190
neglect 142, 168
Netherlands model of
    care 165
neuritic plaques 44–5
neurofibrillary tangles 44, 45
neuroleptics 66, 68
Neuropsychiatric Inventory
    (NPI) 50
neurotransmitters 47, 195
NICE guidance 65, 72
nitrazepam 205
non-steroidal anti-
    inflammatory drugs
    (NSAIDs) 62
noradrenergic system
    47, 195

nursing homes see care homes
nutritional support 190

O

obsessive–compulsive disorder (OCD) 128, 133
occupational therapists 156
olanzapine 70, 92, 151, 197, 200, 206, 208, 209
old age liaison psychiatry 160
old age psychiatrists 157
old age psychiatry, as a speciality 2
'omega' sign 28
overdose 104
oxazepam 204–5

P

palliative care 190
panic disorder 128, 132–3
paranoid illness 144, 198
Parkinson's disease 64, 206
paroxetine 109, 132
Patient Health Questionnaire (PHQ-9) 118
PEG tubes 190
perceptions 5, 28, 78
personality 13, 27, 35, 147
pharmacodynamics 195
pharmacokinetics 194
phobias 128, 133
physical abuse 169
physical examination 6, 30
Pick's disease 49
polypharmacy 196
positron emission tomography (PET) 33
post-stroke disorders 207–9
post-traumatic stress disorders (PTSD) 128, 132
prescribing issues 193
presenilin 46
propranolol 132
pseudodementia 20–1, 99
psychological treatment 115, 117, 133, 190

psychosis
  aggression 198
  delirium overlap 85
  epidemiology 11
  Parkinson's disease 206
  post-stroke 209
psychotic disorder 144
psychotic symptoms 97, 144

Q

QALY 65
quetiapine 70, 92, 151, 197, 206, 209

R

repetition 4
residential homes see care homes
risperidone 70, 92, 151, 199, 206, 209
rivastigmine (Exelon®) 54, 58, 64–6

S

schizophrenia 143
  graduates 144, 152–3
secretase enzymes 44
self-neglect 142
selective serotonin reuptake inhibitors (SSRIs) 109, 132, 197
semisodium valproate 123
senile plaques 44–5
serotonin/noradrenaline drugs 110, 132
serotonin system 47, 195
sertraline 109
services 156
sex hormones 63
sexual abuse 169
sexuality 140
sildenafil 140
simple phobias 128, 133
single photon emission (computed) tomography (SPECT/SPET) 33
sleep disorders 76, 139, 202, 203, 204, 205
social phobia 128
social workers 157
somatization and somatoform disorders 130–1

specialist services 158–162
speech 5, 28, 76
squalor 142
stroke, post-stroke disorders 207–9
stupor 97
subcortical dementias 25
suicide 10, 102

T

tacrine 56
temazepam 139, 205
testamentary capacity 169, 176–7
tetrahydroaminoacridine (THA) 56
thiamine, parenteral 136
thioxanthines 150
thought content 5, 28, 76
trazodone 92, 200
tricyclic antidepressants 110, 132, 196

V

valproic acid 68, 121, 123, 208
vascular dementia (VaD) 25, 38–41, 48, 64
vascular depression 107
venlafaxine 110, 132
visual hallucinations 78
vitamin B_1, parenteral 136
vitamin E 62

W

Wernicke–Korsakoff syndrome 135
white matter 48, 107
wills 169, 176–7

Y

young-onset dementia (YOD) 158–9

Z

zaleplon 139, 205
zolpidem 139, 205
zopiclone 139, 205